Oxf

Shakespeare and (

ᘒ

OXFORD SHAKESPEARE TOPICS
Published and Forthcoming Titles Include:

David Bevington, *Shakespeare and Biography*
Colin Burrow, *Shakespeare and Classical Antiquity*
Michael Caines, *Shakespeare and the Eighteenth Century*
Lawrence Danson, *Shakespeare's Dramatic Genres*
Janette Dillon, *Shakespeare and the Staging of English History*
Paul Edmondson and Stanley Wells, *Shakespeare's Sonnets*
Gabriel Egan, *Shakespeare and Marx*
Sonya Freeman Loftis, *Shakespeare and Disability Studies*
David Fuller, *Shakespeare and the Romantics*
John S. Garrison, *Shakespeare and the Afterlife*
Andrew Gurr and Mariko Ichikawa, *Staging in Shakespeare's Theatres*
Jonathan Gil Harris, *Shakespeare and Literary Theory*
Russell Jackson, *Shakespeare and the English-speaking Cinema*
Alexa Alice Joubin, *Shakespeare and East Asia*
John Jowett, *Shakespeare and Text: Revised Edition*
Douglas Lanier, *Shakespeare and Modern Popular Culture*
Hester Lees-Jeffries, *Shakespeare and Memory*
Ania Loomba, *Shakespeare, Race, and Colonialism*
Raphael Lyne, *Shakespeare's Late Work*
Russ McDonald, *Shakespeare and the Arts of Language*
Randall Martin, *Shakespeare and Ecology*
Steven Marx, *Shakespeare and the Bible*
Robert S. Miola, *Shakespeare's Reading*
Marianne Novy, *Shakespeare and Outsiders*
Lois Potter, *Shakespeare and the Actor*
Phyllis Rackin, *Shakespeare and Women*
Catherine Richardson, *Shakespeare and Material Culture*
Duncan Salkeld, *Shakespeare and London*
Will Sharpe, *Shakespeare and Collaborative Writing*
Stuart Sillars, *Shakespeare and the Victorians*
Bruce R. Smith, *Shakespeare and Masculinity*
Zdeněk Stříbrný, *Shakespeare and Eastern Europe*
Michael Taylor, *Shakespeare Criticism in the Twentieth Century*
Alden T. Vaughan and Virginia Mason Vaughan, *Shakespeare in America*
Stanley Wells, ed., *Shakespeare in the Theatre: An Anthology of Criticism*
Martin Wiggins, *Shakespeare and the Drama of his Time*

Oxford Shakespeare Topics

GENERAL EDITORS: LENA COWEN ORLIN, PETER HOLLAND,
AND STANLEY WELLS

Shakespeare and Collaborative Writing

WILL SHARPE

OXFORD
UNIVERSITY PRESS

OXFORD
UNIVERSITY PRESS

Great Clarendon Street, Oxford, OX2 6DP,
United Kingdom

Oxford University Press is a department of the University of Oxford.
It furthers the University's objective of excellence in research, scholarship,
and education by publishing worldwide. Oxford is a registered trade mark of
Oxford University Press in the UK and in certain other countries

Published in the United States of America by Oxford University Press
198 Madison Avenue, New York, NY 10016, United States of America

British Library Cataloguing in Publication Data
Data available

Library of Congress Control Number: 2023931427

ISBN 978–0–19–881963–9
ISBN 978–0–19–881964–6 (pbk.)

DOI: 10.1093/oso/9780198819639.001.0001

Printed and bound by
CPI Group (UK) Ltd, Croydon, CR0 4YY

For Ada.
And for Dylan.

Acknowledgements

I would like first to thank Catherine Alexander, Jonathan Bate, Terri Bourus, Martin Butler, Hugh Craig, Gwennan Tudor Davies, Michael Dobson, Ruth Easton, Paul Edmondson, Scott Fraser, Andrzej Gasiorek, MacDonald Jackson, Peter Kirwan, Deborah Longworth, Rory Loughnane, Kate McLuskie, Andrew Power, Paul Prescott, Eric Rasmussen, Kate Rumbold, Carol Rutter, Jan Sewell, Adam Sherratt, Peter J. Smith, Tiffany Stern, and Gary Taylor, for helping me get to the point in my career where writing this book was a possibility. I remain grateful and apologetic in equal measure to Emma Smith for allowing me to renege on another writing commitment in order that I might start it. The series editors Stanley Wells, Lena Cowen Orlin, and Peter Holland encouraged me from the beginning, as did Eleanor Collins at Oxford University Press. Jamie Mortimer and Gangaa Radjacoumar were patient and expert title managers through production, and Barbara Ball a superb copy editor. Tamara Atkin, Paul Brown, Claire Bourne, Josh Caldicott, Jennie Challinor, José Pérez Díez, Gabriel Egan, Lorna Giltrow-Shaw, Brett Greatley-Hirsch, David Kathman, Urszula Kizelbach, Randall Martin, Harris Mercer, Eleanor Rycroft, Erin Sullivan, Holger Syme, Kate Welch, and Sara Marie Westh shared ideas and resources generously, or offered expert assistance with queries. Eoin Price commented on drafts of Chapters 2 and 6, and Simon Smith on Chapter 1, while the series editors, Peter Malin, and an anonymous reader assigned by the Press read complete drafts, all making extremely valuable suggestions and saving me from many errors. Any that remain—sadly, the limits of the socially constituted text—are mine alone. Chapters 5 and 6 contain material from my textual introduction to *All Is True* in the *New Oxford Shakespeare: Critical Reference Edition Vol. 2* (2017), and I am grateful to Oxford University Press for permissions. Chapters 4 and 6 contain select passages from my 'Framing Shakespeare's Collaborative Authorship' in *Shakespeare Survey 67*

(2014), with thanks to Svetlana Shadrina and Cambridge University Press for permissions.

My second- and third-year students have been great conversational collaborators on *Pericles* and *Titus*, my MA students on *Titus* and *Sir Thomas More*, and Ellen Roberts and Will Green on matters stylometric. Auditors at the Shakespeare Institute's Thursday Seminar offered helpful comments on early ramblings, and colleagues there and at Birmingham, too numerous to name, have been supportive and sustaining in so many ways. Martin Wiggins helped me enormously with matters of interpretation and factual detail, and Tom Lockwood and Gillian Wright gave me the nudge and the belief I needed, as well as detailed advice and feedback at the proposal stage. My mentor, John Jowett, did the same, and has over the years as here pushed me to hone my work both through direct comment and through the phenomenal standards he sets in his own. My debts to him can never be repaid, though they are obvious throughout this book. Heartfelt thanks also go to my mum for proofreading and cheerleading, John, my dad and siblings, my grandparents, my in-laws, Phil Gray, Dominic Guyver, Lizz Ketterer, Charlie Morton, Matt Stead, Alphonse Sullivan-Sharpe, Yu Umemiya, Jen Waghorn, and Laura Young. Marilyn and Ken Young helped me through a very difficult six months while this work was being written, as did Bonnie Graham, Leon Keogh, Anthony Lakes, the Leach family, Matt Toothill, and Matthew Williams. I must also record my fond remembrance of David Gould, the Shakespeare Institute's beloved groundsman, and of Joy Leslie Gibson, its oldest graduate, who died before this book was finished, and who were always kind.

And, finally, to Erin Sullivan—everything that really matters in my life is a collaboration with you, and I choose that over going it alone, any day, and always.

Will Sharpe

December 2022

Contents

List of Illustrations

Introduction

Did Shakespeare really collaborate? With whom? Why? How do we know? Should it matter? These are all natural questions for a subject with a great deal of fascination for readers and theatregoers alike. And yet it is also a subject with a long and particularly bitter history of division—hardly an encouraging thought with which to begin writing, and the irony that this is about people working together is not lost either. But any ideas about how much co-writing Shakespeare did and how much it mattered to him can only diminish or enhance his canonical integrity and authorial brand in the eyes of the individual. Viewed one way, Shakespeare was a reluctant collaborator, his contributions a few creative offcuts born of necessity or obligation at odd moments of a working life defined by solitary genius. Viewed another, he eagerly sought the collaboration that defined his career trajectory, shaped his virtuosity, and enabled some of the more dynamic, experimental writing he ever attempted. But probably neither is quite right. Rather, as this book will show, both viewpoints shift through the phases of his artistic progression in ways that cannot be easily explained or reconciled.

It is true that the Shakespeare of whom we most readily think was an authorial loner, and the masterworks for which he is most revered—*Romeo and Juliet*, *A Midsummer Night's Dream*, *Hamlet*, *King Lear*, *The Tempest*, and many others—were written without the aid of a co-author. And yet there is complex exchange between Shakespeare the author who wrote apart and the author who wrote together. Though his collaborative contributions have often been dismissed as not distinctively his, as though he was unwilling to share in his best work, from the start we see a real compliance in Shakespeare's attitude to co-writing, his stylistic and narrative voices combining with his partners' in ways that are in fact highly attentive and symbiotic. And though all of his co-written plays have been offhandedly deemed compromised, puzzling, even second-rate examples of Shakespearean drama, we know that to early modern audiences they were

Shakespeare and Collaborative Writing. Will Sharpe, Oxford University Press. © Will Sharpe (2023).
DOI: 10.1093/oso/9780198819639.003.0001

among the most popular plays he ever wrote. Ben Jonson com-
plained of *Titus Andronicus'* continued prominence in the repertory
more than twenty years after it was written, while various accounts,
and a high reprint rate, attest to *Pericles'* vast success on stage and
page.[1] Chapter 3 explores the commercial sensation of the *Contention* (*Henry VI*) plays, written with Marlowe and another, as a
phenomenon both in Shakespeare's career and the early theatres more
widely. If collaboration was, as will be suggested, used aggressively,
even exploitatively in his early career as both learning process and
pathway to solo work, it was also, as in his late career, a spur to innovation and changes of direction, delivering structures and idiolects quite
foreign to anything he produced alone.

Imagining Shakespeare as a figure above the contingencies of
human production, rather than a supreme practitioner within them, is
an unrealistic hagiography, and our growing understanding of collaboration in his work only enhances our appreciation of this. Indeed,
Shakespeare the collaborator and theatre professional—as opposed
to sublime genius—is now almost the stuff of broadsheet orthodoxy, guided by the academy over the almost four decades since
the 1986 Oxford Shakespeare's influential re-evaluation of his working life.[2] That edition's immense bequest was to popularize a set of
contexts for understanding Shakespeare's art more functionally. But
despite the care with which it put Shakespeare back into the collaborative environment of theatre, popular mischaracterizations slowly
arose of collaborative writing as the default mode for early modern playwrights, either in which Shakespeare was entirely implicated,
or against which his exceptionalism stood out. Such thinking has
obscured our more nuanced sense of the motivations for, and particular effects of, collaboration in Shakespeare's work, and of his own
effect on it. The almost consistent co-authorship in which he engaged
at the beginning of his career, for example, differs from almost all
other writers' practices at that time, as Chapters 2 and 3 will suggest.
And collaborative playwri(gh)ting is many different things, for many
different reasons, over many different periods in the early modern
theatres and book trade, so this is as much a story of 'when' as of 'who'.

The present study has the multiple aims of exploring collaboration as a phenomenon within both early modern theatrical and print
culture, with examples of other writers, companies, and stationers

of the period introduced for context and comparison; of finding a way through some of the major disputes outlined in this introduction; and of reappraising Shakespeare's artistic development *through* collaboration. It will, as the canonical basis for its discussion, follow the model posited by the 2016 *New Oxford Shakespeare* (NOS), to date the fullest, most radical treatment of Shakespeare's co-authorial activities in a major edition.[3] Readers will find further examination of this choice in Chapters 1, 6, and 7, and a detailed breakdown of the identities and shares of Shakespeare's collaborators in Appendix 1. While readers will be introduced to some basic examples of attribution method and key debates on reliability and rationale, this book will not attempt to arbitrate on their efficacy, albeit it may be objected that the NOS's are implicitly endorsed. Neither will it dwell exhaustively on stylistic arguments for or against Shakespeare's hand in any of these plays, or on the histories of any individual attributions, though the Further Reading section lists several that do. Nor will it attempt to ascribe any new plays to him. Rather it seeks a fresh understanding of his artistic evolution, aided by the NOS's stylometric conclusions, asking what does it mean for our understanding of Shakespeare's formation as an artist if these attributions are accepted?

As our sense of canon shifts, so does our ability to rethink its contexts—attribution affects biography too—and that is what will be attempted across the central three chapters of this book. While the account is, like every such one, conjectural, it offers readers a chance to reframe the likelihood, and more importantly the significance, of these acts of collaboration. Though a cultural tradition dating back to the 1623 First Folio pictures Shakespeare—quite literally, in that book's case—on his own, it will be a central argument of this book that his formation as a writer happened within, and against, a culture of collaborative writing he helped substantially to create.

What Is Collaboration?

The praise of ancient authors proceeds not from the
reverence of the dead, but from the competition, and
mutual envy of the living.

—Thomas Hobbes, *Leviathan*

Everyone is a collaborator. Everyone must at some time labour, actually or figuratively, with or because of others. The very best in any
field must all undertake to work from the first to some kind of standard, all work 'with' somebody in the formation of their identity,
and often somebody long dead.[1] We only come to understand or
know anything—our craft, our customs, the language we speak, the
technologies we utilize—because others knew it first, lending us the
methods and thoughts that enable our own. And though we might
resent the art of precedent, because it stands for either the conventional or the unachievable, just as we resent the art of those in the
present who outshine us, we find spurs to and partners in creativity
among the living and the dead, whether we seek them or not. They
are in our heads and at our backs when we sit down to write, and in
the struggle to make something new from the shopworn materials of
our learning we are both originator and debtor. Even working against
means working with.

Collaboration, then, means mutuality in enterprise, though the
limits of what we include, or choose to acknowledge in that process

Shakespeare and Collaborative Writing. Will Sharpe, Oxford University Press. © Will Sharpe (2023).
DOI: 10.1093/oso/9780198819639.003.0002

are by no means clearly drawn. At its most fundamental, it underpins the transactional basis of all human communication, a process which:

> relies on recognising each other as rational actors who approach communication with an expectation that we share compatible internal worlds. To speak is not only to exhale and inhale the sounds spat into the world, but to manipulate each other's internal states, to put ideas into another mind and collaborate to create a unified situational perception. The academic study of this phenomenon is called Pragmatics . . . in Gricean terms, even an argument is a collaborative act and even insults require both parties to be evaluating words according to the same values and frames.[2]

In this formulation, collaboration can be simple cognitive processing whenever we speak or are spoken to, or when we read in any context. But Grice's pragmatic optimism about people working together, in harmony or conflict, to ensure successful transference of meaning was not shared by reader-response theory. Roland Barthes' famous postulate of the author's metaphorical death creating the new-born reader on one level posits an act of collaboration between a book's sign systems—to which the notional creator is always subordinated—and the reading interpreter. But reception means compromise, a move towards space separating signifier from signified, where authors cannot communicate in pure form, and perfect collaboration stays beyond reach. Reacting against French philosophy of language, the bibliographer-theorist D.F. McKenzie reconstituted the text as a mechanism both made by, and dispersed among, cultural networks, institutions, and all 'forms of social discourse, past and present'.[3] We are, in other words, all shaped by the many voices we hear and read, alongside the one innate to us—unique, original, yet unavoidably bound in communal energies. When multiplied at the sociocultural level, our collaborators become unmanageable and untraceable, their voices deafening.

Taking this principle into the realm of human creativity, it is easy to see the variety of interchanges that might leave their mark. Collaboration can mean working with or reworking, consciously or unconsciously, anything we see as valuable, which, for Diana E. Henderson, is what we do whenever we perform or adapt Shakespeare today.[4] Tom Stoppard's *Shakespeare In Love* saw its temporarily muse-less muse take inspiration from the life around him for *Romeo and*

Juliet's most famous moments, which, of course, itself begs recognitive collaboration from an audience deeply familiar with them. For a dramatist it could mean using source material, or seeing other writers' uses of form or genre, or hearing words spoken onstage, or ideas gleaned from conversation, or passing advice.[5] Goran Stanivukovic has identified in Shakespeare's early career particularly 'a dramatic culture in which homage, parody, and competition defined the manner of writing plays as much as any definite sense of collaboration'.[6] Some Shakespeare plays are wholesale rewrites of others, like *Richard III*, *King John*, and *King Lear*, albeit so comprehensively reimagined in their dramaturgical and linguistic make-up that they become essentially his. And, more subtly, we see plays with clear thematic debts to others—such as John Fletcher and Philip Massinger's *The Sea Voyage* (1622), which draws extensively on *The Tempest* (1611) for inspiration—that are nonetheless original works.

Ideas about borrowing in Shakespeare's time were complex. When Ben Jonson spoke of Shakespeare 'strik[ing] the second heat / Upon the Muses' anvil', he may have meant revision or drafting as a way to perfecting the 'well-turned, and true-filed lines' for which he was praising him. But he may have been referring to the common concept of *imitatio*, seen as an essential form of linguistic training, as Colin Burrow has explored in depth.[7] Jonson himself spoke of it as the 'third requisite' for a poet, 'to be able to convert the substance or riches of another poet to his own use'. The skill of 'Englishing'—usually translating classical Latin into English, and back again—was a schoolboy staple, intended to build technique by pitting student against source, the text spurring the writer on to ever greater strides in their own embellishment. Shakespeare remained unusually fidgety in his desire to experiment with form on macro and micro levels, his range of grammatical conversion and lexical novelty particularly pronounced, ordinary words often becoming innovative and exotic through simple transference as parts of speech. Such 'copiousness'—following Desiderius Erasmus' 1512 *De Copia*, effectively a manual on rhetoric and style—was also applied to texts in English, seen most obviously in Shakespeare, and most famously, in his close paraphrasing of Thomas North's translation of Plutarch's *Lives* for the 'barge speech' in *Antony and Cleopatra*, in which he transforms the material intellectually as well as poetically and linguistically. Stanivukovic suggests the particularities of Shakespeare's style in using others' rhetorical flourishes, if not their exact words, are where he is 'not simply appropriative and imitative but distinctly Shakespearean'.[8] What to North is a description of place (the River Cydnus), becomes, for Shakespeare, a tributary of the evocative liquid imagery running throughout the play, joining the Nile and its regenerative overflow, molten gold, excess and spilth, the elemental, fortunes in flux—enclosing the fantasy of temporal suspension—and a wider tragic sense of dissolution. Prospero's 'elves of hills' in *The Tempest* similarly reworks Medea's incantation from Book 7 of Ovid's *Metamorphoses* via a pre-existing translation.

The exercise was designed to foster creative independence, which seems paradoxical to modern sensibilities around originality, bringing into sharp relief questions around the extent to which dramatists can be separated from the institutions and things—grammar school, university, print culture, theatres, commercial competition—that shape them. Recent studies have even explored the psychology of memory, and ideas of sublimated intertextual influence, in relation to Shakespeare's work.[9] No one does it alone, then. All human activity takes place within a network of people and protocols, but that fact doesn't preclude originality. Shakespeare and his fellow dramatists used a variety of sources for factual detail and intellectual inspiration in a kind of distant co-authoring, a form of influence the critic Harold Love termed 'precursory authorship'.[10] But source use cannot, and does not, account for art in all respects.[11] Writers reshape things that already exist, that others have written, and that is a kind of collaboration; but sometimes they do so explicitly in partnership with somebody else, and that is quite another.

Legacy and Labour

Collaboration means co-, and it means labour. It was the labour of early modern dramatists, of whom Shakespeare was one, that produced the corpus of plays that today still forms a cornerstone of our cultural and literary heritage; and the labour of the Greek and Roman poets two thousand years earlier who furnished them with the stories and models for writing that shaped their cultural and creative aspiration. And it was the many scribes, translators, and printers, across the wide gulf of time, whose labours ensured it was available to them.

The actors with whom Shakespeare worked, and for whom he wrote, in turn transmitted his words to audiences, themselves collaborating in the imaginative complicity of live performance. And the numerous early modern artisans and labourers in papermills, ink manufacturers, and print shops, making and using technologies that they did not invent, ensured his works' dissemination. That they exist to us at all is merely a consequence of the supply-and-demand network of commercial associations driving the early modern marketplace.

The era in which Shakespeare lived and worked was characterized by the principle of intellectual collaboration with the cultures of the past. We tend to think of Shakespeare as a Renaissance dramatist, a word that signals rebirth. Though Shakespeare would not have known it by that word—'rinascita' first appeared in Giorgio Vasari's *Lives of the Artists* (c.1550), but not in English until the nineteenth century— he would have been very aware of the 250-year cultural legacy of reclaiming and reworking the techniques and pagan ideas of classical antiquity that characterized his age. Francesco Petrarch's rediscovery of Cicero's letters to Atticus, Quintus, and Brutus in the library of the cathedral in Verona in 1345 is a transhistorical, transcultural act of collaborative interchange, seen as the intellectual spark of humanist thought. Humanism sought in the political and artistic cultures of ancient Greece and Rome the eloquence, reason, and sound provincial government it hoped would better the modern world. Its language was Latin, and Ciceronian rhetoric, designed to stir the logical mind and the emotions in equal measure, central to Erasmus' curriculum in the *studia humanitatis* (humanities), formed in broad terms the foundations of Shakespeare's art as a poet-dramatist.[12] Petrarch's extraordinary influence goes in two directions: as a researcher, he produced thousands of pages of scholarly work in Latin looking back to the ancients, but as a poet, through some ten thousand lines only of vernacular Italian verse, he envisioned modernity. His most enduring and important achievement was to capture the autonomous individual spirit, suffering and joyous alike, within the artificial strictures of the sonnet form. He did not invent lyric poetry, nor the sonnet, nor the vernacular tradition in European poetry; he merely took what he needed from pre-existing systems to build the machinery of self-expression he sought to perfect. It was a Marconi moment, a genuine technological shift in the analysis, and descriptive possibility, of interior experience, and the sounds were heard in courtly circles all across Europe for the two hundred years that followed.

The innovations of, first, Sir Thomas Wyatt, and then Henry Howard, Earl of Surrey, are seen as forming the moment at which the spirit and techniques of the humanist, vernacular lyric were imported into England and English. Wyatt had discovered Petrarch's verse on a diplomatic voyage to Italy in the 1520s, and, in translating it, inflected it with his own rougher, more cynical sensibilities, giving to English an intensely inward form of poetic possibility. Man's life was at the centre of Wyatt's poetry, the personal, political voices adopted through the solipsism of his love lyrics imbued with violent images of betrayal and sexual possession, of loss of faith in others. His writing seems rawer and more brutally honest, more allied to the immediacy of drama, than the labyrinthine, elusive Petrarch, even when translating him:

> I find no peace, and all my war is done;
> I fear and hope; I burn and freeze like ice;
> I fly above the wind, yet can I not arise;
> And nought I have, and all the world I seize on.
> (Sonnet 134, ll. 1–4)

The varied rhyme scheme of Wyatt's great disciple Surrey, with its overflowing enjambment, rendered a sense of natural speech that took the English lyric in radically new directions—a plain speaking voice seeming affectless in a form announcing its own technical excellence. Between them they rediscovered Petrarch's interiority and repackaged it, giving it new spirit and function, and Shakespeare built on these immense foundations. Surrey translated Virgil's *Aeneid* into blank verse, the first recorded use in English of a form that would massively influence the drama, its early genealogy traceable from 1560s' Inns of Court plays to Christopher Marlowe's mighty line in the professional public theatres of the late 1580s. A growing pride in the English vernacular led variously to the retransmission and commissioning of major works of poetry and history, new and classical alike; Arthur Golding's translation of *Metamorphoses* (1567), North's *Lives* (1579), George Chapman's *Iliad* (1598), John Foxe's *Acts and Monuments* (1563), Edward Hall's *Union* (1550), and Raphael Holinshed's *Chronicles* (1577). Through his career Shakespeare used every one of these books—the ancient, the modern, the ancient made modern through translation.

Stephen Greenblatt's famous study, *Renaissance Self-Fashioning*, espoused the idea of cultural 'improvisation', the ways people find of working with the affordances and constraints of what is around them.[13] Shakespeare inherited the diverse learning of the world around him and made his art from it. We see influences on him and other playwrights among the living in direct commercial and artistic competition, and the long dead in the materials that helped shape the narratives, structures, and complex moods of their works. Ben Jonson's *Sejanus* (1603) and Philip Massinger's *The Roman Actor* (1626), for example, were part of a subspecies of play in the early seventeenth century focusing on the corruption of imperial Rome. They are so dependent on Tacitus and Suetonius respectively, not only for historical details, but also for the rigorous scepticism towards power and the ruthless realism of its depiction, that, in both factual and intellectual terms, it is hard to see them as purely sole-authored creations. Massinger's use of Juvenal's *Satires* also extends to tonal as well as narrative borrowings. Though early modern drama was inescapably 'English'—in its dominant language, cultural frames of reference, religious worldview, allusions, and predominantly 'Elizabethan' costuming aesthetic even in Roman-set plays—it was still, in its form, structure, genre, in many cases source and subject matter, even design of select theatre buildings, heavily reliant on ancient precedent. But though creativity receives from and re-energizes pre-existing forms, such reciprocity is probably still more about absorption or assimilation than actual collaboration.

Jonson, in the 1605 quarto of *Sejanus*, further fashioned his own deeply literate authorial persona by acknowledging scholarly debts in pedantic marginal notes. In this case he was applying to a play written by himself techniques of annotation already well established in other contexts by editors of pre-existing texts, the Bible most obviously. Many early modern books were 'edified' by such marginalia, supplied by translators, compilers, conveyors, witnesses, and annotators inviting readers to interact with or interpret texts in ways that were not immediately self-evident.[14] In Jonson's case the debt is going the other way: he is signalling, as author of the primary text, the breadth of his own research in writing it. But were those annotators supplying textual apparatus, like modern editors, really collaborators with their authors, or glorified transmissional functionaries, processing the text like the labourers who physically assembled it? Unlike writers for early modern professional theatres, whose job was to create content inventively, early modern print shops disseminating that work were tasked with the job of reproducing it mechanically.[15] But when compositors—workmen employed to set type—unwittingly generate readings diverting from copy, especially ones that make a kind of sense in context, do they become creative and effectively collaborative, even if these variants are the unintended consequences of mistakes?[16] Or when a scribe, proofreader, or compositor, in their role as professional agent of textual transmission, corrects error in their copy, is 'collaborator' overstating their role?

Gabriel Egan emphasizes the distinction between the more general collaborative milieu of the print trade and direct co-authorship—the material production of text versus its artistic creation through playwriting. Gary Taylor's locution 'artiginality' provocatively stresses the interface between artisanal and artistic practices in the vocation of 'playwrighting', but again distinguishes authorial and non-authorial labour.[17] Jack Stillinger, though, argued that even single-authored texts are inescapably multi-authored, due to proofreading and correction by others, or in authors changing their text in reaction to comments or criticism.[18] The 1980s' sociology of text movement, led chiefly by Don McKenzie and Jerome McGann, pushed at the idea of distributed authorship to figure any act of textual creation as essentially collaborative. Eoin Price has argued that the title pages of printed plays could be the work of multiple agents: of authors, playing companies, and stationers, and building from this we might suggest a kind of meta-collaborative authorship on top of the text contained within the book, in ways that affect its readerly signification and reception.[19] Heather Hirschfield describes the multifariousness of the terms 'collaboration' and 'collaborative authorship', as increasingly:

used to designate a range of interactions, from the efforts of two writers working closely together to the activities of printers, patrons, and readers in shaping the meaning and significance of a text.[20]

We are, of course, always in danger of being pedantic or fetishistic in seeing the ways people routinely interact in the world as forms of collaboration. The impulse is no doubt part of a continued reaction against the work of the New Bibliography—the influential early-twentieth-century academic movement dedicated to a more rigorous, 'scientific' approach to textual study—whose primary points of investigative focus were, as Hirschfield notes, ultimately 'who penned what lines, or who set what copy'. Jeffrey Masten has argued the same impulses lie behind compositor analysis as behind author attribution, both ongoing legacies of New Bibliographic thought privileging the author in ways that can feel uncomfortably ideological.[21] But to move from more permissive definitions of collaboration to the specific sense of two or more dramatists authoring a play, the author figure is needed. We must also note that 'dramatist' and 'play' implicitly involve 'theatre', a series of institution-specific practices that further complicate 'authorship' and 'collaboration'.

Theatrical Collaboration

Theatre is an environment in which collaboration is normal, even expected, but that statement, in the context of this book, requires some disruption of the term. Shakespeare was a collaborator in the precise sense of co-writer of plays and in the general sense of compliant worker within a socially embedded profession; the extant texts of his plays the ghosts of collective processes we will never see. Shakespeare was an actor—the Folio identifies him as one in a paratextual list—an inherently cooperative job, giving life and nuance to the lines he had learned as he interpreted them in performance. Evelyn B. Tribble's work on early performance, drawing on the field of 'distributed cognition', suggests that actorly memory, perception, and physical coordination were socially constituted, dispersed within theatre companies' particular methods, dynamics, and practices, even among the audience relationships they cultivated.[22] Gary Taylor describes Richard Burbage as Shakespeare's main collaborator, the mutuality between actor and playwright intimate and vibrant, while Nora Johnson's account sees an almost symbiotic co-dependency in the actor–dramatist relationship.[23] *Hamlet*'s reference to clownish improvisation, to actors speaking 'more than is set down for them', often taken to be a dig at the recently departed Will Kemp, is well known, and the broad complexion of certain roles undoubtedly owed something to the particular talents and personalities of individual actors, who collaborated with the text in an improvisational way.[24] Simon Smith has also shown how composers and musicians worked with, and beyond, texts to generate new performative meaning through song, which was itself located in documents requiring transcription.[25]

Shakespeare was a sharer—core members of the acting company responsible for buying playbooks and properties, who 'shared' in the company profits after rent and hired actors' wages were paid—entailing joint administrative responsibilities in the running of a theatrical business. Roslyn L. Knutson has shown how carefully companies planned their repertories with dramatists, and Holger Schott Syme has demonstrated how much they played a role in commissioning plays on particular topics, with dramatists needing to script and structure their plays to match theatre conditions and the skills and capacities of individual actors and apprentices (boys who played female roles).[26] But all plays needed licensing, and reading before they could be licensed, and finishing before they could be read, and vetting by the company before they were finished. Direct actorly input certainly took place at the earliest readings of the finished play to the company, or even at the earliest stages of commissioning, where companies would request a play and dramatists would deliver sample material that we might understand today as proof of concept.[27] A letter to the theatrical entrepreneur Philip Henslowe from the Admiral's actor Robert Shaw tells him 'we haue heard their booke and lyke yt', meaning a finished play—*2 Henry Richmond* (1599) by Robert Wilson and collaborator(s)—had been approved for purchase.

Egan suggests Shakespeare's intimate access to the company for whom he was writing would have made it easier for him than other dramatists to hone a play as it transitioned from authorial tables to stage platform.[28] There are instances of playwrights being paid to make pre-licensing alterations to plays for one reason or another, as Henry Chettle was in 1602 for *1 Cardinal Wolsey* (1601). Company dynamics were not the only issue: plays needed to pass the censor. The dramatist Robert Daborne attests to labouring intensively over the ending of a play, as well as reworking a scene from the third act, which 'they now have in parts'.[29] This has been taken to mean he was altering a licensed play the company was already learning.[30] But it has also been argued he was revising a scene in an unfinished, unlicensed play—whether for artistic or legal reasons is not clear—preparing parts as he wrote, which actors would not learn until licensing.[31] Egan also points out that plays were sometimes licensed before the company bought them, meaning more pressure on the dramatist to get it right.[32] We do not know when, or how, Shakespeare first became a sharer in his company, but probably by 1594 and the formation of the Chamberlain's Men. After he did, he no longer needed to worry about his plays being accepted, though as Chapter 3 suggests, that may never have been a particular problem for him.

It is important to remember, when assuming a wide reciprocal creative relationship between company and dramatist(s), that when writers were writing, actors were busy performing in other plays. We might imagine Shakespeare—as in *Shakespeare in Love*—keeping the company happy with a steady drip of scenes to rehearse while he finished a play off, or imagine actors filling in the blanks with their own suggestions or speeches in a kind of a whole-company writing in the process of a play's initial composition. But those things did not happen. They would not wait around for a new play to be ready, but keep rotating the repertory in the meantime. Time was money. Much of what we would call rehearsing for an early modern acting troupe involved conning 'parts' (individual cue scripts) in private anyway, which itself was not viable until a play was licensed for performance. And if a play was to be added to or substantially rewritten based on company input, it needed relicensing, a legal issue costing money they would be loath to pay without good reason.[33] Typically the impetus for change was revival, to revamp old plays with 'new additions', the two potential remedies for stale plays being time—waiting a couple of years for a new generation of audience, or for the older one to forget—and/or reworking. Sometimes this was done by *the* author, but more often by *an* author, becoming a revising co-author as we see Shakespeare doing in Chapter 4. All of his additions to *The Spanish Tragedy* are discrete insertions easily accommodated into both playbook and existing actors' parts as additional slips.

Tiffany Stern's account of rehearsal describes minor actorly changes in performance diverging from the promptbook, likely to result from any combination of part-based learning, minimal whole-company rehearsal, and actorly grandstanding.[34] She gives as an example Q1

Henry V (1600), a corruptly transmitted text preserving material apparently recalled from performance, in Fluellen's 'looke you' and 'God's plud', verbal tics amounting to little more than space-fillers. But such material is typically local, and, for the most part, distinguishable from authorship, especially where we have multiple versions of texts for comparison. Several sources describe actors' omissions in relation to authorly permission or chagrin, though by the point of performance, companies, or actors, owned the plays they were performing, and were not obliged to please authors. Stern also notes that while a play was essentially tested in its first performance, any alterations in response to performance had pragmatic limits. A play that was too heavily altered would necessitate extensive work recopying the promptbook and all the parts, the latter also needing to be learnt by the actors.[35] This was another logistical cost–benefit ratio.

Changes to licensed material were overwhelmingly likely to have been limited, by pragmatics and law, to cuts, typically resembling the 'internal' cuts seen in speeches from Q2 to F *Hamlet*, and those made to the manuscript of Thomas Middleton's *The Lady's Tragedy* (1611), the only extant playbook of a King's Men play during Shakespeare's time with the company. These were simple omissions of lines within long speeches, leaving the final line intact because it was a cue used in parts.[36] They were practical—because a play was too long, or a part deemed excessively hard to learn—and not necessarily, or even likely, made by authors. The ecology of performance, then, could bring about limited revisions in the form of cuts amounting to a 'collaborative' reworking of the play. Cuts in which a theme or idea is excised, either partially or thoroughly—as in Folio *Lear's* excision of Quarto references to French involvement in the final battle—are usually taken as authorial revision. But Eric Rasmussen observes that the manuscript playbook of *Charlemagne* (*c.*1618), an anonymous Jacobean play surviving as a single manuscript, shows cuts around the theme of fortune, in which 'the distinction between pragmatic theatrical cutting and literary revision begins to blur'.[37] Some of the alterations are due to censorship—George Buc, the Master of the Revels, also annotated it—but otherwise the cuts, according to the play's editor, John Henry Walter, were simply about reduction of performance length.

Walter's conclusion depends on the annotator not being the author, which he assumed in his 1938 edition, ascribing the changes to a bookkeeper, and Paul Werstine's comprehensive analysis of playhouse manuscripts concluded that evidence for 'collaboration' in terms of consultation between playhouse bookkeepers and dramatists was minimal at best.[38] Scribes or playhouse functionaries were far more likely to have been called upon than original authors to ready a play for the stage, such as Hand C in *Sir Thomas More* who is clearly attuned to the play's thematic and intellectual content in a discerning way (see Chapter 4). For every play, the vast majority of which survive only in print, we must determine the nature of the underlying manuscript. Who is/are the likely agent(s) behind it, in authorship and/or transcription? How do we account for changes between versions? If there is evidence of theatrical annotation or cutting, who, and what, is prompting it? What constituted the roles of the various categories of theatrical personnel identified or inferred, and how plausible are they? These issues dominated the work of the New Bibliography, and have been long discussed and disputed, Werstine, the most assiduous critic of its assumptions, showing that old distinctions between categories of 'foul papers' (messy, authorial) and 'theatre manuscripts' (clean, scribal) were more fluid than the New Bibliography assumed. John Jowett summarizes the New Bibliographic model—as imagined by its leading figure, W.W. Greg—in the following stemma:

Author's papers > theatre manuscript > actors' parts/ backstage plot > performance[39]

Greg assumed all authors' papers were 'foul' and that theatre companies routinely paid professional scribes to make copies, which we now know was not the case. Authors made clean transcripts of their work for final presentation to the company, which were only sometimes re-transcribed for theatrical use—in other words, step 1 in the stemma involved two stages, the latter sometimes used for step 2. Thomas Heywood's transcript of his play *The Captives* (1624), for example, is, despite its untidiness, marked up for performance. A single document, authorial or scribal, could acquire many marks indicative of censorship, revision, and performance as it evolved through time and use. The *John of Bordeaux* (1591) manuscript, which may originally have been by a single author, is in four different hands, including a scribe, two revisers, and Henry Chettle, who wrote twelve lines in Scene 17 of the play.[40] And yet it also contains some theatrical annotation, perhaps undermining expectations we might have of a text meant for theatrical use.

It is still largely possible, and desirable, to distinguish between 'the first makers of the text as a semantic system' and the influence of 'those who subsequently reproduced it, whether through theatrical performance or the production of new physical documents', which is not to decontaminate the revered author but to understand accurately how any given text came to exist in the form it is.[41] Jowett reminds us that there was always a stage at which a play took the pre-theatrical form of an authorial draft; this 'directly or indirectly prior authorial manuscript is a necessary thing: the observation that no such document survives to the present is completely immaterial to the postulate that such documents historically existed'.[42] James Purkis, though, has argued that the later functions of theatrical annotation are a kind of indivisible mode of collaboration, complicating the categories of 'authorial' and 'theatrical' manuscript.[43] Stephen Orgel's influential essay 'What is a text?' stated that early modern plays were 'basically collaborative', though again mainly invoking various processes either before or after the stage of originary, 'foul paper' authorship.[44] Orgel's essay dates from the early 1990s, when a necessary and radical re-evaluation of the theatrical text—and a wider reaction against the New Bibliography—was taking place. Features once thought of as a kind of contamination were being refigured in terms of the inescapably collaborative textual shaping of theatre. But by the late 90s, Pauline Kewes was describing as 'mistaken' the impulse to 'conflate the categories of joint writing and multiple agency'.[45] And while Werstine and Purkis notably continue to urge the socially constituted nature of theatrical texts, the last twenty years of stylometrically informed editing have pushed to see distinctions between authoriality and other kinds of agency reasserted.

We might say that even if theatrical agents did 'revise' plays in their work, they are intervening in authored material, not creating it. Or object that if a scribe is an agent of textual change if he makes mistakes or imposes grammatical preferences, he is an incidental one whose influence can usually be identified in any case. Or that if a censor can alter a text, it is only through demands for cuts that are not creative, and/or rewrites that he will not supply. Or that if a playhouse annotator describes the actions and properties required to perform a text through inscription that is itself 'text', it is extrinsic to the spoken, compositional text. But methodological differences remain at an impasse. Those who claim to wish only to identify authorship as a realistic phase in the process of playmaking are always in danger of being perceived as venerating it. And at the risk of that charge, this book now makes a distinction between interventions assignable with confidence to non-authorial agents in the theatre and printing house—the latter discussed in Chapter 6—and authorship. It recognizes the many ways in which plays were shaped by the collective needs of performance, by multiple people working on and with texts for specific ends beyond the point of authorial composition. But it hereafter focuses primarily on the joint writing of plays, assuming that in order for there to be a text to use as a working theatrical document in the first place, someone had to write it. Or they had to do so in collaboration with someone else.

Authorial Collaboration

Authorial collaboration in early drama is when two or more people plan and write a play together. In the main, dramatists seem to have written agreed portions separately, in 'structural' or 'parcelled' collaboration; nothing indicates continuous, close collaboration was ever standard practice. As Taylor contends, '[T]he solitary executive act of formulating strings of hundreds or thousands of words, and putting them down on paper, for the first time', was the 'early modern norm'.[46] Attribution study reinforces the idea of collaborative plays really only existing as unified wholes at two distinct stages, and in two distinct forms: as the authors' plot at the start, and as a gathering of individual shares at the end, typically then transcribed either by one of the collaborators or a professional copyist. Even if collaborative dramatists got their sections back after the transcript had gone to the company, they were useless on their own. Holger Schott Syme has suggested that collaborative authors' ability to make a name in print may partly have been governed by the fact that they never had a complete play to sell. Dramatists' relinquishment of rights in a sold script was only expected, not binding, though typical policy seems naturally to have been to not risk alienating clients in publishing their assets in any case. This is all speculation, but aligns with the patterns and processes we can reconstruct to suggest separate working practices among collaborators. Nothing, as we will see across Chapters 3–5, suggests Shakespeare was any different in this: his collaborations all indicate remote work in one way or another.

The previous section mentioned that Shakespeare became a sharer, but it is perhaps the single most important detail in understanding him as a working dramatist. Sharers were actors who co-owned the theatre company in a syndicate of around ten members, all of whom took a share of the daily performance takings. Being one was highly profitable, and Shakespeare even came to own shares in the Globe and Blackfriars playhouses themselves. Such stakes were not dependent on being a theatre professional in the same way—company sharers shared the labour as well as the cost—but were another lucrative income stream, attesting to Shakespeare's financial savvy. Not all actors were sharers, but most sharers were actors. Most dramatists were not actors, and no dramatist during Shakespeare's lifetime was attached to a company specifically *as* a dramatist, Shakespeare included, though his value as one no doubt aided his progress to sharer status. While most writers sold their plays to whichever companies wanted to buy, Shakespeare's, from 1594, at least, all stayed in-house. For a modern analogy, Shakespeare was tenure-track, his colleagues adjuncts, whose main limitation on earning was individual burnout. None made much money out of playwriting: George Peele died a pauper's death, and Middleton was racked with financial problems through a long career working for at least seven companies.[47] Marlowe's other professional activities are notoriously murky—spy, forger of money—while George Wilkins kept a brothel. Of all Shakespeare's collaborators Thomas Heywood is the only other actor-sharer, in Worcester's/Queen Anne's Men from 1602–3 to 1619 when Anne died, after which he was attached to no one company. But he was a sharer around the time he and Shakespeare contributed to *Sir Thomas More* in 1603–4. Richard Tarlton, Samuel and William Rowley, Robert Armin, and Nathan Field, were other actor-sharers who also wrote plays, Samuel Rowley the only one active in both in 1603–4. His brother, William, a popular comic actor who wrote most famously in collaboration with Middleton, was the most productive writer of these other names, but his sharer's status seems to have first come 1609–12, and the majority of his dramatic output in the late 1610s–early 1620s. The prolific and regular nature of Shakespeare and Heywood's work suggests they also stood apart from the rest in working primarily as dramatists.

Some playwrights were contracted exclusively by companies, but that was not the same, or as profitable, as sharing. Richard Brome's contract with the Salisbury Court company in the 1630s is 'the only such . . . we know of from the pre-civil war period', though is likely not the only or first judging by some other writers' patterns of work.[48] John Fletcher wrote exclusively for Shakespeare's company, the King's Men, from 1614 to 1625, staying afloat over the nine years in which he was likely contracted working voraciously and mainly in collaboration with Philip Massinger. Massinger continued to supply elsewhere during Fletcher's tenure, but worked exclusively, and more slowly, for the company as a solo author when he took over as 'ordinary' dramatist after Fletcher's death. A combination of payment for work and pensions and gifts from patrons had seemingly made him prosperous enough to afford to do so, and he may also have been trying to dissociate himself from the practice, both as a reflection of his upward social mobility and the negative associations attaching to collaboration by the mid-1620s (see Chapter 2). But unlike Shakespeare, both he and Fletcher still produced and sold goods about which they had no say after sale. The instances of sometimes fussy authorial revision we see in Shakespeare's plays—in *2 Henry IV*, *Hamlet*, *King Lear*, for example—were enabled by his continued ownership of them. And all his plays, through public and court performance, kept turning a profit for him long after any collaborators had been paid off. Shakespeare may have been contracted separately for his playwriting, the company perhaps stipulating a certain number of plays per year (he typically produced two in solo authorship). Brome's contract mentions three, though he objected that may be beyond him. We know that Heywood as a sharer in Worcester's Men was paid for several plays in 1602–3, as a hired playwright would have been, including a fee of £6 for his masterpiece, *A Woman Killed with Kindness*. While we have no evidence of Shakespeare's payment arrangements within his company, he was probably paid an initial lump sum for his plays in addition to the performance profits he got from them as sharer.

Shakespeare must have started as an actor, which he remained until at least the early 1600s. The 1616 Folio of Ben Jonson's *Works* names him in cast lists for performances of *Every Man in His Humour* and *Sejanus*. But in his early career he was highly unusual—and uniquely valuable—as an actor who was also a prolific, and successful, collaborative dramatist, working within, and for, his acting company with writers outside it. When Robert Greene, in his *Groatsworth of Wit* (1592), first attacked Shakespeare as an 'upstart crow, beautified with our feathers', his ostensible point was about a lowly player enjoying reflected glory—either presuming he could learn to write through the playwrights' lines he spoke onstage, or through direct authorial collaboration—his buried one, an anxiety about artistic cachet and reduced earnings. Indeed, Greene had died in poverty by the time these words were published. His plays, like almost all others, were bought for small, one-off payments on the open market, his contingent of dramatists freelance literati with university credentials, a proud sect—'*our* feathers'—of intellectuals who nonetheless struggled to make ends meet through their work. Gentlemen-scholars by virtue of their university degrees, their literary achievement and status intimately connected, they could or would not take up regular trades, which thrust them into financially penurious relationships with the theatre companies and stationers to whom they sold.[49] For a mere player to outshine and out-earn a university writer was a deep insult. Playing had only been legitimized for around twenty years, since the 1572 'Act for the punishment of Vagabonds'—strolling players, masterless men without a patron—regularized theatrical practice, authorizing and professionalizing playing companies with the noble patronage that brought greater security and earning potential.

Shakespeare may initially have earned more than his early rival dramatists through actor's wages supplementing his pay for plays, but his sharing arrangements brought financial security and the luxury of time, meaning he did not need to finish plays quickly. Even his extraordinary productivity during 1594–99, no doubt to help build a repertory for the Chamberlain's, is still comparatively sluggish, writing on average one play, alone, every four months. But for most hired playwrights, anything more than a few weeks was not financially viable. The estimated annual cost of living and rent in London in 1600 was around £50, ten times what Henslowe was paying for a play at the time, with collaboration a good way of keeping on the clock.[50] Gary Taylor, though, has critiqued the idea, chiefly espoused by Brian Vickers and Jeffrey Knapp, that collaboration was about speed of production. He cites Vickers' urging of inconsistencies and structural defects in plays as indicative of collaboration, dramatists rushing out material in uncoordinated projects that was not an ideal, but nonetheless 'normal', way of working. If one dramatist could write an act in a week, then five theoretically could write a play in the same time. Taylor, though, points out that the speed theory only works for fewer plays than the number of dramatists. Five plays written by single authorship is as quick as five in collaboration, removing the need to co-author in a production-line model.

Taylor further suggests that collaboration was a bad business model for writers being paid less than if they were to work alone, and that the motive 'must be qualitative, and therefore phenomenological'.[51] Jeffrey Masten saw collaboration within the 'cultural geography' of the playhouse, in living arrangements, social organization, the ephemera of material existence, institutional practices, codes, and ceremonies around birth, marriage, and death, and the language used to understand them and to bind, most commonly, men, together, massively disrupting assumptions about it as both an early modern idea and a practice.[52] Combining book and theatre history, Foucauldian and queer theory, and studies of early modern identity more generally, Masten saw collaboration as a normal, even ideal, way of working in a culture that effaced proprietorial authorship. He argued an ambivalence to individualism among co-authors, a principle carried over into his own editing of collaborative drama, which did not attempt to signal authorial shares.[53] For Masten, literary collaboration was just one facet of a culture among writers in which everything, especially language, was shared, blurring the lines between sole and co-production, (modern) notions of homo-sociality and sexuality, and our sense of the working and living relationships early modern playwrights enjoyed.

One major objection to this line of thought for Taylor is that it shrinks the particular agency behind individual acts of collaboration; 'the cooperative mentalité of early modern playwrights' in this pre-Enlightenment, pre-bourgeois-capitalist model, he asserts, means 'Shakespeare collaborated because he didn't know any better'.[54]

It also undermines the historical reality of acts of labour, Taylor describing attribution in terms of 'the fundamental ethical principle of giving people credit for the work that they have done'. Yet for Masten, apportioning shares in this way reinforces a paternalistic, patriarchal way of understanding, and determining, past and present cultures, linked indissolubly to the model of single authorship. The idea of 'credit' is also, he argues, anachronistic, ideas around individual intellectual property not yet formed in the period. Both Masten and Taylor attend to the historical evidence for authorial collaboration through completely different paradigms. The starting assumption for attribution study is that at some point, however authors conceived of their ownership—authorial copyright did not exist—and however dead they now are in the Barthesian or the biological sense, they once had to sit down and write something. And, in collaborative projects, that had to be organized differently to single authorship.

Shakespeare the Collaborator

Nothing from Shakespeare's own lifetime identifies him as a collaborative author. The 1634 title page and Stationers' Register entry for *The Two Noble Kinsmen*, and a 1653 entry for 'The History of Cardenio, by Mr Fletcher & Shakespeare', never published, are the only apparently objective, albeit posthumous, early statements we have. Almost all identifications of Shakespearean co-authorship, then, have been made on the basis of internal evidence—detailed analyses of language—as Chapter 7 discusses in more detail. As noted in the Introduction, this book follows the 2016 *New Oxford Shakespeare*, for which the present writer edited Shakespeare and Fletcher's *All Is True* (*Henry VIII*), in assuming Shakespeare's part authorship of the works in the following list. The adoption of NOS attribution is further founded in work I have done detailing historical arguments for *Arden of Faversham*, *Edward III*, *The Spanish Tragedy*, *Sir Thomas More*, and *Cardenio* (*Double Falsehood*) as legitimately part-Shakespearean.[55] I diverge in certain respects from the NOS chronology, though, part-informed by other arguments I have made on the shape and order of Shakespeare's murky career beginnings, so agreement is neither blind, nor an assertion of settled fact in all cases.[56] The list also proposes distinct categories of collaboration: direct, synchronous denoting two or more authors actively planning and writing in partnership; indirect, asynchronous describing consecutive work, or 'finishing off' an incomplete play; and 'diachronic' collaboration—popularized by Jeffrey Masten, whose influential work, opposed to attribution-based study, features prominently in this study—meaning the later revision/adaptation of a previously completed play:

Direct (synchronous)
Arden of Faversham (1590), *2 Henry VI* (1591), *3 Henry VI* (1591), *Timon of Athens* (1605–6), *Cardenio* (1612), *All Is True* (*Henry VIII*) (1613), *The Two Noble Kinsmen* (1613)

Indirect (asynchronous)
Titus Andronicus (1592), *Pericles* (1607–8)

Revision/Adaptation (diachronic)
1 Henry VI (1592/1594–5)*, *Edward III* (1592–3/1593–4)*, *The Spanish Tragedy* (1587/1599)*, *Sir Thomas More* (c.1600/1603–4)*, *Macbeth* (1606/1616), *Titus Andronicus* (1592/1616), *Measure for Measure* (1603–4/1621), *All's Well that Ends Well* (1605/1622)[57]
*Plays revised by Shakespeare; the others by Middleton

   Shakespeare's part-authorship of *Titus Andronicus*, *Timon of Athens*, *Pericles*, *All Is True*, and *The Two Noble Kinsmen* is by now widely accepted, with *1 Henry VI*, *Edward III*, and *Sir Thomas More* increasingly so. Sir Brian Vickers, a prominent attributionist and the NOS's most high-profile opponent, acknowledged all eight as Shakespeare collaborations, making detailed cases for the former five in his influential study, *Shakespeare, Co-author*. Shakespeare's hand in *1 Henry VI* has never been in doubt, but its status as a co-authored play, and Shakespeare's precise role in it, has shifted massively. Vickers has identified Thomas Kyd as Shakespeare's collaborator on *1 Henry VI* and *Edward III*, and as the sole author of *Arden of Faversham*. Kyd is most famous as the main author of *The Spanish Tragedy*, which, according to Vickers and the NOS alike, Shakespeare revised. The NOS's main controversies lay in its consolidation of arguments, which are not new, for Marlowe's co-authorship of the *Henry VI* plays; for Shakespeare's of *Arden of Faversham*; and for Middleton as adapter in *All's Well that Ends Well*. But Marlowe's proposed collaboration with Shakespeare was the undoubted cause célèbre for which the edition is now most (in)famous.⁵⁸ Though long-suggested, the claim's attachment to a flagship complete works, aided by the massive developments in computer-based attribution of the last twenty years, saw it resonate more widely than had ever before been possible. Disrupting the single-authorial unity of *Parts 2* and *3* of *Henry VI*—the epic historical saga that in many ways defines Shakespeare's career beginnings—not only changes our perception of Shakespeare the 'upstart crow', but also, as will be seen, of Shakespeare the willing collaborator.

Even with their inclusion, only five commonly acknowledged Shakespeare plays seem to be true, direct collaborations, co-conceived and co-created from beginning to end of the writing process: *2* and *3 Henry VI*, *Timon of Athens*, *All Is True*, and *The Two Noble Kinsmen*. And yet *Arden of Faversham* seems to have been written in direct collaboration, likewise the lost *Cardenio*, with even the revisions to *The Spanish Tragedy* and *Sir Thomas More* looking increasingly like small-scale collaborations within themselves, further troubling the idea of Shakespeare's aversion to the practice if we accept his hand in them. Ben Jonson's 1605 *Sejanus* first quarto includes a prefatory note in which he claims to have replaced the contribution of 'a second pen' from the version originally acted in 1603, whom the NOS editors propose was Shakespeare. He could have been involved as house dramatist, revising the play to make it more stage-worthy, as Anne Barton argued, or finishing an incomplete play Jonson sold to the company, as the NOS suggests.⁵⁹ The next chapter discusses other instances of this practice, though the ambition of Jonson's 1605 text makes this seem less likely. Their case for the circumstantial, external evidence of Shakespeare's involvement is intriguing, not least Jonson's apparent deference to the collaborator's 'genius' as both dig and humblebrag, his deeply scholarly revision carrying implied critique of Shakespeare's popularist approach to Roman history.⁶⁰ Shakespeare was certainly involved as an actor, and as participant in a repertory milieu seen in his next solo tragedy for the company.⁶¹ *Sejanus*'s caustic examination of power has also been seen as an influence on the iconoclasm that would pervade Shakespeare's Jacobean work. But as the NOS acknowledges, nothing of a collaborator's share remains, and the hypothesis remains untestable and thus not taken further in this study's discussion of Shakespeare's mid-career collaboration.

Marlowe, Middleton, Fletcher, and, on a more micro-level, Heywood, are the only authors we can propose as having directly worked with Shakespeare on the basis of extant writing. Middleton, Shakespeare's collaborator on *Timon*, is the writer most linked to him through 'diachronic' collaboration. His presence in *All's Well* is a claim barely ten years old at the time of this book's publication, and his supposed role in that time has been argued variously from collaborator to adapter. Arguments for Middletonian adaptation in Shakespeare's mid-career sole-authored works *Measure for Measure* and *Macbeth* are long held and well established, popularized by the 1986 *Oxford Shakespeare* in particular, though they still garner notable resistance.[62] The NOS also sought to consolidate arguments for his hand in *Titus*'s 'fly scene' (3.2), added, like all the others, after Shakespeare's death. Eight plays in the Shakespeare canon evidence co-authorship by adaptation over a twenty-eight-year period; some Shakespearean revision of others' work, some posthumous revision of Shakespeare's. Often motivated by the common theatrical practice of updating older plays for the purposes of revival, it is an important distinction in modes of production. Even though we end up with co-authored plays, they could still have been completed in single authorship before revision, even by someone no longer alive at the point of secondary contribution. In fact, Middleton's work on Shakespeare's solo-authored plays only became possible after Shakespeare's death. Shakespeare seemingly never allowed another writer to adapt his work while alive, though frequently, carefully revised it himself. But for writers who had sold their work for a fee, adaptation by others was normal.

Kyd had been dead for around five years when Shakespeare revised *The Spanish Tragedy*, and Marlowe for a year when Shakespeare reworked the *Henry VI* plays they originally wrote in direct collaboration. The Arden edition of *Edward III* suggests it was a collaborative play, possibly involving Marlowe, which Shakespeare revised late 1593–4.[63] Diachronic adaptation in *Titus* complicates its co-authorial picture, but it, like *Pericles*, shows signs of having been begun by others (Peele and Wilkins, respectively) and finished off by Shakespeare. Though we could urge the trans-temporal nature of all writing, with collaboration a special instance of that, the distinction between finishing an unfinished play and revising a finished one is here upheld as categorical.

The distribution of authorship in *Titus* and *Pericles* points to asynchronous work, but what that tells us about Shakespeare's approach either to the individual co-authors, or to collaborative work in general, is less clear. The two come at such different times in his career, with such apparently different sets of circumstances attached to them. A long-standing difference between our understanding of late Shakespearean collaboration and early has been—with the exception of Peele in *Titus*—an inability to identify securely any of Shakespeare's first collaborators, though this is changing. In a direct collaboration, opening the play, setting its narrative and structural framing as Marlowe did in his work with Shakespeare, and Shakespeare with Middleton and Fletcher, is frequently interpreted to denote the senior partner. Suzanne Gossett notes that Fletcher, with whom Shakespeare collaborated on the final plays of his career, wrote *The Two Noble Kinsmen*'s subplot and Shakespeare the main, but also that Fletcher frequently handed Massinger, his junior, opening and closing sections.[64] Varied approaches to playmaking from person to person, even specialisms, are most likely reflected in this, and hierarchy does not seem to have been a priority for Shakespeare in any of his collaborative projects. All of his direct collaborations show a kind of interwoven pattern of work between the writers, suggesting this is the way, when he did collaborate, that he preferred to structure the work (Appendix 1).

The dates attached to the list of plays earlier in this section show co-authorship quite strikingly bookending Shakespeare's career, seemingly neither his priority nor his preference for the main part of his writing life. Over a career spanning twenty-three years, Shakespeare actively collaborated during only six of them (1590–2, 1606, 1612–13), and only exclusively so for the final two. *1 Henry VI*, of which Shakespeare's revision is thought to constitute around 10 per cent of the extant text, *The Spanish Tragedy*, *Sir Thomas More*, *Timon of Athens*, and *Pericles* contain the only contributions he made to multi-authored texts in the main part of his career as his company's principal dramatist. But in urging collaboration as a secondary pursuit for Shakespeare, the line between statement of fact and ideological position is easily crossed, and usefully signalled. Gordon McMullan has warned against the early/late dichotomy as privileging Romantic notions of 'the author'.[65] He also saw in the term 'co-author'—which

Vickers' book did much to popularize—a built-in resistance to 'collaboration as a more responsive paradigm for the way early modern drama came into being than the singular "life, mind and art" focus of Romantic authorship'.[66] This is a similarly aimed, albeit differently rooted, critique to Masten's in its aim to disperse the author figure, a non-specific idea of 'collaboration' seen as more appropriate to early play production than parsing collaborative wholeness into individual authorial shares and canons. The opposite view is that collaboration *is* co-authorship, authorial shares intrinsic to the work in practice, which attribution helps us better understand and celebrate. These difficult distinctions will be a main focus of Chapter 7, though it is worth noting that no early modern writer referred to themselves as a co-author or collaborator, terms not current until the nineteenth century, so the semiotic battleground is a modern one in any case.

The next chapter examines the history and methods of joint playwriting in the early theatres, and will start to consider Shakespeare's role in helping develop them. We will see collaboration not as subordinate, ideal, or necessary paradigm, but a way of working that, for Shakespeare and others, was as varied, distinct, even difficult, as it was uniquely enabling.

2

Stage

Companies and Collaboration

All that survives is not all that was. It is important to remember this when analysing practices of, and attitudes towards, single and co-authorship in the London repertories across Shakespeare's dramatic career. Shakespeare excepted, the Chamberlain's/King's company to which he was attached for the majority of his working life is not at all well documented, and Pembroke's Men, the first company to which he is linked even less so. His main rival company, the Admiral's Men, on the other hand, is another matter entirely thanks to the survival of the manuscript collection of memoranda known as Philip Henslowe's 'diary', the records of the everyday business transactions Henslowe oversaw for the various companies he managed—Lord Strange's, Sussex's, the Admiral's, and Worcester's Men—from around 1591 to 1604.[1] Though patchy, they still give us far more information than we would otherwise have, showing that a large number of plays written from 1597 onwards, many of which were apparently never printed, were collaborative. Without Henslowe we would have no reason to assume that early repertories were so large or collaboration so prevalent.[2] It is hard to overstate how unusual was the degree of early modern collaborative playwriting—in any period of the London theatres from the Restoration to the present day we do not see a fraction as much.

And yet a large number of very early, pre-diary plays associated with Henslowe's companies that were printed—perhaps because they were

Shakespeare and Collaborative Writing. Will Sharpe, Oxford University Press. © Will Sharpe (2023).
DOI: 10.1093/oso/9780198819639.003.0003

exceptional hits—suggest, based on modern attribution, that from 1587 to 1592 single authorship was the dominant practice. Trying to know how, or, indeed, if it moved from one model to the other—many plays both extant and lost are only sole-authored as far as we know— is of course to reconstruct from partial remains. We cannot really pin down Shakespeare's earliest activities within the ever-shifting, mysterious, and complex arrangements of the pre-1594 London adult companies, a task far beyond the scope of this study. Pembroke's Men, Shakespeare's first known affiliation, existed in its first incarnation from May 1591 to either autumn 1593, when Andrew Gurr argues they broke, later reconstituting and breaking again in 1597. Or they lasted right through to 1597, as Holger Schott Syme suggests.[3] Gurr's famous argument that a 1594 settlement granting exclusive rights to the Admiral's, around since the 1570s, and Shakespeare's newly formed Chamberlain's, represented an effective duopoly on playing in London's public venues has since been decisively overturned.[4] It really only gave them exclusivity to perform at court during the Christmas and Shrovetide revels, and the theatrical scene probably remained every bit as diverse as it had been.

What follows is a chronological list of all the known plays by dramatists associated with the adult professional theatres in London up to 1594: Robert Greene, Thomas Kyd, Thomas Lodge, Christopher Marlowe, Anthony Munday, Thomas Nashe, George Peele, William Shakespeare, Robert Wilson, and the ever-troublesome Anon.[5] John Lyly, who wrote exclusively in sole-authorship for boy companies, is the notable exception. The list comprises 57 plays, 47 of which are non-collaborative.[6] Of the ten that are collaborative, five involve Marlowe, five Shakespeare, four Nashe, two Greene, one Lodge, and one Peele, clustering most thickly around 1591–2, and most consistently around the subject of Henry VI (collaborative plays in **bold**):[7]

The Three Ladies of London (1581, Wilson, Leicester's Men)
Campaspe (1583, Lyly, Oxford's Boys)
Fedele and Fortunio (1583, Munday, Children of the Chapel Royal)
The Arraignment of Paris (1584, Peele, Chapel Royal)
Sappho and Phao (1584, Lyly, Oxford's Boys)
Galatea (1584, Lyly, Children of Paul's)

The Hunting of Cupid (1585, Peele, survives partially in extracts)
The Famous Victories of Henry V (1586, Anon., Queen's)
The Spanish Tragedy (1587, Kyd)
Tamburlaine (1587, Marlowe, Admiral's)
Alphonsus, King of Aragon (1587, Greene, Queen's?)
Tamburlaine Part 2 (1587, Marlowe, Admiral's)
Endymion (1588, Lyly, Paul's)
Suleiman and Perseda (1588, Kyd)
The Wounds of Civil War (1588, Lodge, Admiral's)
Doctor Faustus (1588, Marlowe and collaborator, probably Nashe)
The Battle of Alcazar (1588, Peele)
The Woman in the Moon (1588, Lyly, Paul's)
Dido, Queen of Carthage (1588, Marlowe and Nashe, Chapel Royal)[8]
The Three Lords and Three Ladies of London (1588, Wilson, Queen's?)
Friar Bacon and Friar Bungay (1589, Greene, Queen's)
The Troublesome Reign of King John (1589, Peele, Queen's)
Mother Bombie (1589, Lyly, Paul's)
The Jew of Malta (1589, Marlowe, Strange's?)
A Looking Glass for London and England (1589, Greene and Lodge)
Midas (1589, Lyly, Paul's)
King Leir and His Three Daughters (1589, Anon., Queen's?)
The True Tragedy of Richard III (1589, Anon., Queen's)
Love's Metamorphosis (1590, Lyly, Paul's)
Fair Em, the Miller's Daughter of Manchester (1590, Anon., Strange's)
James IV (1590, Greene)
John a Kent and John a Cumber (1590, Munday)
The Two Gentlemen of Verona (1590, Shakespeare)
Arden of Faversham (1590, Anon. and Shakespeare)
David and Bathsheba (1590, Peele, Queen's?)
Orlando Furioso (1591, Greene, Queen's and, almost simultaneously,
   Admiral's)
Edward I (1591, Peele)
Mucedorus (1591, Anon.)
Locrine (1591, Anon. adapting older play by Charles Tilney?)
**First Part of the Contention (1591, Marlowe, Shakespeare, and Anon.,
   Pembroke's)**
George-a-Greene (1591, Greene?, Sussex's)
**Richard Duke of York (1591, Marlowe, Shakespeare, and Anon., Pem-
   broke's)**
Selimus (1591, Greene?, Queen's)
John of Bordeaux (1591, Greene?, Strange's?)

Titus Andronicus (1591–2, **Shakespeare and Peele, Pembroke's?**)
The Old Wife's Tale (1592, Peele, Queen's)
Harry VI (**1592, Nashe, Marlowe, and Anon., Strange's**)
The Cobbler's Prophecy (1592, Wilson, Queen's?)
Edward II (1592, Marlowe, Pembroke's)
The Taming of the Shrew (1592, Shakespeare, Pembroke's)
Collaboration between **Greene and Nashe**, possibly lost/never written,
   possibly non-dramatic, or possibly *A Knack to Know a Knave* (1592,
   Strange's)
Edward III (**1592, Anon. collaboration possibly involving Marlowe**)
Richard III (1592, Shakespeare, Pembroke's?)
Summer's Last Will and Testament (1592, Nashe)
The Massacre at Paris (1593, Marlowe, Strange's?)
Cornelia (1594, Kyd)
The Taming of a Shrew (1594, Anon.)

John Jowett has argued that the practice of authorial collaboration was 'resisted in the period when Shakespeare most vigorously
practised it . . . At this [early] stage of his career he was collaborating more regularly, and more insistently, than anyone else at all',
an important suggestion we can nonetheless qualify with the emerging exception of Marlowe.[9] And Marlowe himself only begins to
stand out on account of his hand in the Shakespeare history plays,
the two authors seemingly driving the early culture of collaboration, and not, in Shakespeare's case at least, exploiting a regular
working practice as a means of induction to dramatic authorship.
Collaboration, in other words, was not 'normal' when Shakespeare
began doing it. The otherwise anonymous plays in the list are also all
associated with Shakespeare in one way or another, either through
his part-authorship, as source texts he adapted, doubtful attributions to him, or probable compilation or reconstruction of his work.
Locrine was described as '[n]ewly set forth, overseen, and corrected by
W.S' on its 1595 title page, and, despite the unlikelihood of Shakespeare's involvement, appears to contain multiple hands as a result of
diachronic collaboration (see Chapter 6).

Peele is not known to have otherwise collaborated, and the authorial
distribution in *Titus Andronicus* may suggest he had started out planning to write it alone. But outside the plays attached in one way or
another to Shakespeare, *Doctor Faustus* and *Looking Glass for London
and England* seem like the only exceptions to the sole-authorship

norm at this time. Of course, the list may only look the way it does because attribution work has not yet been carried out on all early modern plays, especially those furthest away from Shakespeare's gravitational pull. But as things stand, this is the picture. By the late 1590s–early 1600s, though, that picture was practically reversed. Shakespeare was the only one from this list still alive and writing to be producing sole-authored drama with any consistency. Robert Wilson and Anthony Munday, the other two dramatists left from the 1580s–early 1590s—who had written sparsely and exclusively in sole-authorship—were by the end of the decade prolific collaborators for Henslowe's companies:

Munday (early career)
Fedele and Fortunio (1583)
John a Kent and John a Cumber (1590)
Munday (late 1590s–1600s)
***Mother Redcap*, with Michael Drayton (December 1597)**
The Downfall of Robert Earl of Huntington (February 1598, printed 1601)
***The Death of Robert Earl of Huntington*, with Henry Chettle (February 1598, printed 1601)**
Valentine and Orson, with Richard Hathway (July 1598)
***Sir John Oldcastle Parts 1 and 2*, with Wilson, Drayton, and Hathway (November 1599–Spring 1600)**
***Sir Thomas More*, possibly with Chettle (*c.*1600), revised by Chettle, Thomas Heywood, Thomas Dekker, and Shakespeare (*c.*1604)**
***The Rising of Cardinal Wolsey*, with Drayton, Chettle, and Wentworth Smith (12 November 1601)**
***Two Shapes*, with Dekker, Drayton, Thomas Middleton, and John Webster (May 1602)**
Wilson (early career)
The Three Ladies of London (1581)
Phyllida and Corin, Felix and Philomena, Five Plays in One? (1584)
The Three Lords and Three Ladies of London? (1588)
The Cobbler's Prophecy (1592)
Wilson (late 1590s–1600s)
***Earl Godwin and his Three Sons Part 1*, with Chettle, Dekker, and Drayton (March 1598)**
***Piers of Exton*, with Drayton, Chettle, and Dekker (March 1598)**
***Black Bateman of the North Parts 1 and 2*, with Chettle, *Part 1* with Dekker and Drayton also (May–June 1598)**

The Funeral of Richard Coeur de Lion, with Chettle, Drayton, and Munday (June 1598)
The Madman's Morris, with Dekker and Drayton (July 1598)
Hannibal and Hermes, with Dekker and Drayton (July 1598)
Chance Medley, with Munday, Drayton, and Chettle (August 1598)
Catiline's Conspiracy, with Chettle (August 1598)
Pierce of Winchester, with Dekker and Drayton (July–August 1598)
Henry Richmond Part 2, with unknown collaborator(s) (November–December 1599)
Sir John Oldcastle Parts 1 and 2, with Drayton, Munday, and Hathway (November 1599–Spring 1600)
Owen Tudor, with Drayton, Hathway, and Munday (January 1600)
Fair Constance of Rome Part 1, with Dekker, Drayton, Hathway, and Munday (June 1600)

The Chamberlain's and Admiral's appear, on the basis of the surviving evidence, to have diverged in practice by the turn of the century. One had a shareholder–dramatist producing plays alone and taking his time over them, the other a freelance, piecework model supplying the rapid turnover we see in Henslowe's account books. Of course, Shakespeare could not produce enough alone, so his company would also have bought plays in. We cannot know how many of those would have been collaborative; Henslowe's records for these years are the only source of our knowledge of extensive collaboration within a repertory which may have been anomalously large. Diary records of performances from 1594 to 1597 suggest that companies normally needed between about 14 and 18 new plays a year, about one every three weeks, though things apparently became more urgent in the late 1590s, with a sharp spike in commissioning at this time: 37 in 1598, dipping slightly to 29 in 1599, still double what had been normal, before stabilizing back to 19 in 1600, and 18 in 1601.[10] These two years may have been atypical, either in a changed repertory policy to present more plays, or in a stockpiling of scripts, perhaps with an eye on financing the planned building of the Fortune theatre in Clerkenwell, to which the Admiral's moved in November 1600. But this period in the diary represents the first major visible instance of the practices of collaboration shifting in line with evolving modes of company organization.

The Big Picture

In Shakespeare's theatre only men were allowed to be professional playwrights. Jane Lumley, Baroness Lumley (1537–78), Mary Sidney, Countess of Pembroke (1561–1621), and Elizabeth Cary, Viscountess Falkland (1585–1639) who wrote *The Tragedy of Mariam* (1605), all had to work solely in the milieu of aristocratic closet drama. Female writers, most famously Aphra Behn (1640–89), wrote professionally after the Restoration when sole-authorship predominated, and while certain adaptations—*The Counterfeit Bridegroom* (1677), for example, adapting Middleton's *No Wit/Help Like a Woman's* (1611)— are attributed to her, she is not known to have collaborated directly.[11] Katherine Philips' tragedy, *Horace*, unfinished at the time of her death in 1664, was served a fifth act by Sir John Denham for its 1668 performance, making Philips the first, albeit involuntary and diachronic, female co-author of the professional theatre.[12] But pre-Restoration, collaboration was about male bonding. The early days of the professional theatre had thrived on individual authorship from pseudo-revered outsiders, a hyper-masculinized personality cult of university-educated classicists whose writing was largely non-collaborative.[13] The extent to which the practice began to change through Shakespeare, the outsider, and Marlowe, Cambridge alumnus and theatre's ultimate *enfant terrible*, is something we are only now coming to realize through more complex investigations into authorship attribution. But how we get from there to the Henslowe picture is less clear.

We know audience takings for Marlowe's plays, the major component of the Admiral's dramatic back-catalogue, had begun to dwindle even by 1594.[14] By then, Marlowe, Greene, and Kyd were dead. Peele, like Greene, would die in poverty, in late 1596, retired from the stage, and, unlike Shakespeare, having failed to secure noble patronage as a poet. A lack of experienced, popular dramatists may then have forced Henslowe's companies to help develop and regulate playwrighting apprenticeships through collaboration in the latter half of the decade.[15] It may even have been a move to make the profession of working dramatist more sustainable, though some kind of hierarchy seems to have been normal, judging by the four kinds of collaborator Jonson describes in claiming a play: 'From his own hand, without a coadjutor [an equal partner, literally a Bishop's assistant],/Novice [an apprentice], journeyman [a hack], or tutor [an experienced writer, tutoring an apprentice]'.[16] Neil Carson notes that informal syndicates of collaborators grew to work for Henslowe under the Admiral's: Drayton, Hathway, Munday, and Wilson being one and Chettle, Day, Dekker, and William Haughton the other, working in various combinations within, but rarely across, themselves. Paul Brown has further noted correlation between proximity of residence and collaboration.[17] At the start of Shakespeare's career, most dramatists lived in scattered locations around the city. Marlowe and Kyd shared lodgings, but did not collaborate. But the late 1590s–early 1600s, a time of intense institutional collaboration for Henslowe's companies, saw Drayton, Hathway, Munday, and Wilson all living in the parish of St Giles, Cripplegate, near the new Fortune theatre, suggesting moves to enable daily working practice.

Henslowe's accounts mark the earliest appearances of such luminaries of the Jacobean generation of playwrights as Thomas Dekker, Thomas Heywood, Ben Jonson, Thomas Middleton, and John Webster, all seemingly developing their craft in this way. Yet there is no discernible pattern to help us understand whether this was part of an institutional apprenticeship model, or the self-directed action of writers adapting to serve particular companies' repertory demands. By 1602 Henslowe had interest in both the Admiral's and Worcester's. Dekker and Jonson's first plays were sole-authored, the latter's for Pembroke's before appearing in Henslowe's pages as a collaborator, while Middleton wrote a sole-authored play, *The Chester Tragedy*, almost immediately after his first collaboration, *Caesar's Fall*, in 1602.[18] Middleton and Webster briefly joined the Drayton–Munday syndicate for the Admiral's, Hathway moving to partner Wentworth Smith and John Day, with whom he wrote for both companies, Wilson having died in 1600. Carson also identified a syndicate between Chettle, Dekker, and Heywood within Worcester's 1602–3, of great significance for our understanding of the *Sir Thomas More* revisions discussed in Chapter 4.[19] Jonson's break-out comedy, *Every Man in His Humour* (1598), was sole-authored for the company most associated with the practice, Shakespeare's Chamberlain's Men, at the same time as his Henslowe collaborations. Crucially, the so-called and contemporaneous 'war of the theatres', a battle for authorial supremacy between Jonson, Dekker, and John Marston, may also have been part-founded on a stance against Henslowe's mode of production.

Hamlet's 'little eyases' sequence (2.2.339–69) is the most famous allusion to a theatrical trend at the turn of the century for the troupes of boy players returning to the London stage, whose repertories, rife with sexual innuendo and biting political satire, were becoming popular enough to pose a serious commercial threat to adult companies in the very early 1600s. Their repertories at first asserted sole-authorial individuality, reflecting the social and intellectual exclusivity to which they aspired. There was an excoriating moral impetus to all this, the companies conceiving of themselves and of their audiences as constituting 'the artistic and moral heart of the nation', presenting plays designed to 'punish the immorality of the members of the civic establishment', which may in part have involved an anti-populist, anti-collaboration reaction to Henslovian audiences and practices, for whom, and under which, most of these dramatists had worked.[20] Robert Armin, Lording Barry, George Chapman, John Day, Dekker, Jonson, Marston, Middleton, and Edward Sharpham all wrote many unaided plays for children's repertories. Jonson's *Poetaster* (1601), for the Children of the Chapel Royal, insults Dekker as the kind of collaborative author or writer of revisions on demand—'parcel poet', 'play-dresser', 'dresser of plays'—familiar from Henslowe's accounts, while Dekker turned Jonson's own phrase back on him in *Satiromastix* (1602), his rejoinder for Shakespeare's Chamberlain's, which transferred to the Children of Paul's by the following year.

But within a few years the practice gained traction within children's companies, led by two of Henslowe's collaborators. Dekker and Webster's *Westward Ho!* (1604) is the first collaborative venture we know of for a boy company repertory, along with its follow-up, *Northward Ho!* (1605), for Paul's. John Fletcher cut his teeth on two collaborations for boy companies, *The Woman Hater* and *Cupid's Revenge*, with Beaumont, and *The Faithful Shepherdess*, solus, during 1607–8, before re-joining Beaumont to write *Philaster* (1609) for Shakespeare's company. From 1611 to 1613, he was involved in a run of six collaborations in a row for the company, three—*A King and No King* (1611), *The Maid's Tragedy* (1611), and *The Captain* (1612)— with Beaumont, and three—*Cardenio* (1612), *All Is True, or Henry VIII* (1613), and *The Two Noble Kinsmen* (1613)—with Shakespeare

in what was Shakespeare's only exclusively collaborative phase. Beaumont and Fletcher's tenure with the King's coincided with the last
five or so years of Shakespeare's career. Shakespeare stands out as
the most active collaborator before Fletcher's arrival, especially if the
NOS is correct about *Sejanus*, though Fletcher seems to have regularized the practice within the company. Massinger, first detected
as a playwright in 1613—collaborating with Fletcher on *The Honest
Man's Fortune* for Lady Elizabeth's—partook massively in the culture
of collaboration driving the King's repertory after Shakespeare's death.
He and Fletcher were by far the King's most productive co-authorial
pairing, working on 18, possibly 19, plays together from 1615 to 1623.
But Fletcher was also the company's key co-author when Shakespeare
was there. Before him its repertory shows little evidence of collaboration, as shown in the following list of the known plays—28 solo
Shakespeare plays excluded—acquired by the Chamberlain's/King's
from 1594 to Shakespeare's death in 1616:

*A Larum for London, Every Man Out of His Humour, Thomas Lord Cromwell,
Satiromastix, The Merry Devil of Edmonton,* **Sejanus,** *The Fair Maid of Bristow,*
The Malcontent (revisions), *The London Prodigal, A Yorkshire Tragedy,* **Timon
of Athens,** *Volpone, The Revenger's Tragedy, The Miseries of Enforced Marriage,
The Devil's Charter,* **Pericles,** *The Atheist's Tragedy (?),* **Philaster★,** *The Alchemist,
Catiline, The Lady's Tragedy,* **A King and No King★, The Maid's Tragedy★, The
Captain★, All Is True (Henry VIII)★, The Two Noble Kinsmen★,** *The Duchess
of Malfi, Valentinian, Bonduca,* **Love's Cure★,** *The Widow,* **Love's Pilgrimage★,
Beggar's Bush★,** *The Witch, The Mad Lover, The Devil is an Ass*

★ = co-authored by Fletcher

The Henslowe picture from 1604, the end of the diary, to 1613 is
fairly scant, seen mainly in plays that found their way into print, a
small portion of the number that must have been written. Middleton
and Dekker's *1 The Honest Whore* (1604) survives in Henslowe's records
and print for the Prince's (as the Admiral's became). The two reunited
for *The Bloody Banquet* (1610), and, most famously, *The Roaring Girl*
(1611), also for the Prince's, the former finding its way into print eventually, the latter immediately. Dekker is all over the diary in the late
1590s as a collaborative author of lost plays, though two sole-authored
hits from 1599—*The Shoemaker's Holiday* and *Old Fortunatus*—were
printed, and survive.[21] Worcester's Men became Queen Anne's in

1603, Heywood their major visible author through the 1600s into the 1610s, exclusively solus in the extant repertory, though we see him as a collaborator in the diary, the *Sir Thomas More* manuscript, two plays with Rowley in the early 1620s, and as supplier of a new prologue and epilogue for the 1633 first imprint of Marlowe's *Jew of Malta*.[22] He may well have been the theatre's ultimate collaborator, claiming to have had 'an entire hand or at least a main finger in two hundred and twenty plays', though this is unverifiable.[23] Middleton, first seen writing both on his own and in collaboration for Worcester's Men in 1602, became a regularly employed sole-author for boy compa-nies, chiefly Paul's, up to 1607, producing for them some of his more enduringly popular comedies. He also worked with the King's Men as a tragic writer during this time, writing *A Yorkshire Tragedy* (1605) and *The Revenger's Tragedy* (1606) solus, and co-authoring the one major identifiable collaboration of Shakespeare's mid-career, *Timon of Athens* (1605–6). He had a later run of sole-authored plays with the company, *The Second Maiden's Tragedy* (1611), *The Widow* (1615), and *The Witch* (1616), the latter probably around the time he adapted *Macbeth* for them (Chapter 4). He also wrote alone and in collabora-tion for Lady Elizabeth's, for whom he and William Rowley produced arguably the greatest work of collaborative authorship of the early theatres in *The Changeling* (1622).[24]

Dekker and Webster were both members of the Merchant Taylors' company. Dekker had been writing for Henslowe for four years when he likely provided Webster with a collaborative way into professional drama. But after several collaborations for Henslowe's companies, the job of adapting *The Malcontent* for the King's in 1604, and his boy-company work with Dekker, we hear nothing of Webster from 1605 until 1612, when he wrote *The White Devil* for Queen Anne's at the Red Bull. Dekker was to spend nearly seven years in debtors' prison from 1612 to 1619, arrested in part at the suit of Web-ster's father, to whom he owed £40, possibly for coaches for his 1612 pageant for the Merchant Taylors' company, *Troia Nova Tri-umphans*.[25] But he had worked for the Red Bull company in 1611, possibly smoothing the way for the commissioning of Webster's first sole-authored play, one of the masterpieces for which he is remem-bered. The Red Bull has somewhat simplistically been associated with a 'drum and trumpet', popular repertory, perhaps explaining why the play was a commercial failure there, Webster publishing it in high dudgeon later that year.[26] Its follow-up, *The Duchess of Malfi* (1613), for the King's, and *The Devil's Law Case* (1617)—sporadic, monumental statements of single authorship—suggest the scale of Webster's individualist artistic ambition, which, *The White Devil*'s preface suggests, had taken him a long time to realize. He returned to Queen Anne's for *Devil's Law Case*, maybe running out of steam or ideas afterwards, or maybe not wanting to waste any more time on uncomprehending audiences, and an unstable business on which he was not reliant.[27]

Theatrical market pressures in the early 1620s, though, seem to have forced some breakdown in the distinction between playhouses and repertories, between elite and popular, with heightened collaboration between authors and entrepreneurs needed to help fuel demand, which apparently drew Webster back in.[28] His last known play was *A Cure for a Cuckold* (1626), with Rowley, for the newly formed Queen Henrietta's. While this may seem like yet another play in a long list, it may be especially significant, considering the company and the timing. The 1625 regime change, when James I died and his son Charles was crowned, led ultimately to the end of the early theatres in their 1642 Civil-War closure. Charles began straight away to alienate Parliament with lavish, state-funded court masquing. A massively changed sociopolitical climate, a copious established repertory, a nostalgic vogue for older plays, more exclusive playgoing conditions, and a rise in the perception of plays as poetic works, leading to fewer commissions, all saw sole-authorship venerated above the 'aura of hack-work' around collaborative writing.[29] New fashions hit the theatres hard, and from 1626 collaboration fell sharply and definitely away. Kewes notes it amounted to 6 per cent of all professional plays in the 1630s, as against 30 per cent in the 1600s, and that the Restoration theatre all but repudiated the practice.[30] *The Late Lancashire Witches* (1634) by Heywood and Richard Brome, and *The Country Captain* (1640) by William Cavendish and James Shirley—both for the King's, the company most invested in the practice over the previous two decades—stand out as the only professional collaborations of which we know from 1630 to 1640.[31] Otherwise, the new generation of writers, and the remnants of the last—Aston Cokain, William Davenant, Shackerley Marmion, Thomas Randolph, Shirley, and John Suckling, with Brome and Heywood particularly prolific among them—worked alone.

We know of many more collaborative plays, lost and extant, than have been named in this account; a full list can be explored via the open-access *Co-Authored Drama in Renaissance England* database.[32] Crudely, though, the main evolutionary phases in professional collaboration were the earliest days, when Shakespeare drove the practice after, and with, Marlowe; a vigorous late-1590s'–1600s' Henslovian phase of commissioning for the Admiral's and Worcester's, continuing through Dekker and Middleton, before Dekker's lengthy incarceration in 1613; the volte-face mid-1600s' boy-company adoption of the practice, initiated by Dekker, and bleeding over into the King's via Fletcher late in the decade; and, lastly, the Henslovian Lady Elizabeth's/King's Men Fletcherian phase. The latter continued consistently through the Jacobean era with Massinger et al., re-intensifying for other repertories in the early–mid-1620s, before effectively dying off around 1626.[33] But, in truth, it would be foolish to try to parse the practices of the early theatres so neatly. Our picture comes from the evidence of all that is, which is not the same as all that was.

Logistics and Pay

In the period up to 1597 Henslowe acted mainly as owner–landlord of the Rose playhouse. His records deal mainly with incomings from performances, his outgoings for things like nails, boards, lath, sand, lime, tiles, poles, wages for workmen, carpenters, painters, and carmen. But from 1597 until 1604 he also acted as banker–manager for the Admiral's, and Worcester's from 1602, his outgoings now mainly things like painted cloth, props, costumes, payments to tailors, property makers, and to dramatists. Just as artisans were contracted in, to supply the building of, repairs to, and necessaries for the stage, so freelance writers were contracted to supply labour and materials in the form of authorship and playbooks. In the 1590s the Admiral's paid an average of around £5–6 per play, though Henslowe's later correspondence suggests that by 1613–15 the going rate was more like £20. In his later 1590s' phase as money-man, Henslowe starts to give an unusually rich record of author payments in the diary, and we begin to be able to attribute plays very definitely. The first clear information comes in a payment of 14 October 1596 'for hawodes bocke'—a book, or play, by Thomas Heywood—though he began to keep more consistent, detailed records of author payments from late 1597. Munday and Drayton's *Mother Redcap* that year is the first collaborative pairing he records, and thereafter we also begin to see the extent to which these plays were being written collaboratively.

Henslowe's main role in the commissioning of drama at that time amounted to holding the company's money, releasing sums of it at their request to pay whichever writers they wished to supply them with a new play, or with revisions to an old one. But by the 1610s, the period of his more detailed correspondence in managing Lady Elizabeth's— the newly created company he installed in the Hope playhouse he built in 1613—his role was more impresario–controller, taking a more active role in the commissioning of scripts. Repertory matters had formerly been left up to the companies he managed, and there was no especial reason for him to have taken on the extra headache then. Theatre was also by no means his most lucrative venture: he owned many properties as landlord, and even became Master of the Bears. It seems, then, at least part of his continued, changing involvement was simply the love of show business. But though his artistic input increased, the basic model of commissioning, which the diary helps us reconstruct, stayed the same. Ben Jonson, on 23 December 1597, was advanced 20 shillings for an unknown play, having 'showed the plot unto the company'.[34] A writer or writers delivered a plot and/or scene breakdown, along with their initial research, to persuade the company a good play was available. They could then be given the go-ahead to finish, typically paid in instalments ('in earnest'), with a final payment on delivery, which members of the company authorized, and Henslowe released up front. Sometimes it was more than a plot. The Admiral's actor Samuel Rowley recommended Henslowe buy a play for the company on the strength of their having heard 'five sheets' of it.[35] A 'sheet' is a bifolium, a large folio piece of paper folded once to make two leaves or four pages, and later typically cut, detachable leaves being more practical for use in a theatrical document.

Dramatists averaged about 100 lines per leaf in surviving manuscripts, 1,000 lines or so being about right for a couple of acts.[36] This was a hefty dramatic sample, though less than a finished 'book' (a whole play). They might sell as much as this, or as little as a few completed scenes, to a company, along with a skeletal plan for the rest, which might be the agreed extent of their involvement. Or the play could be taken from them for whatever reason and handed over to another dramatist. Either or both of these scenarios may be evident in *Titus Andronicus* and *Pericles*. Thomas Nashe and Jonson's *The Isle of Dogs* (1597) seems to evidence the former, though the circumstances are unusual. Jonson and two leading Pembroke's actors were charged with 'lewd and mutinous behaviour' and imprisoned for staging the play, and all theatres closed by Privy Council order of 28 July 1597, shortly after the first performance.[37] Nashe, who fled London to escape incarceration, later described his involvement:

> I having begun but the induction and first act of it, the other four acts without my consent, or the least guess of my drift or scope, by the players were supplied, which bred both their trouble and mine too.[38]

His disavowal of collaboration is understandable—his co-author had been jailed—so he offers no reliable insight into regular practice. He elsewhere likens his contribution to a monstrous birth he was 'glad to run from', perhaps meaning he abandoned the play, or that he sold it to a company, despite misgivings, as a regular transaction, knowing or assuming someone would finish it. Jonson may have gone rogue in finishing it, though Nashe could likewise have been catering from the start to the burgeoning taste for comic satire following Jonson's own *The Case Is Altered* (1597)—also for Pembroke's, who broke and amalgamated with the Admiral's that autumn—and, especially, Chapman's revolutionary *Comedy of Humours* (1597) for the Admiral's. But the incident remains one of the first externally evidenced acts of professional co-authorship of the early theatres. Something similar may be happening in Dekker, Webster, John Ford, and William Rowley's *Keep the Widow Waking* (1624, lost). Dekker, in a court case concerning the real-life events on which it was based, deposed to having written 'two sheets of paper containing the first act . . . and a speech in the last scene of the last act of the boy who had killed his mother'. The latter is a moment of dramatic significance, structural importance, and political sensitivity, probably suggestive of a particular skill on Dekker's part.[39] Authorial shares in a collaboration were usually apportioned either by specialism, genre, character(s), moment, speech, scene, act, or plotline. Dekker may have originally sold the first act for others to develop, with a sketch of a speech to be used later in the play, or they may have brought him back in to help as the play progressed. It may equally suggest pre-arrangement in plotting and therefore planned collaboration. Both *Widow* and *Isle of Dogs* are extreme cases in the controversies they stirred, but Nashe's and Dekker's protestations at least suggest that selling an act on the understanding it would be given to others to finish was as normal as writing entire plays in collaboration.

The speed at which dramatists worked varied greatly, the diary showing a play's typical completion in around four to six weeks, though could be slower or quicker, collaboration notwithstanding. Michael Drayton promised a play in a fortnight, and Chettle and Day the lost *Henry I* in twenty days.[40] This evidence is of payments only, from which we must reconstruct our sense of work-rate. We also cannot know how much preplanning was done in any individual case, or if/when dramatists were handed plots to work to with specific instructions for scenes. Beyond Henslowe, Gary Taylor notes Jonson's *Volpone* was written, according to Jonson, in five weeks, or 85 lines per day, and Middleton's *Game at Chess* in a little under five at 53 lines per day.[41] Shakespeare never had to produce material as quickly as Henslowe's contractors, but his output is still impressive. Of his full collaborations, *Timon* looks the quickest, written February into March of 1606 (see Chapter 4). His three plays with Fletcher average one every six months, though the individual writing phases would have been shorter. His average play length is 2,000–3,000 lines, about 10–15 sheets, meaning about 10–16 weeks each for the three plays in a year he sometimes managed. His contribution to *Sir Thomas More* would have taken about a week at that rate. Perhaps he wrote in bursts of creativity, though the degree to which his work is imaginatively engaged in careful research seems to suggest steadier work. Research typically involved either big, expensive books—it has been suggested companies had libraries for dramatists to use—or small, cheaper books, which writers probably paid for themselves.[42] It could affect patterns of work in collaborative plays, with one writer using a mutual source text while the other(s) worked on something else for the subplot, or writers using competing sources for different parts of the main plot, as in *All Is True*.

Sometimes a dramatic collaborator could contribute only to the structure or ideas of a play without writing any of its dialogue. Francis Meres describes Anthony Munday as 'our best plotter', while Thomas Fuller records an anecdote of Beaumont and Fletcher '[m]eeting once in a tavern, to contrive the rude draft of a tragedy', again most likely referring specifically to this particular facet of a dramatist's professional skill.[43] 'Plotting' involved a level of intense investment in research for subject matter, in working out scenic form, and in logistical planning of the apportionment of writing. It was a more technical exercise than simply working out a story, especially important in a collaboration where writers needed guidelines on what, and how much, to write. Often playwright(s) and plotter were one and the same, but a collaborator's contribution could be limited to that phase of work. Evidence for plotting *as* collaborative share comes from Henslowe's later correspondence, in a collaboratively written letter in which Nathan Field, Robert Daborne, and Philip Massinger claim to be working on a play with Fletcher (the letter mainly begs for an advance for Field's release from debtors' prison). The play was probably *The Honest Man's Fortune*, written early to mid-1613, which survives in manuscript and as a printed text in the 1647 Beaumont and Fletcher Folio. In other letters, Daborne complains bitterly about receiving less money than Massinger despite 'deserv[ing] as much', claiming to have 'spent a great deal of time in conference about this plot'. Henslowe was by now seemingly paying writers according to the scale of their involvement, and Daborne is dismayed that his role as plotter is valued less than a minor collaborator's share.[44] We are in part able to surmise all this through attribution study, with the pioneering work of Cyrus Hoy, who did not detect Daborne's hand in the play, breaking down the authorial shares thus:

Field—Acts 1 and 2; Act 3, Scenes 1b (after Montague's entrance) and 2; Act 4
Massinger—Act 3, Scene 1a (to Montague's entrance)
Fletcher—Act 5, Scenes 2 and 3
Field and Massinger—Act 3, Scene 3
Field and Fletcher—Act 5, Scenes 1 and 4[45]

No author's plots survive, their existence only inferable by the kinds of evidence just described. And without Henslowe's correspondence, we would not know about Daborne's collaborative input here. Beyond plotting, the play seems to evidence all three major kinds of collaborative authorial labour: by distinct unit of act or scene; by blended authorship within scenes, which may sometimes have been one author revising another (3.3, 5.1, 5.4); and by takeover (3.1). We might assume only the first of these to be typically accounted for in plotting, the other two more reactions to circumstance once writing was under way, though the various evidence suggests either was possible. Field apparently wrote the majority of *The Honest Man's Fortune* and partakes in all three kinds of work; Fletcher the first and second only; and Massinger the second and third.[46] Fletcher makes a much larger overall contribution to *All Is True*—where he shares with Shakespeare, both by discrete unit of act and scene, and by takeover in the lengthy centrepiece 3.2, which seems planned—than he does here, possibly because he was working on them simultaneously and prioritizing one over the other.

The manuscript is a transcript by King's Men bookkeeper, Edward Knight, when *Honest Man's* passed into the company's ownership in 1624–5. Clarity for theatrical use was undoubtedly the prime motivation for copying, though at a pre-theatrical stage transcription by a main author was the best way a collaborative work could be assembled, checked for inconsistencies, and modified. Individual authors could employ features such as blank space for the later working out of staging issues, or marginal cue lines to signal linkage between authorial sections, but once transcribed, those links disappear. Jonson seems to have copied the final draft of *Eastward Ho!*, and stylistic indicators suggest Beaumont did the same for *Philaster*.[47] The original text of *Sir Thomas More* is an authorial fair copy by Anthony Munday of what seems to be a collaboration between him and Chettle, around the time of particularly active co-authorship between the two.[48] Munday's transcription would have been an entirely normal, pragmatic effacement of collaboration, the document's usability in the early theatre being of primary importance. Chettle's underlying contribution to a document that came in many other ways to be so revealing of collaborative practices must now be argued via the same attribution methods used on printed plays.

There is no record in Henslowe of the apportionment of particular sections of a collaborative play to individual writers—information he did not need to record or even know—in the 1596–1604 diary period. The closest we get are payments for revisions to old plays, but again *what* is added is never specified. It is possible payment was divvied-up among the dramatists themselves, though Grace Ioppolo suggests the many examples we can see in the diary show it was more typical that 'each dramatist took full payment for his individual share, not when the entire book was completed, but when he had finished his "part" or portion'.[49] Dramatists going separately to Henslowe for payment probably reflects the way they had worked on the play: together, but apart. Their labour was a cheap resource within a company's overall financial operation. Andrew Gurr estimates the Admiral's expenditure on playbooks 1597–99 was £150 —11 per cent of £1,377 total costs— for about 30 plays.[50] Companies made most profit from playing in London (touring was harder), and being able to present a large repertory of plays to regular audiences. It was in the acquisition of large numbers of plays that literary expenses became significant, though those costs were more than recouped from performance. Gurr's example shows £290 available at year's end for sharer profits. But the wealth did not trickle down. Authors, especially collaborative ones, saw little financial reward for their work.

Struggle and Success

We tend, now, to see writers' canons as things that just *are*, without the difficulties that brought them into being. But things happen to people—circumstantially, logistically, emotionally, psychologically, physiologically—that hinder them from working. For a playwright in the early theatres, work meant steadily churning out plays on a strict industrial time schedule. At the best of times, writing is hard, linked to a confidence and creativity that comes and goes, and dramatic co-authorship must sometimes have been about motivation, or, indeed, help. When we see a co-authored scene in particular, while possibly revision, specialism, or even close collaboration, we could equally be seeing a writer jumping in when another was flagging and holding things up. Early modern writing was logistically tricky in the first place, trimming pens and candles—the latter a sign that much work took place in dim light—and mixing ink regularly, but far harder logistical burdens were placed on professional dramatists. Payment was eked out as and when work was delivered, an uncertain way of living that forced many into penury, and Neil Carson's analysis of the diary shows that plays written in collaboration were statistically likelier to get finished.

Robert Daborne in a letter of 1614 admits struggling to finish a play because he had caught a cold, and elsewhere begs for advances in return for dramatic dribs and drabs.[51] He records waiting for 'the book [Henslowe] promised', probably a source he needed to be able to continue working. In 1613, he was contracted to supply five plays on his own—*Machiavel and the Devil*, *The Arraignment of London*, *The Bellman of London*, *The Owl*, and *The She Saint*—all lost. *Machiavel and the Devil* was delivered piecemeal.[52] A series of letters between Henslowe and Daborne discuss breakdown by act, scene, and sheet, as well as Henslowe's expectation that authors supplied 'fair' copies of their work, obviating the need for him to pay scribes.[53] More burden of expense and time was thus placed on dramatists. Scribes were expensive, but copying was time-consuming, and time to write the most valuable commodity. Daborne, though, seems to have found the cost–benefit ratio too uneven, promising at one point to send '2 sheets more fair written', and the 'last scene perfected', hinting at the additional labour dramatists took on to keep their employers happy and their profit margins wide.[54] Dramatists also paid for the tools of their trade—paper, pens, ink, pen-knives, candles all cost money—and while paper was not nearly as expensive as is often thought, a 25-sheet quire costing fourpence (around £2–3 today), a London lodging in which to use it was a big drain.[55] A fee of £20 for a full play in 1613 converts to around £2,700 today: not bad, but after rent and living expenses, and the fact that it may have taken 3–4 weeks' intense work to earn it, not great either. Daborne struggled to stay afloat, and we finally see Cyril Tourneur being given an act of *The Arraignment of London* to help it along.

Human limitations aside, there was the unreliable nature of the work to contend with—plague could strike, theatres could close, and plays could be unsuccessful. Playwrighting was a trade without a guild, and the financial protection they offered in times of hardship.[56] Employment structures kept most dramatists one mishap away from ruin, and imprisonment for debt barred access to the very environments and materials in and with which livelihoods were made.

In such a vicious circle things spiral quickly downwards. Henslowe bailed Dekker out of jail in 1598, and the Field correspondence in 1613 shows the piecework payment model continuing to disadvantage playwrights. Dekker embarked on another, largely collaborative, playwriting career after his 1619 release from prison, mainly with Day and Ford, for a theatrical scene much changed from the one in which he had last worked. Henry Chettle's constant need for cash as a dramatist is seen through the huge number of plays to which his name is linked, and the many diary records of Henslowe advancing or lending him petty sums, including payment of his expenses in the Marshalsea in January 1599 and money to get a play out of pawn in 1603. His imprisonment could have been the end result of a protracted period of writer's block, from which he apparently suffered in 1598.[57] The experience was a powerful motivator. Immediately after his release he wrote *Troy's Revenge* solus in just nine days, and had a hand in seven of twenty new Admiral's plays in 1599–1600, collaborative history plays a particular specialism. Alone or in collaboration, adaptability, finding a way to work, was key.

Chettle is now most (in)famous for his involvement in calling Shakespeare an upstart crow. In 1591 he had embarked on a short-lived professional partnership with the disreputable printer and stationer, John Danter, for whom, in September 1592, he prepared Greene's text, and perhaps two short passages and certain descriptive stage directions in the 'bad' quarto (Q1) of *Romeo and Juliet* in 1597.[58] Danter, incidentally, had printed an authoritative text of *Titus Andronicus* in 1594 (Q1), which, like Q1 *Romeo*, lacked any authorial information on its title page. Q1 *Romeo* potentially marks Chettle's transition from an insalubrious stint in the print industry to the theatre. Henslowe links him to some 49 plays from early 1598 to 1603, thirteen of which were sole-authored. For all the rest, he worked occasionally as a reviser, but usually as a collaborator. Of his solo efforts, only *The Tragedy of Hoffman* (1603), and, of his many collaborative plays, only *The Death of Robert, Earl of Huntingdon* (1598), *Patient Grissil* (1600), and *The Blind Beggar of Bethnal Green* (1600) survive in print, none naming him as an author. His other extant dramatic work—apart from a twelve-line speech in the *John of Bordeaux* (1591) manuscript, probably from an early 1600s' revival—is his contribution to *Sir Thomas More*, in direct co-authorial relation to Shakespeare.

As a full-time dramatist, his ability to live was entirely contingent on his ability to feed the stage, a crushing process that helped bring his erstwhile acquaintance Robert Greene to destruction.

Admittedly, Greene's personality had been a factor. He had a successful side-gig as a pamphleteer, trading on salacious stories of his own lifestyle, including habitual overspending on clothes—and sumptuary laws kept the price high—gambling, drinking, and prostitutes. That which had nourished him, destroyed him. His final letter to his wife, itself published in a pamphlet, begs for £10 to satisfy the debt to his 'host', 'but for [whom] I had perished in the streets'.[59] Greene spent the last months of his life desperately penning pamphlets for quick cash, and, like everyone else, away from the theatres, closed by plague and Privy Council order from 23 June to 29 September (Michaelmas) 1592, by which time he would be dead. The closure lasted much longer in the end, but the temporal distance of a couple of months allowed him an extended, bitter reflection on the theatrical livelihood that was 'so mean a stay' it could not support Peele, described as driven, like Greene, self-confessedly, to 'extreme shifts' through poverty. In the posthumously published *Groatsworth*, Peele is warned, along with Marlowe and Nashe—other than Lodge, the three 'university' dramatists writing for the adult, public stage—about collaborating, not so much with each other as with parasitic actors turned dramatist.

Shakespeare was not the only 'upstart crow'—neither Munday, Wilson, nor Kyd were graduates, the former two also actors—but was the most immediate threat, already earning prodigious success in collaboration with two of the dramatists Greene names. The address explicitly positions them as sole theatrical authors with a skill set and style in danger of being plagiarized by a predatory, imitative Shakespeare, seeking to infiltrate through collaborative associations that were not yet usual ways of working. Jowett observes that Shakespeare distinguishes himself from Marlowe in his early writing by developing exceptionally powerful female roles (see next chapter), which Greene seems partly to acknowledge in (mis)quoting York's gendered insult of Margaret from *3 Henry VI*.[60] But the attempt to mock Shakespeare is caught in the obvious paradox that in the context of what is now thought to be a collaboration with Marlowe, the moment was instantly recognizable and associable with Shakespeare precisely because it had stood out as distinctive and original.[61] Shakespeare's writing was both attention-grabbing and threatening, his structural craft honed in, and reputation enabled by, collaboration, his poetic and dramaturgical innovation unexplained by it.

Greene, ironically, was then one of very few dramatists to have written in collaboration, perhaps influenced by Marlowe. He wrote *A Looking Glass for London and England* with Lodge, and talks about a 'young juvenal, that biting satirist, that lastly with me together writ a comedy', who may have been Nashe.[62] And the *Groatsworth* itself is to an unknown extent co-authored, a fact swept under the paratextual rug—not only because of the obvious need to conceal libellous plagiary-cum-identity imposture, but also because the pamphlet's sensationalism depends on it all being in Greene's voice. As a snapshot into Shakespeare's early career, we see a moment of change against which an anxious rival seeks to act in the heat. Greene had form in this area. In the 1588 romance, *Perimedes the Blacksmith*, he scathingly attacked Marlowe's success, using a line from *2 Tamburlaine* to land an allusive blow, in the same way as the Shakespeare reference here. But here it is Chettle who is implicated in attacking other living writers through the dead Greene's authorial voice, beautifying himself with his feathers. It was a risky move. The retractions and denials he made in the hurriedly composed *Kind-Heart's Dream* (1592) seem to indicate that it backfired, but his and Greene's put-downs were too little too late in any case. Shakespeare's name had by then been made through a visionary and influential project, already altering profoundly both the course of his career and the culture of collaboration in the early English theatres. Whether or not he could have anticipated the effect, Shakespeare, at this moment, *chose* to involve himself with Marlowe; or perhaps Marlowe chose to involve himself with him.

Shakespeare: 1590–4

Marlowe

Christopher Marlowe was the first great collaborator of the early
professional theatres. And then came Shakespeare. Well, almost.
Marlowe could not have collaborated without a partner—Nashe on
Doctor Faustus in 1588—and despite his *Groatsworth* protestations,
Greene the following year worked with Thomas Lodge on *A Looking
Glass for London and England*, the only early play we know written in direct collaboration not to involve Marlowe, Shakespeare, or
Nashe. Over the entire span of the early professional drama up to
1594, no one else collaborated with any consistency, or no one we
can name—the anonymous dramatist identified in *Arden of Faversham*
and the three parts of *Henry VI* may well be the same person, as this
chapter will discuss. Marlowe's influence as a dramatist, through his
'mighty' line and the dynamic psychology of his tragic leads needs
no rehearsing. *Doctor Faustus* inspired a slew of superstition plays,
Greene plundering it for his *Friar Bacon and Friar Bungay* and possibly the lost two-part *Fortunatus*, and the debts to it in Munday's *John
a Kent and John a Cumber* are plain. *Looking Glass* essentially blended
the Tamburlainian and the Faustian as a Middle Eastern, biblical tale
of power and divine retribution, and Lodge had already individually
ripped off *Tamburlaine* in *Alphonsus* and *Wounds of Civil War* respectively. A clear echo of the crassly racialized, boastful evils of *The Jew
of Malta*'s Barabas and Ithamore resounds through Aaron the Moor
in Peele and Shakespeare's *Titus Andronicus*:

Shakespeare and Collaborative Writing. Will Sharpe, Oxford University Press. © Will Sharpe (2023).
DOI: 10.1093/oso/9780198819639.003.0004

BARABAS   As for myself, I walk abroad o' nights,
And kill sick people groaning under walls:
Sometimes I go about and poison wells;
And now and then, to cherish Christian thieves,
I am content to lose some of my crowns,
That I may, walking in my gallery,
See 'em go pinioned along by my door.

(2.3.176–82)

AARON. . .   Oft have I digged up dead men from their graves
And set them upright at their dear friends' door,
Even when their sorrows almost were forgot,
And on their skins as on the bark of trees
Have with my knife carvèd in Roman letters,
'Let not your sorrow die, though I am dead.'
But I have done a thousand dreadful things
As willingly as one would kill a fly,
And nothing grieves me heartily indeed
But that I cannot do ten thousand more.

(5.1.135–44)

The Virgilian, mythic *Dido* held less sway on the repertory, though *Tamburlaine*'s impact in the vogue for conqueror plays is infamous. Its brutal depictions of power saturate the mood of the *Henry VI* plays, as well as offering the only precedent for a multi-part structure. That the *Henrys* are inspired by Marlowe—the originator of two-part epic tragedy in the professional theatres—is well known; but that they are partly *by* Marlowe is an old, often-dismissed idea that has resurfaced in a major way in the last decade. The texts printed as *The First Part of the Contention* in 1594 and *Richard Duke of York* in 1595 respectively—which differ significantly from the texts renamed *2* and *3 Henry VI* in the 1623 Folio—were assumed, in a line of thought going back to the late eighteenth century, to have been imprints of plays by Marlowe and/or Robert Greene, with Shakespeare, the 'upstart crow', brought in as patcher of their work. The meaning of Greene's notorious jibe remains unclear, Edmond Malone taking it to signify bit-writer, his *Dissertation on the Three Parts of Henry VI* (1787) hugely influential on thought around the *Contention* plays as not wholly Shakespearean.[1] John Semple Smart in 1928 was the first to suggest 'upstart crow' referred more probably to an actor turning dramatist, which Smart's student, Peter Alexander, built on in asserting the two texts as 'bad' versions of Shakespeare plays. For our current purposes this amounts to a conflation of issues: one critical orthodoxy urges largely non-Shakespearean, possibly collaborative, authorship to explain poetic badness; another urges transmissional badness to assert sole Shakespearean authorship. But to simplify a theory with which this book agrees, they now look like badly transmitted versions of good collaborative work.

From the time Shakespeare became a Chamberlain's man in 1594, his playwriting activities over time become fairly easy to chart. His earlier career is another matter entirely. We will likely never know for certain how, or when, he got started, and if it was determined by collaboration, though the two-part *Contention* is the main chronological anchor point. The 1595 octavo of *Richard Duke of York* (O) names Pembroke's Men as the company that owned and performed it, an affiliation seemingly confirmed by Q1 *Titus* (1594). While O is a text of dubious authority, buyers of plays would still be expected to recognize company ascriptions as correct. While we do not know when or how Pembroke's came into existence, John Dover Wilson's hypothesis, accepted by Andrew Gurr and Martin Wiggins, suggests May 1591, when both the Admiral's and Strange's companies, who had been using James Burbage's Theatre in Shoreditch, broke away after an argument between Burbage and Edward Alleyn's brother, John. Edward joined Strange's, relocating them to the Rose, with the remaining Admiral's departing on tour, leaving the Theatre empty. Burbage's son, Richard, the aspiring tragic lead, persuaded a number of players—including Shakespeare—to stay there with him, and the Earl of Pembroke to take them under his patronage.[2] The huge asset Burbage could boast was his father's playhouse, ready for use, which probably housed all of Shakespeare's plays up to *Much Ado about Nothing* in 1598.[3] Q1 *Titus* names Derby's, Pembroke's, and Sussex's in that order, changed in Q2 (1600) to Pembroke's, Derby's, and Sussex's, which Wiggins suggests is a correction.[4] Henslowe showcased Sussex's at the Rose between December 1593 and February 1594—when Derby's were on a lengthy provincial tour—during which time they performed *Titus*. Sussex's featured some members of

Derby's, Henslowe perhaps able to mine their respective repertories for proven crowd pleasers (assuming *Titus* had come to Derby's via Shakespeare).

Lawrence Manley and Sally-Beth Maclean, though, argue that the plays we attach to Pembroke's by title-page evidence were probably written for Strange's *c*.1590, at the Theatre, which the NOS avers.[5] They further suggest *1 Henry VI* is a prequel Shakespeare part-authored in early 1592 while planning work on *Richard III*, not as commercial competition for Pembroke's plays, but as commercial continuity of the sequence with Strange's. But nothing links Shakespeare to Strange's. *Arden*'s 1592 title page lacks attribution of any kind, meaning we cannot use it to attach the play either to Shakespeare, or, more unusually, to any company. Assuming the Pembroke's evidence is correct, and *Harry VI* (*1 Henry VI*) appeared as a competitor-prequel in early 1592—Henslowe records the first performance on 3 March—then the *Contention* plays must date between May 1591 and then. The start of this time frame looks the likeliest for Shakespeare and Marlowe to have begun work, though it could conceivably be even earlier, and it is possible both plays were completed by the autumn of 1591. We might observe that sequels generally depend on initial success, though there is a sense that a two-parter was planned from the start.

Marlowe was both a pioneering dramatist, and an itinerant one. He had written *1* and *2 Tamburlaine* (1587) unaided for the Admiral's, and *Doctor Faustus* (1588)—with the Admiral's by 1594 at least—in collaboration with Nashe. *Dido, Queen of Carthage* (1588) followed, for the Children of the Chapel Royal, the 1594 quarto naming Nashe as collaborator, which recent stylometric analyses have discounted. But the question remains live, and their collaboration here would only augment what we know of their co-authorial activity. Beyond the possibility of inconclusive stylometry, it is theoretically possible this is an instance of a title page recording a non-authorial collaborative contribution (plotting), though we cannot know that.[6] *The Jew of Malta* (1589) was written solus, either for Strange's or the Admiral's, though Strange's owned it by 1592. Early 1592 marked a return to writing for Strange's, and with Nashe, along with another unknown writer on *1 Henry VI* (*Harry VI*), a loose prequel to the saga that had brought

Pembroke's such success.[7] Marlowe may also have contributed lines to *The Taming of the Shrew*, presumably when he returned to Pembroke's with *Edward II* in the summer of 1592.[8] The sole-authored *Massacre at Paris* was his last work for the stage, probably for Strange's in early 1593. He may also have co-authored *Edward III*, probably for Pembroke's, as it does not appear in Henslowe's records as either an old or a new play. Taylor, Nance, and Cooper attribute the Mariner's speech at 3.1.141–84 to Marlowe, while Proudfoot and Bennett note similarities in the play to *Massacre at Paris*, suggesting the possibility of Marlowe's involvement as a collaborator 1592–3, and arguing for Shakespeare as adapter 1593–4.[9] Wiggins—noting the Earl of Derby is a character, and Warwick, a late addition into the play, has lines reassigned from Audley's rather than Derby's part—argued for original composition in collaboration in the latter range, placing the play with Derby's, as Strange's became in September 1593 (Ferdinando Stanley, Lord Strange, became Earl of Derby following his brother's death that month).[10] It has also been noted that the closest connections in the Shakespeare sections are to *Richard III*, the Sonnets, and *Lucrece*, perhaps confirming 1593–4.

Much hinges on *Richard III*, which has proven notoriously tricky to date and place with a company, containing as it does flattering portraits of both Stanley, Earl of Derby, Strange's ancestor, and the Earl of Pembroke. It was either, as Manley and Maclean argue, for Strange's in 1592 and later revised for Pembroke's, or, as Wiggins suggests, begun for Pembroke's in 1593 and finished for Derby's, explaining the expanded Stanley material that way. Shakespeare could well have been hedging his bets with patronage in late 1592. Plague had shut the London theatres down from 23 June 1592, and Pembroke's were forced to tour, possibly going bust from the slender takings of provincial playing in summer 1593. Six months separate the authorship of *Shrew* and his likely beginning work on *Venus and Adonis*—the nondramatic comic poem that secured Henry Wriothesley, the Earl of Southampton's, private patronage in a time of theatrical dearth—in early 1593, offering a likely time frame for *Richard III*'s composition. If the play did come with him to the Chamberlain's in spring 1594, he had clearly had to shelve it during the long closures. The Chamberlain's is the only company associated with it, on the Q1 imprint of 1597, probably around 2–3 years after first performance as was normal, though Syme—who suggested the possibility that Pembroke's survived in 1593, continuing to own and perform the tetralogy until their eventual split in 1597—hypothesized it could have been a company assertion having just re-acquired it.[11] While Shakespeare most likely was with Derby's in late 1593, shortly before returning to Wriothesley with *Lucrece*, this study assumes his revision of *Edward III* as his only new work for them.

Marlowe's apparent lack of playwriting activities between 1589 and 1592 had for a long time left an odd, even mysterious, biographical gap, fuelling speculation about the extent of his covert lifestyle as a spy and forger. But it also gives a plausible time frame for him and Shakespeare to have worked together. According to Charles Nicholl, the only glimpse we get of Marlowe between *The Jew of Malta* and his arrest in Flushing for coining in early 1592 is a mention of him writing plays in a 'chamber' in mid-1591.[12] These could be lost plays; recognized Marlowe plays written earlier than we thought; or hitherto unrecognized contributions to plays we already recognize as being by someone else. According to a letter from the governor of Flushing of 26 January 1592, Marlowe had just been arrested and sent back to England 'to be tried', putting him in London a little over a month before the first recorded performance of *Harry VI*, of which the NOS assigns him a share. Until the *New Oxford Shakespeare's* high-profile assertion in 2016 that he co-wrote all of what became the *Henry VI* trilogy, his tally of two collaborative plays in seven had looked fairly unremarkable. Five in ten, on the other hand—perhaps even six in twelve, if the *Shrew* and *Edward III* ascriptions are right—looks unusually prolific for the early 1590s.[13] While long recognized as a mould-breaking and widely copied dramatist, Marlowe's influence on playwriting *practices* in the period has received less consideration. Stylistically, a wealth of data in the *Contention* plays all points in Marlowe's direction, but even impressionistically, the end-stopped intensity of his verse can be felt in the writing:

> Therefore to arms! And, father, do but think
> How sweet a thing it is to wear a crown,
> Within whose circuit is Elysium,
> And all that poets feign of bliss and joy.
> Why do we linger thus? I cannot rest

> Until the white rose that I wear be dyed
> Even in the luke-warm blood of Henry's heart.
> (*3 Henry VI*, 1.2.30–5)

The interplay here of idea, image, and syntax—a clear echo of *Tamburlaine Part 1*'s 'That perfect bliss and sole felicity, / The sweet fruition of an earthly crown' (2.7.28–9)—is so distinctly Marlovian as to suggest either rip-off, parody, or authorship, and stylometric testing by Hugh Craig and John Burrows on a range of linguistic features eliminates the candidacy of all other working dramatists in 1591.[14] The *Contention* plays were almost certainly written that year for Pembroke's by Marlowe, Shakespeare, and another unknown dramatist, revolutionizing collaborative playwriting in the process.

Collaboration: *Arden of Faversham* and *Henry VI*

If, as many attribution studies indicate, Shakespeare really is involved in *Arden of Faversham*, consistently dated 1590 or earlier, then his playwriting activities must pre-date Pembroke's. Wiggins suggests *Arden* 'may have been associated with members of Pembroke's' before its 1592 printing—which names neither company nor authors (see Figure 1)—but we cannot assume it to have been theirs; members of Pembroke's were previously members of other companies. Greene attests to Shakespeare's early career as an actor, but his beginnings as a dramatist must have involved writing a play either whole or in part for a company, with Strange's or the Admiral's the likeliest affiliation. It has been suggested, with the attrition rate for plays in the 1580s, that Shakespeare must have written even earlier lost works, though we cannot know that.[15] But the idea of authorly training on the *Contention* plays, as Greene tried to suggest, only really works if we assume Shakespeare had not written anything before them. The relative priority of *Arden* and *The Two Gentlemen of Verona*—which this study proposes were the first two plays on which he worked— is impossible to establish. Neither is in Henslowe, so apparently did not remain in the Strange's or Admiral's repertory if written for them. There is in fact no evidence for *Arden*'s ownership by any company, and *Two Gentlemen* only comes into the Chamberlain's/King's orbit with its appearance in the 1623 First Folio. *Two Gentlemen*, notoriously hard to date, seems very early even on impressionistic grounds, and

THE
LAMENTA=
BLE AND TRUE TRA-
GEDIE OF M. AR-
DEN OF FEVERSHAM
IN KENT.

Who was most wickedlye murdered, by
the meanes of his disloyall and wanton
wyfe, who for the loue she bare to one
Mosbie, hyred two desperat ruf-
fins Blackwill and Shakbag,
to kill him.

Wherin is shewed the great mal-
lice and discimulation of a wicked woman, the vnsatiable desire of filthie lust
and the shamefull end of all
murderers.

Jmprinted at London for Edward
White, dwelling at the lyttle North
dore of Paules Church at
the signe of the
Gun. 1592.

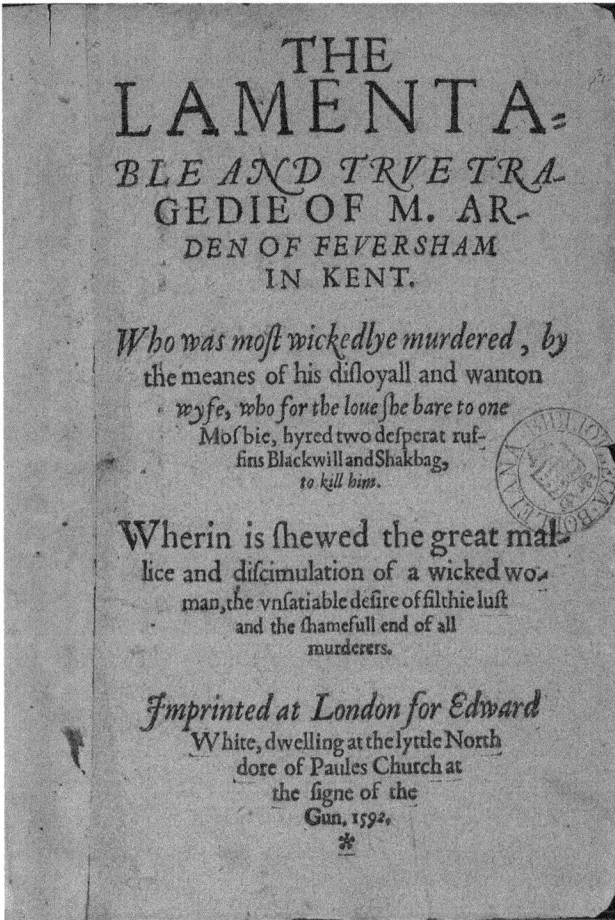

Figure 1 *Arden of Faversham*, Q1 (1592), Mal. 208 (3), title page. The earliest imprint of a play containing Shakespeare's writing. The Bodleian Libraries, University of Oxford www.digital.bodleian.ox.ac. uk Under a CC-BY-NC 4.0.

pause-pattern analysis of the verse links it closely to the other earliest works including the *Contention* plays, after which there seems no real room for it in Shakespeare's artistic chronology.[16] If it was his debut, it was solo-authored, precociously sharp, contiguous with 1580s' Lylian euphuistic comedy, and it got him noticed. The London theatre scene at the turn of the decade was a small world, and Shakespeare's nascent talent, combined with a pushy opportunism, would have quickly marked him out. As with *Venus and Adonis* and *Lucrece*, if comedy opened the door for him, he soon turned to 'graver labour', lighting on Holinshed for his tragedy of *Arden*, either paired with, or more probably seeking out, a collaborator—not so much about learning to write as about determined assimilation into a profession.

If, on the other hand, *Arden* came first, it was perhaps helped by an exceptional skill shown in early poetry writing—Francis Meres in 1598 first spoke of Shakespeare's 'sugared sonnets', modern scholarship dating his earliest efforts to the late 1580s—which carried over into acting work and/or script doctoring for the company. If Shakespeare was aiming to become a kind of informal in-house dramatist, the guidance of an experienced writer was perhaps prerequisite to the company trusting him with his first project. But the solo authorship of *Two Gentlemen*, and the fact that collaboration was not at this moment common in the professional theatres, suggests Shakespearean innovation more than regular practice. And if he was seeking to infiltrate a body of established writers and stamp a reputation as an impressive new talent among them, it is also notable he was not giving up his day job. This, then, was not so much about determined assimilation into the dramatist's profession, as about attempted realignment with his own company, carving a niche for himself as a writer with the security of a player's, and, ideally, a sharer's income.

Arden and *Two Gentlemen*, whichever way round they came, had proved Shakespeare really could write, and the formation of Pembroke's in May 1591 may even mark his beginning as a sharer, secured by his growing value as a proven actor–dramatist who could furnish the company, at the least, with a two-part planned historical epic with Marlowe and another. Early 1591 could then have been the planning, even composition phase for the first of the *Contention* plays. We cannot know if Marlowe saw in Shakespeare a reason to want to write plays again, or if Shakespeare went looking for him, but Shakespeare's work on the *Contention*s sees him as the main influence on an ambitious, in-house, collaborative venture, not infiltrative contributor to established writers' projects. Was he already helping to model, even drive the evolution of the business-minded model of collaborative repertory production that seems to have become a reliable, even 'normal', system for Henslowe by the late 1590s? Judging by his later authorial career, and the Chamberlain's company's otherwise scant records, it never became a main mode of commissioning for them, and Jowett has highlighted a calculated drive at individualism behind Shakespeare's early activities as actor seeking to turn playwright, stating that these 'acts of collaboration *enable* his acts of sole-authorship and are entirely necessary'.[17] *Arden* was, it seems, the pivotal work of his early career; a tactical use of collaboration launching a nearly two-year period of hugely successful, highly innovative, co-authored tragic writing. Shakespeare's rapid, determined rise, plus his decade-long project of adapting Holinshed—which he would soon use for something grander than histories of local murder—to the stage may suggest *Arden* began with him. And if he was using collaboration to become something more for himself, he seems to have seen his *Arden* collaborator as a prime mover in his ambitions.

That person is either someone we do not know, or someone we do whose dramatic work we do not. They may have been a more established dramatist, though Wiggins notes a theatrical naivety, casting doubt even on *Arden*'s status as a professional play.[18] Thomas Kyd has been the longest standing, most vigorously championed candidate as sole author in recent decades, with a concurrent theory refuting his presence at all in favour of an anonymous collaboration probably involving Shakespeare.[19] Thomas Watson is the most recently proposed collaborator in the latter scenario, Gary Taylor using the 62 lines of Watson's 'The Poet's Speech to Her Majesty', from the 1591 royal entertainment at Elvetham, as a control sample to make the case, though a rebuttal claiming statistical distortion quickly followed.[20] While Watson's plays are all lost, he is in some ways a more likely candidate than Kyd, or Marlowe, whose extant plays are a poor match.[21] Michael J. Hirrel has written of Watson's considerable influence on the drama, describing him as 'the most important playwright in English none of whose plays survive', and suggesting he 'may have been among the first to intermix comedy and tragedy in single plays'.[22] This is hugely relevant to *Arden*'s innovations, from the pitch-black humour of the bungling assassins Alice hires and their repeated failed attempts on Arden's life, to the terrible tragic shift when they finally succeed. Watson seems to have been forced into jobbing playwrighting having squandered his inheritance. His employer, William Cornwallis, wrote that 'twenty fictions and knaveries in a play' was his 'daily practise and his living'.[23] Watson was imprisoned for manslaughter from September 1589 to February 1590, defending Marlowe in a street fight, putting *Arden* later than that if 1590 is correct. Taylor notes similarities between the non-Shakespearean sections of *Arden* and the unidentified collaborator's sections in the *Contention*s, leaving open the possibility Watson is the common denominator, facilitating Shakespeare and Marlowe's co-authorship. Watson and Marlowe were demonstrably close; both were involved in government service abroad in the 1580s, and may have shared London lodgings in 1589. Marlowe repaid his life debt in acting as literary executor after Watson's death in late September 1592, around the same time the *Groatsworth* was entered in the Stationers' Register.[24] Like Greene, Watson lived as an inveterate rogue; though unlike him he may have seen an asset, not a rival, in a young Shakespeare.

Arden was unusual—visionary, even—in rooting itself in provincial, domestic, English history. Much tragedy we know of before it and up to the early Jacobean period deals with high politics of some kind, mainly classical subject matter. *A Warning for Fair Women* (1597) takes up the mantle, and some lost collaborative domestic tragedies can be seen in the diary, including Jonson and Dekker's *Page of Plymouth* and Haughton and Day's *Cox of Collumpton*, both 1599, suggesting a revival of interest around that time. Heywood's 1603 masterpiece *A Woman Killed with Kindness* was the pinnacle, inspiring a Jacobean wave, including Shakespeare-apocrypha regular *A Yorkshire Tragedy* (1605–6). But *Arden* seems a genuine archetype. It shuns classical allusion, its epilogue boasting proudly that 'no filèd points [classical affectations] are foisted in', though Catherine Richardson has noted 'a significant strand of classical views on love in the play' which might itself point towards the Ovid-inspired Watson.[25] Shakespeare's attributed share of Scenes 4–8 is about a fifth of the play, a block of five consecutive scenes, remarkably similar in dramatic function and scenic distribution to his NOS-assigned share in *2 Henry VI*. Scenes 1–3 comprise nearly a thousand lines, the same number again making up 9–19, while 4–8, though amounting to only 410 lines between them, are according to Richardson the place 'where action stops for its motivating emotions to be bodied forth'.[26] Taylor, citing David Edgar, has urged Shakespeare's relative lack of skill in exposition, suggesting he prospers best when focusing his attention not on openings but on 'scenes of intense conflict'.[27] Indeed, Richardson notes how the *Arden* collaborator deals with logistical complexities, freeing Shakespeare up to focus on 'a different concept of how language and gesture combine to advance characterization in performance'.[28] And in *Arden* and *2 Henry VI* Shakespeare is fulfilling this same function.

The NOS's first securely attributed Shakespeare scene in *2 Henry VI* features a hyperextended soliloquy for the Duke of York in which he plots rebellion, and a speech of powerful grief for the title character, immediately finding a new level of dramatic urgency. Henry's powerlessness to intercede in his innocent uncle's murder is also figured through metaphorical imagery characteristic of Shakespeare's part in these plays:

> And as the butcher takes away the calf
> And binds the wretch, and beats it when it
>   strays,
> Bearing it to the bloody slaughter-house,
> Even so remorseless have they borne him
>   hence;
> And as the dam runs lowing up and down,
> Looking the way her harmless young one went,
> And can do nought but wail her darling's loss,
> Even so myself bewails good Gloucester's case
> With sad unhelpful tears, and with dimmed
>   eyes
> Look after him and cannot do him good,
> So mighty are his vowèd enemies.
> His fortunes I will weep; and, 'twixt each groan
> Say 'Who's a traitor? Gloucester he is none.'
>   (3.1.198–222)

Shakespeare shows an unusual level of ambition in his contribution, both in overt displays of rhetorical and dramaturgical power, and in the 'disruption' that is 'substantially grounded on his feminization of the actions of history'.[29] His value as a collaborator who could handle a play's dramatic core with potent originality may in part have lain in what his co-authors perceived as a particular interest and skill in writing women's parts, something shown throughout his early work. It has been suggested that Peele's predilection for female-warrior characters—Tamora in *Titus*, and the Queen in *Edward I* in early 1591—influenced Shakespeare's portrayal of Margaret. Yet the 1593 quarto of *Edward I* seems to be a revised text, clumsily expanding the Queen Eleanor material, most likely to exploit the success of powerful queen roles in the wake of the *Henrys*, suggesting the influence may go the other way.[30] Marlowe, across the first two acts of *2 Henry VI*, writes four speeches of 20 lines or more: three for male characters, and one 23-line speech for Margaret. The unknown collaborator pens a 30-line lament for the Duchess of Gloucester on her way to prison for her part in the Hume rebellion, along with one other speech of 21 lines for Hume himself. But in Shakespeare's Act 3 alone there are seven such speeches, of which Margaret is given two, notably length-ier and weightier—one of 38 and one of 49 lines—than anything seen in her role, and in most of the male roles, up to that point.[31] Only York, the play's leading part, has had a speech approaching 40+ lines, Shakespeare's two for Margaret showing the complexity in female characterization defining his contribution. Alice is also an unusually large role for a boy actor, around 600 lines, against the 200–300 aver-age for apprentice actors in early 1590s' professional companies, a major part of its demands coming in the so-called 'quarrel' scene 8 penned by Shakespeare, including the single longest speech for the character in the play at 29 lines. A further symmetry of dramatic situation in Shakespeare's writing across the two plays lies in the rela-tionship between Margaret—*Contention*'s second-longest role—and Suffolk, lost in obsession, making a cuckold and tragic figure of Henry as Alice does Arden:

> QUEEN . . .   O, could this kiss be printed in thy hand,
> That thou mightst think upon these, by the seal,
> Through whom a thousand sighs are breathed for
>   thee.
> So, get thee gone, that I may know my grief;
> 'Tis but surmised whiles thou art standing by,
> As one that surfeits thinking on a want.
> I will repeal thee or, be well assured,
> Adventure to be banishèd myself.
> And banishèd I am, if but from thee.
>
> (*2 Henry VI*, 3.3.329-37)

ALICE ...   Nay, hear me speak, Mosby, a word or two;
I'll bite my tongue if it speak bitterly.
Look on me, Mosby, or I'll kill myself;
Nothing shall hide me from thy stormy look.
If thou cry war, there is no peace for me.

(*Arden*, 8.109–13)

Randall Martin established that *Contention* and *Richard Duke of York*, and their Folio counterparts, *2* and *3 Henry VI*, were all based on lost versions, of which the former are imperfect reports, and the latter Shakespearean revisions, though Jowett has since refined the argument to take in original collaboration, which Martin did not believe.[32] Martin's other major contribution was in identifying the nature and sequence of revision based on source use—the 1595 octavo of *Richard Duke of York* (O) indebted to Edward Hall's chronicle account, with unique and revised passages in *3 Henry VI* (F) clearly following Holinshed's—and suggesting Shakespeare revised the plays when they came with him to the newly formed Chamberlain's in 1594. The revisions forge more coherent links with *Richard III*, reworking elements of Margaret's role in *Part 3*—including in scenes otherwise attributed to Marlowe—pertaining especially to her as mother, linking more strongly with her bereavement in the sequent play.[33] And Richard was the major element of which Shakespeare took control in *Part 3*; again, his focus was on the play's middle, the character's famous soliloquy at the close of Act 3 a sign of the character's dramatic centrality beginning to take precedence over matters of historical narrative. It marks a key moment of transition for the audience's understanding of Richard's 'authentic' self, and the development of the tragedy away from a dynastic scale to the more intensely personal psychodrama, with Richard and Henry at the centre, that it becomes. In his revisions Shakespeare was thinking both of the internal dynamics of the play and of the wider narrative sequence as a whole, though it was the audacious, bold, virtuoso mapping of Richard's impulses that had also most defined his great achievement as an emergent playwriting voice in 1591.

His *Arden* contribution is similarly interested in psychological worlds within worlds—pauses, almost, from dramatic action—that are strong enrichments of character. Arden's Scene 6 speech relating a dream to Franklin anticipates Clarence's in *Richard III* in its divination of death, rich in the images of hunting, predation, and butchery that suffuse both *Richard III* and Shakespeare's writing in the *Henry*s, their final lines extremely similar in language and idea:

> This night I dreamed that, being in a park,
> A toil was pitched to overthrow the deer,
> And I upon a little rising hill
> Stood whistly watching for the herd's approach.
> Even there methoughts a gentle slumber took me
> And summoned all my parts to sweet repose;
> But in the pleasure of this golden rest
> An ill-thewed for'ster had removed the toil
> And rounded me with that beguiling snare
> Which late, methought, was pitched to cast the deer.
> With that he blew an evil-sounding horn,
> And at the noise another herdman came
> With falchion drawn, and bent it at my breast,
> Crying aloud, 'Thou art the game we seek.'
> With this I waked, and trembled every joint
> Like one obscurèd in a little bush
> That sees a lion foraging about,
> And, when the dreadful forest king is gone,
> He pries about with timorous suspèct
> Throughout the thorny casements of the brake,
> And will not think his person dangerless,
> But quakes and shivers, though the cause be gone.
> So, trust me, Franklin, when I did awake,
> I stood in doubt whether I waked or no,
> Such great impression took this fond surprise.   (6.6–30)

Michael's speech in Scene 4 has a similar tonal intensity, and the set piece between Alice and Mosby in Scene 8 again develops interiority through a secretive adulterous complicity, further fragmented by a mistrust even within that relationship:

> ALICE   It is not love that loves to murder love.
> MOSBY   How mean you that?
> ALICE   Thou know'st how dearly Arden lovèd me.
> MOSBY   And then?

ALICE   And then—conceal the rest, for 'tis too bad,
Lest that my words be carried with the wind
And published in the world, to both our shames.
I pray thee, Mosby, let our springtime wither;
Our harvest else will yield but loathsome weeds.
Forget, I pray thee, what hath passed betwixt us,
For now I blush and tremble at the thoughts.
MOSBY   What, are you changed?

(8.58–69)

If Shakespeare was a precocious talent who helped mastermind an experimental project redefining the interplay between private and national contexts in English tragic-history writing, he in turn benefited from the professional fast-tracking of collaboration, aggressively using its lessons and opportunities to ascend. We see Shakespeare, who Taylor notes 'did not write the opening scenes of any of his Elizabethan collaborations', most clearly in Act 3 of *2 Henry VI*, and might suppose a pecking order, the senior partner leading— just as Shakespeare speaks first in his two extant collaborations with Fletcher—the junior employed to fill gaps in the middle.[34] Yet while Marlowe began both parts, it is still entirely possible, given the literal and figurative centrality of Shakespeare's contribution, that he initiated the subject matter. Marlowe had not written an English history play before, though a serious, focused use of chronicle material defines both dramatists' subsequent approaches to the genre. These were by no means the first plays to use chronicle material: the Queen's Men's playwrights of the 1580s used Holinshed, Hall, and Stowe on such plays as *The Famous Victories of Henry V*, *The Troublesome Reign of King John*, and *The True Tragedy of Richard III*, and, post-Armada, a slew of plays on English history, mainly 'pleasant' histories, appeared in the form of comedies such as *Fair Em, the Miller's Daughter of Manchester*, *James IV*, *Edward I*, and *George a Green, the Pinner of Wakefield*. But in the *Contention* plays, the English history play becomes something more.[35] They seem to represent the biggest single collaborative venture of the early theatres in scale—*Contention* has more than 60 speaking parts, against the 30–40 that had been more common for earlier history plays—and authorial organization. They seem to be the first plays for commercial performance written by more than two dramatists. Whoever they were, if indeed they are the same person, the anonymous collaborator's parts here and in *Arden* are both substantial and original. If it is Watson, personal associations may help explain Marlowe's presence in the *Contentions*. Yet it is also possible Marlowe saw a particular talent in Shakespeare and wanted to work with him to help him create something genuinely new, requiring a coherent, planned, and massively ambitious approach to the creative opportunities of collaborative authorship.

Laurie Maguire lists 41 'bad' quartos from the early theatres. Of the 20 printed in the 1590s, most of which display very limited textual 'badness', only three seem manifestly wholesale corrupt transmissions—a view Maguire did not share—patched together by apparently spurious means for the purposes of sale: *Contention*, *The Taming of a Shrew*, and *Richard Duke of York*. *A Shrew* (1594), which contains many textual borrowings from Marlowe's plays, and *Richard Duke of York* also bore ascriptions to Pembroke's Men, suggesting both commercially attractive performance associations, and a supply and demand problem with the company's authorized versions.[36] Readers apparently wanted them, though the company—or perhaps the remnants of it—did not want to supply them. Q1 *Contention* (1594), shown in Figure 2, seems to be the first such corrupt text of a play to be printed from the period of the early professional theatres, with several garbled passages, substantially different staging information, and over 400 lines not found in the more authoritative Folio *2 Henry VI*.[37] *Richard Duke of York* likewise has many speeches with no equivalent in the collaborative play preserved in F, at times even borrowing from itself in ways that suggest patching by a non-authorial agent; someone, presumably the same person, also worked in other material including lines from George Peele's *The Battle of Alcazar* (1588).[38] Neither imprint bears Shakespeare's name, though this unique publishing phenomenon at this early stage in his career seems perhaps less about his authorial involvement as about the plays' exceptional popularity.

The collaborative venture that was the *Contention* plays had an immediate, transformative impact, Greene's barbed commentary revealing Shakespeare's writing as a major force in that. By *Part 3* it is the dominant contribution, in length, overall control, and, the *Groatsworth* backhandedly suggests, artistic distinction. If

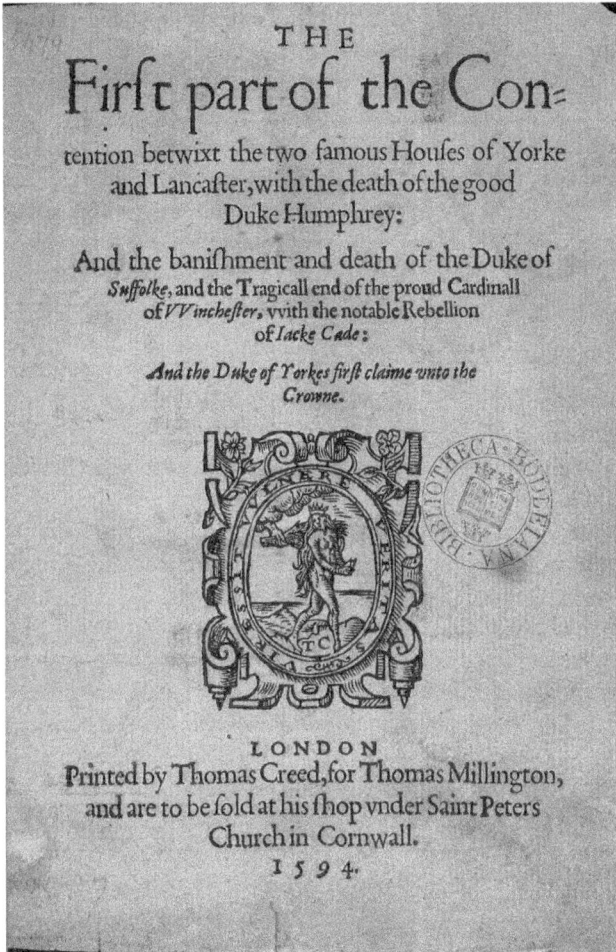

THE

Firſt part of the Con=

tention betwixt the two famous Houſes of Yorke
and Lancaſter, with the death of the good
Duke Humphrey:

And the baniſhment and death of the Duke of
Suffolke, and the Tragicall end of the proud Cardinall
of *VVincheſter*, vvith the notable Rebellion
of *Iacke Cade*:

*And the Duke of Yorkes firſt claime vnto the
Crowne.*

LONDON
Printed by Thomas Creed, for Thomas Millington,
and are to be ſold at his ſhop vnder Saint Peters
Church in Cornwall.
1 5 9 4.

Figure 2 *The First Part of the Contention*, Q1 (1594), Bodleian, Arch. G e.17, title page. The first imprint of which we know of a corruptly transmitted text of a play from the early professional theatres. The Bodleian Libraries, University of Oxford www.digital.bodleian.ox.ac.uk under a CC-BY-NC 4.0.

Shakespeare was seeking even at this early stage to transcend the collaborative associations from which he was benefiting, *Richard III* then looks not so much an unplanned consequence of the collaborative history-play writing that offered his first major opportunities, as a teleological aim from early in the process, especially if it was written in late 1592 when Marlowe was still alive. But the carefully cultivated, ambitiously pursued collaborative associations of Shakespeare's earliest work radically alter our sense of his formation as a dramatist, and of his influence on authorial practices in the professional theatres.

Co-authorship: *Titus, Edward III, 1 Henry VI*

Shakespeare may have been done with direct collaboration after *Part 3*. *Titus Andronicus*, it seems, began with George Peele, modern comparative stylistic and stylometric analysis giving him the first act and beginning of the second.[39] Chapter 2 has noted plays bought by companies on the strength of an opening act, and it is possible Peele did the same, offering about 3 sheets' worth (657 lines) to Pembroke's, with Shakespeare tasked with finishing it off, which he did over the remaining 1,671 lines. It may have been a planned collaboration, though the authorial pattern of unbroken, consecutive stints differs markedly from Shakespeare's earlier partnerships. J. C. Maxwell, in refuting collaboration in the play, which he dated 1589–90, argued Peele, an established dramatist, would not have taken or been given the subordinate role with a young Shakespeare. But if Wiggins is right about the title-page evidence, and the play began with Pembroke's, then late 1591–early 1592 seems likelier, and the power dynamic weighted towards Shakespeare, now a more successful writer both in popularity and financial arrangement. Peele seems to have been on the way down and out of playwriting, with *Titus* certainly among his last writing for the stage. He may simply have sold the act, perhaps wanting to move on to *The Old Wife's Tale*, which he wrote solus for the Queen's in early 1592. Or the project may have been taken away from him. With the younger man so much in the ascendancy, the real potential the company may have seen in the work was in where Shakespeare might take it. Given Peele's struggles, which Greene would document later that year, as a takeover it seems opportunistically ruthless.

Peele's influence over Shakespeare's part is strong. He not only develops the private, insular revenge narrative; invents the characters of Aaron, Tamora, Chiron, and Demetrius; and, in 2.1 and 2.2, the plot mechanism of the hunt in which Lavinia will be raped and mutilated, but his 'high-level classical education' was also 'responsible for the play's ingenious syncretism'; that is, its seamless merging of different political cultures within Roman history.[40] Brian Vickers details Peele's part as a 'cross-section of a thousand years of Roman history' drawn from minor historians such as Herodian, with further use made of literary sources in Livy and Virgil, for, among other things, the unhistorical Roman practice of human sacrifice initiating the cycle of bloodshed.[41] It is a fictive vision of late imperial decadence, Saturninus and Bassianus—the names drawn from Herodian—torn between hereditary and elective monarchy, the threatening Goths symbolic of 'all the enemies of Rome'.[42] The play can more profitably be thought of as classical revenge fantasy than the 'Roman' works in which Shakespeare lucidly figures precise historical fault lines, from the Livy-indebted overthrow of the Tarquins by the early Republic's founders in *Lucrece*, to the move from Republic to empire of his later Plutarchan tragedies, *Julius Caesar* and *Antony and Cleopatra*.

Put another way, *Titus* is the Shakespearean tragedy most *like* a classical tragedy. Shakespeare bases his section not on historical account but on his favourite Roman writer, Ovid, though clearly led by Peele, who is first to invoke Ovidian carnage through the myth of Hecuba and Polymester at 1.1.139–41, setting the fantastical political parameters and revenge motif from a mishmash of chronicle and poetic source. From this, Shakespeare took the theme of mythic transformation made flesh to an extreme tragic bourn, not seen anywhere in his sole-authored work, refiguring the Ovidian trope of raped women turning into birds, animals, or trees as a violent, real-world mimesis. Yet while the play has been noted as a foundation for much in later Shakespeare, from the fascination with Ovid to the violence of Gloucester's blinding, it is nonetheless Peele's imaginative framing enabling the bizarre, bloody excess attempted here.

While no single main source can be identified, *Titus*, unlike *Arden*, positively feasts on classical allusion. Ovid's *Metamorphoses* supplies the tale of Procne and Philomela, in which Tereus and Procne's son is

killed, boiled, and fed to the father, while Seneca's *Thyestes*, in which
Thyestes' two sons are killed by his brother, Atreus, and served up
for the father to eat, is another intellectual source. Latin tags from
Senecan tragedy, a practice well exemplified by Kyd, appear in both
authors' sections, and Colin Burrow has written of the resemblance
of the hunt that opens Peele's 2.2 to the beginning of *Hippolytus*,
both aesthetically, and in the prefiguration of destructive carnality it
summons.[43] Burrow further notes that the apparently benign natural world as a space for sexual violence is a common Ovidian theme
(Seneca himself was heavily influenced by Ovid). Peele also evokes
Virgil in the naming of Lavinia, Aeneas' chaste bride-to-be at the
foundation of Rome's imperial history, though the spectre is raised
precisely to effect haunting contrasts, and Virgilian tropes of suffering have been seen in Shakespeare's language in the play, as formative
as Ovid on its ideation.[44] Livy's tale of the rape of Lucrece, which
Shakespeare was to rework at much greater length within a couple of
years, helps further feed the play's classical, intertextual voracity, and
Shakespeare seems to be alluding also to *The Spanish Tragedy* in the
line Titus speaks to his mutilated daughter:

> Or shall we bite our tongues, and in dumb shows
> Pass the remainder of our hateful days?
>
> (3.1.131–2)

Kyd's masterwork ends with Hieronimo biting out his own tongue
when grief and revenge become unbearable and inexpressible, and
Lukas Erne has also pointed out how *Titus* follows closely *The Spanish Tragedy*'s structure.[45] *Titus* has been long dismissed as a vulgar,
unworthy part of Shakespeare's juvenilia, yet there is more innovation in its bending and shaping of disparate, poetic source material,
more formal experimentation in its black-comedy hybridity than such
judgements comprehend. Though an out-of-time fantasia—reflected
even on the micro level in semi-abstract moments of temporal suspension, like Marcus' lengthy soliloquy as he contemplates Lavinia's
rape—its focus is powerfully on both the expressiveness and inex-
pressiveness of poetic language in the face of the kind of horrors
the stage had not yet attempted. In a dizzying moment of language figuring its own violent loss as elemental power swallowing

the sense, Titus allows his and Lavinia's desperate predicament to consume him:

> If there were reason for these miseries,
> Then into limits could I bind my woes.
> When heaven doth weep, doth not the earth
>   o'erflow?
> If the winds rage, doth not the sea wax mad,
> Threat'ning the welkin with his big-swoll'n face?
> And wilt thou have a reason for this coil?
> I am the sea. Hark how her sighs doth blow.
> She is the weeping welkin, I the earth.
> Then must my sea be movèd with her sighs,
> Then must my earth with her continual tears
> Become a deluge overflowed and drowned.
>   (3.1.218–28)

The play takes us beyond conventional expression to the bodily rhetoric that must take over when words fail or are denied us, through Lavinia—Shakespeare's other early tragic heroine, her somatic reactive presence the play's starkest dramaturgical experiment—and through Titus' laughter at the limit of his pain. And just as both are in their various ways metamorphosed, classical generic boundaries are perverted by a savage comedy that seeps in from all sides to make a monster of the play. Yet Shakespeare also crafts some of the most impressive expressions of grief and empathetic suffering he ever wrote, and certainly that had been heard on any English stage by 1592. He began to engage in a career-long preoccupation with finding practical, human, stageable actions as ways of dramatizing Ovidian moments of transformation, rooting them in the psyche, the acting out of lived experience, decisions to act and react. Such ideas are occasionally present in direct allusion and reference—even in the appearance of the *Metamorphoses* on stage in 4.1—but they are also embedded in the very warp and weft of dramatic action and speech, in dialogic and performative grief, human mutability in the face of pitiless or arbitrary cosmic forces and worldly mechanisms of power and justice. We see the principles that drive and define this strange, deeply poignant, Ovidian black comedy repeated in Shakespeare's evolving work on the changes wrought on individual inner lives by powerful emotional forces. Yet the play's tone is something he never tried to recreate, in many ways because it is so rooted in its early 1590s' moment, in satirical dialogue with the excessive blood-and-thunder tragedy all around it. And, more significantly, because it was so uniquely rooted in the artistic vision of its co-author.

After *Titus*, early Shakespearean co-authorship falls markedly away. His additions to *Edward III* around eighteen months later were mainly to the subplot scenes involving the Countess of Salisbury, at 1.2.90–627 and 2.1. Proudfoot and Bennett suggest that Shakespeare's work here was almost certainly replacing lost material by an unknown author, and this book agrees with other studies identifying Shakespeare's authorship of 4.4 as a further feature of his overall reworking. As with *Arden*, the Countess scenes feature a lengthy, disturbing dialogue between a male and female character, that, impressionistically, can feel less like Shakespeare than the data suggest, though consistent with his writing of strong female roles and charged male–female dialogue in his early work. A seemingly un-Shakespearean feature is the use of 'pleasant' historical source material in William Painter's *Palace of Pleasure*, though Jean Froissart's *Chronicles*, which Shakespeare used in his account of Richard II's deposition, gives details. The scene 4.4 from the martial main plot seems richer in characteristic technique, imagery, and idea; its treatment of persuasion renewing hope, for example, anticipates ideas and stylistic flourishes in *Henry V* :

> He that hath far to go, tells it by miles;
> If he should tell the steps, it kills his heart.
> The drops are infinite that make a flood,
> And yet thou know'st we call it but a rain.
> There is but one France, and one king of France,
> That France hath no more kings, and that same
>   king
> Hath but the puissant legion of one king.
> And we have one, then apprehend no odds,
> For one to one, is fair equality.   (4.4.57–65)

The Countess scenes draw complex connections between literalized Petrarchan metaphors of love as siege, the writing of poetry, and its empty devices—there is even an allusion to the 'many pens' memorializing Lucrece's tale, another early work depicting sexual assault,

on which Shakespeare may already have been working—and authorial collaboration. Shakespeare had already dramatized co-authorship
as linked to sexual violence in *Titus*, Lavinia writing 'stuprum Chiron
Demetrius' in the sand, prompted by both her father and uncle and
the onstage Ovidian source she references, yet co-authorship there
was crucially and necessarily singular.[46] Marcus and Titus supply the
means, but are unable to write, share, or fathom what she alone knows.
In *Edward III* the King's letter-writing, for which he suborns Lodowick, highlights 'a dramatic trope of invention, or rather a temporary
crisis of invention, and of the capacity for rhetorical persuasion, both
of which are metonymies for playwriting'.[47] It is also a depiction of
nondramatic collaborative writing within the context of a collaboratively written drama, where again co-authorship, in practical terms, is
single authorship: Edward merely supplies the need, and Lodowick
the labour and invention. What was explored in *Titus* for its terrible
poignancy is arguably here reconfigured as a satirical metacommentary on a mode of working that, for Shakespeare, had by then served
its purpose.

If May 1594 was the moment of his *Henry VI* revisions, the final
act of co-authorship of his early career, it was likely brought about
by the commercial impetus for the Chamberlain's to stage all three
parts and his debuting *Richard III* together as a sequence. His work
on *Part 1*—presumably acquired from Derby's—involved some bol-
stering of the Act 4 military plot, as with *Edward III*, and the addition
of the famous Act 2 'Temple Garden' or 'rose-plucking' scene, deftly
bringing the otherwise fantastical, French-obsessed prequel in line
with the English domestic blood-feud underlying Henry's, and England's, tragedy, in the two-part epic he had co-created. Shakespeare
was both stamping his authority on the plays in revision and presenting himself as a powerfully original sole-authorial voice. In *Richard
III* he began to construct drama around a physically and imaginatively
dominant central figure, an assertion of intent to find new possibil-
ities in writing for a main actor in a structural method common to
his later tragedies—*Titus* and the *Henrys* are far more democratic in
their character distribution. It was the only play of the first tetralogy
he wrote alone, a watershed moment in the culmination of a collaborative sequence in sole-authorship. But the theatres were closed when
it came. Shakespeare's autonomy as a dramatist, ironically, was most
secured away from the stage.

The only surviving instances of Shakespeare editorializing are two early statements about creativity. His dedications to Henry Wriothesley in *Venus and Adonis* and *Lucrece*—reproduced in any modern edition—frame individual authorship within a model of private bequest, declaring love and duty to a patron as both prime motivation for the work and the reason for its quality. Such disingenuous attempts to downplay his role and distance himself from commerce were unsustainable—the poems were now being sold within the 'marketplace of print', and the signed dedications are themselves statements of proprietary authorship.[48] *Venus* was the first publication to name Shakespeare as an author, it and *Lucrece* the only printed examples of his solo authorship until *Richard III* was published in 1597.[49] Before that, only uncredited collaborations in *Arden*, *Contention*, *Titus*, *Richard, Duke of York*, and *Edward III* (printed 1596) were in circulation. But *Venus*, not owned by a theatre company, was the first publication over which Shakespeare had control. It was printed by his boyhood Stratford friend, Richard Field, a London stationer known for careful, prestige work, and, Jowett argues, can be understood in part as a rejoinder to the pamphlet satires of the early 1590s, a transient, sensationalist milieu of literary culture in which Nashe, Chettle, and Greene were major protagonists.[50] Though lacking prestige, their works nonetheless traded on distinctive authorial identities, inimical to sharing or collaboration, and Greene's *Groatsworth* had directed scorn at Shakespeare the actor-collaborator a few months earlier. But now Shakespeare was firing back. Of his early work, only *Arden* had perhaps been published while Greene was still alive, the *Henry*s' success still solely the preserve of the stage. With *Venus* and *Lucrece*, he became a name in print. Though they likewise took the form of cheap quartos promoting individual authorship, they were also stunning, audaciously brilliant artworks; even had Greene still been alive to offer a retort, it is clear he was being left behind. The work he would have needed to produce to remain a serious rival to Shakespeare would have been beyond him.

It is worth noting that Shakespeare's name appears on the title page of neither publication—another way in which he stands aloof— though that did not stop it getting around. When the theatres reopened in 1594, he was a famous poet, nobly connected and wildly popular in print; if he was a tried-and-trusted dramatist before the closure, growing in reputation and even starting to outshine those with whom he had shared, everything was different now. There are seven acts of dramatic co-authorship in the first four years of Shakespeare's career, and seven more over the remaining nineteen. From 1594 he began writing consistently alone, within and for his new company. It would be another twelve years before he would write another play in full, direct collaboration. But whatever associations it now held for him, and however he may have sought to dissociate himself from the practice, there was something particularly calculated, needful, and indeed revolutionizing, about his earliest collaborative writing for the public stage.

Shakespeare: 1599, 1603–6

Heywood and Revision: *The Spanish Tragedy* and *Sir Thomas More*

It is perhaps a strange feature of this book in general that it deals
so entirely in less familiar Shakespeare. In more familiar terms, then,
from the time he became a Chamberlain's man to his collaboration
with Middleton on *Timon of Athens* in 1606, he, unaided, wrote *The
Comedy of Errors, Love's Labour's Lost, Romeo and Juliet, Richard II,
A Midsummer Night's Dream, Love's Labour's Won (?), King John, The
Merchant of Venice, 1 Henry IV, The Merry Wives of Windsor, 2 Henry
IV, Much Ado About Nothing, Henry V, Julius Caesar, As You Like It,
Hamlet, Twelfth Night, Troilus and Cressida, Measure for Measure, Othello, All's Well that Ends Well,* and *King Lear.* Over twelve years it seems
Shakespeare chose, and managed, to work entirely alone. But through
consolidated scholarly analyses, we are beginning to see a new collaborative relationship emerging within that run of work. Henslowe's
diary shows 1598–1604 as a time of intensely, even predominantly
collaborative playwriting practices among the Admiral's and Worcester's companies, while Shakespeare, with the Chamberlain's, had gone
the other way. But if he sat down, sometime around 1599, to work
on revisions to *The Spanish Tragedy* with Thomas Heywood, it was the
first time he had worked actively with another dramatist since *Richard
Duke of York* in 1591.

Claims for Shakespeare's authorship of the five passages that first
appeared in the 1602 Q4 imprint of *The Spanish Tragedy*, going back
to Coleridge in 1833, have only gained serious traction since Warren
Stevenson's work in the 1960s, followed by Hugh Craig's in the 1990s,

Shakespeare and Collaborative Writing. Will Sharpe, Oxford University Press. © Will Sharpe (2023).
DOI: 10.1093/oso/9780198819639.003.0005

and Craig, Brian Vickers, Douglas Bruster, John V. Nance, and Gary
Taylor's over the last decade. The passages are:

> Addition 1: 54 lines, inserted between 2.5.45 and 46
> Addition 2: 11 lines, between 3.2.64 and 66, replacing 3.2.65 and part
> of 66
> Addition 3: 47 lines, between 3.11.1 and 2
> Addition 4: 160 lines, at start of 3.13
> Addition 5: 49 lines, replaces 4.4.166–87, retaining some lines from Kyd's
> original text.

Stevenson, Craig, Vickers, and Bruster have given all five to Shakespeare, while the Arden editors ventured only that there are 'sufficient
grounds to link the author of the fourth addition with Shakespeare'.[1]
Stylistic and tonal differences across them have long been noted, and
while Taylor and Nance allow the 'painter's part' in Addition 4 as
Shakespeare's, Taylor argues for Heywood's authorship of Addition
1, with further investigation needed for the rest.[2] Heywood is most
notable for picking up on the pioneering work of the *Arden of Faversham* playwrights in his masterpiece, *A Woman Killed with Kindness*,
for Worcester's Men in the early months of 1603, lifting the genre
of domestic tragedy to its highest heights, and possibly influenc-
ing Shakespeare's *Measure for Measure*.[3] Heywood's *Apology for Actors*
(1612)—incidentally our only contemporary source of knowledge for
Thomas Kyd's authorship of *The Spanish Tragedy*—supplies one of the
very few records we have of Shakespeare reacting privately to something, perhaps suggesting some degree of intimacy.[4] His *Age* plays also
have relationships with Shakespeare's late plays, *The Golden Age* (1611)
featuring a giant eagle like the one in *Cymbeline* (1610), perhaps
showing them working 'together' in intertextual homage, even sharing ideas or props. A sequence of staged battles in *Coriolanus* seems
influenced by *1 Edward IV* (1599), usually attributed to Heywood,
and he may also have contributed to the text we know as Q1 *Hamlet*
(1603), though in that instance almost certainly without Shakespeare's
approval.[5]

The *Spanish Tragedy* additions mainly focus on the play's protagonist Hieronimo's madness: the first imbues the moment he finds his

son Horatio's hanged body with a powerfully irrational denial absent from Kyd's original scene, taken up by the second's short dialogic interjection in which his behaviour becomes aggressively cryptic, and in which dramatic and psychological complexity are explored with extraordinary economy. The repeated collocation 'a thing of nothing' (Add. II, 9–11) echoes Hamlet's obfuscatory wording (3.5.22–4), but here conveys absurd understatement in its yoking of opposites, the triviality of a son's murder:

> LORENZO   How now, Hieronimo?
> HIERONIMO   In troth, my lord, it is a thing of nothing,
> The murder of a son, or so—
> A thing of nothing, my lord.   (Add. 2, 8–11)

The mood is developed through Additions 3 and 4, the former a speech meditating on the grief of losing a child, hinting at the private revenge Hieronimo, official arbiter of justice as Marshal of Spain, will enact:

> Well, heaven is heaven still,
> And there is Nemesis and Furies,
> And things called whips,
> And they sometimes do meet with murderers.
> They do not always 'scape, that's some comfort.
>   (Add. 3, 39–43)

Addition 4 is a dialogue of some 180 lines in which Hieronimo challenges a painter, another bereft father petitioning for justice, to capture impossible images of abstract suffering. Addition 5 sees Hieronimo exulting in his revenge, joining up with Kyd's infamous tragic motif of the character's self-muting self-mutilation in biting out his tongue. Shakespeare, as in *Titus* and *Edward III*, again links imagery of writing with violence, expanding the moment in Kyd's play where Hieronimo uses a penknife, an author's tool, to kill the Duke and himself, furthering the association of these ideas in his co-authored work. By the late 1590s, late 1580s' plays like *The Spanish Tragedy* were coming to be associated with antiquated bombast, and the additions make Hieronimo a more psychologically interesting character than the admittedly rhetorically interesting one of the substrate text. But if Taylor is right, the emphasis of Shakespeare's reworking takes its cue from Heywood's. Complex, difficult evidence surrounds the play's early auspices and performance history, as does that linking it to Shakespeare's company by the turn of the century.[6] Burbage's 1619 epitaph explicitly credits him with having played Hieronimo, and the 1601 satire *The Second Return From Parnassus* has him speak some of Hieronimo's lines, so the 1602 text may have been the acting version of the Chamberlain's company, expanded for its star actor. John Marston's *Antonio and Mellida*, dated autumn 1599 by Wiggins, parodies the so-called 'Painter' scene of the fourth addition, providing a further suggestion of a *terminus ad quem*. The play seems likely, though, from 1587 to 1597 to have gone from the Admiral's, to Strange's, to the Chamberlain's. If all the additions were indeed part of a single phase of revision, Heywood—contracted as an actor with Henslowe in early 1599, and writing for the Admiral's as a free-lance dramatist—was supplying another company in working with Shakespeare here. And Shakespeare was to pay back in kind.

When he made small-scale revisions to *Sir Thomas More* in c.1603–4 as part of a wider coordinated project in which Heywood was heavily involved, the two worked demonstrably closely together on it. The *More* revisions are significant as the only dramatic writing Shakespeare ever contributed for a different company after 1594, his involvement in the project a cause of long-standing bewilder-ment among scholars, especially considering its deep controversy. But Heywood's position as shareholder in Worcester's, the company most likely attempting to revise it, may help explain things. Hey-wood was the other main actor–sharer–dramatist on the London scene by then—around the same time Shakespeare was working on *Measure*, his first full play as a King's man—aligned more closely with Shakespeare's working practices than almost any other play-wright. It seems possible that as a small sect within the profession the two were mutual admirers, and again that Shakespeare's part in the *More* revision may have been a favour among friends. Shakespeare was not collaboratively authoring plays with Heywood, but work-ing semi-collaboratively on sets of additions and revisions to them. Nonetheless, these two projects represent significant deviations from what had become a deeply entrenched authorial *modus operandi*, even deviating from Shakespeare's earliest practices as a collaborator. They most resemble his revisions on *Edward III* and *1 Henry VI*, perhaps reflecting Heywood, 'prolific as bit-writer', in impetus and rationale.[7] But Heywood looks like Shakespeare's closest writing partner at either end of a five-year period not usually associated with Shakespearean co-authorship.

Sir Thomas More tells the story of the famous Catholic martyr, rising from his position as Sheriff of London to the Lord Chancellorship of England through exceptional service in quelling the 1517 'ill May Day' riots which Shakespeare's main contribution dramatizes.[8] Like all plays, it was submitted for approval, but unlike most we know of, it had fallen seriously foul of the Master of the Revels Edmund Tilney's criteria for acceptance, with major revision ordered before it could be staged. The manuscript in which the play survives comprises twenty folio leaves of paper, two more if we include its vellum wrapper, and contains the writing of Anthony Munday (S), Henry Chettle (A), Thomas Heywood (B), an as-yet-unidentified scribe (C), William Shakespeare (D), Thomas Dekker (E), and Tilney himself.[9] As far as we can tell, A, B, C, D, and E's contributions were made three to four years after Anthony Munday, almost certainly the main author, prepared the Original Text (OT) which Tilney marked up when it was submitted for licensing.[10] The play partakes in a distinct Admiral's sub-specialism of plays about Henry VIII's chancellors from *c.*1600 to 1601, many involving Chettle and Munday, Chettle's potential co-authorship of the OT perhaps suggesting his instigation of revision.[11] Worcester's came onto Henslowe's books mid-1602, when they moved into the Rose, with some Admiral's plays passing over into their repertory. Perhaps *More* was first given to Chettle, heavily involved in the earliest stages of the revision, to try and give it a second chance at passing the censor. He was demonstrably working with Worcester's 1602–3, as were Heywood and Dekker, the three even identified by Carson as a playwriting syndicate within the company.[12] This fits the unusual circumstances of the revision remarkably well: an old play handed to a trusted in-house team, one of whom was able to recruit outside help in the form of Shakespeare.

Worcester's had become Queen Anne's by the time of the revisions, all London companies having been brought under members of James' family following his March 1603 accession. The Queen's took in some members of the Chamberlain's as actors, the majority of whom went on to form the King's, perhaps further explaining

Shakespeare's link.[13] There was likely no especial reason for the company returning to the play beyond trying to salvage it as a commercial property, perhaps on the assumption that the changed political order might now allow it. Hand C was a go-between, whose role it was to make sense of, in some cases transcribe, and give shape and structural coherence to the dramatists' contributions. Whether or not he can be regarded as a collaborative revising author is open to question. Appendix 1 details the sequence of events at all different stages of revision, the manuscript breaking down as follows. The likely writer behind Hand C's transcriptions is given after the oblique stroke (Additions III and V are slips pasted over deleted material on to fols. 11b and 14a of the OT respectively):

Fol. 1—*Wrapper*
Fol. 2—*Wrapper*
Fol. 3—Original Text*
Fol. 4—Original Text
Fol. 5—Original Text*
Fol. 6—**Addition I** (Chettle)[14]
Fol. 7—**Addition II** (Heywood, Hand C/Chettle)
Fol. 8—**Addition II** (Shakespeare)
Fol. 9—**Addition II** (Shakespeare)
Fol. 10—Original Text*
Fol. 11—Original Text/**Addition III** (Hand C/Shakespeare)
Fol. 12—**Addition IV** (Hand C/Dekker)
Fol. 13—**Addition IV** (Hand C/Dekker, Dekker)
Fol. 14—Original Text/**Addition V** (Hand C/Shakespeare rev. Heywood)
Fol. 15—Original Text
Fol. 16—**Addition VI** (Heywood)
Fol. 17—Original Text*
Fol. 18—Original Text
Fol. 19—Original Text
Fol. 20—Original Text
Fol. 21—Original Text
Fol. 22—Original Text
*—contains Tilney's annotation/marks for deletion

Additions I, II, and IV all replace at least one missing leaf, though Shakespeare's Addition II D is the only one without equivalent OT material remaining.[15] It should be noted that not everyone accepts that Hand D, who must have been a professional dramatist, is

Shakespeare, though stylistic and thematic impressionism accounting for how the writing 'behaves' like him, along with suggestive spelling and collocation evidence, is manifold in the passage.[16] The *Spanish Tragedy* additions, with one exception, were not intended to replace material, but to augment it, slotted into otherwise unchanged scenes in an allowed, licensed text. The case of *Sir Thomas More* is quite different, and we cannot fully appreciate Shakespeare's contribution without first understanding the need for it.

Sir Thomas More: Censorship and Revision

The cause of the May Day uprising—the continental Protestant exiles living in the city oppressing unopposed the rights and liberties of London citizens—is the part in which Tilney is most active as an annotator, and most concerned as a censor. Curiously, though, the play's central section, dealing episodically, anecdotally, even comically at times, with aspects of More's life and character, is the most heavily revised, and not at Tilney's behest. This material drew as much on popular tales of More's wit and wisdom as on the more familiar historical sources—Holinshed, especially—supplying the narrative outline.[17] The endgame moves to a notably tragic key, covering, from fols. 17 to 22 (Scenes 10–17), the arc of More's arrest, imprisonment, and execution. Tilney's intervention here is quite minimal, though whether more is implied is a moot question. Either way, the link between censorship and revision throughout the play is by no means easily established.

The copy Munday originally submitted was a clean authorial transcript, ready for licensing and use in the theatre, although neither happened. The revised manuscript as it survives, with its many annotations, crossings out, paste-downs, marginal insertions, alterations to staging, and additional leaves is a mess which Tilney probably never saw. Tilney had heavily censored the early portion of the manuscript dealing with the insurrection, his hand mainly absent from the final part of the play, and much depends on the interpretation of his instruction at the head of fol. 3a:

> Leave out the insurrection wholly with the cause thereof
> and begin with Sir Thomas More at the Mayor's ses-
> sions, with a report afterwards of his good service done

> being Sheriff of London upon a mutiny against the
> Lombards—only by a short report and not otherwise, at
> your own perils. E Tilney.

Taken one way it is a very conditional licence, as Greg thought.[18] Taken another, it is a final verdict, denying licence until conditions are met. Taken another, it is an order made in the course of reading, further annotation and the possibility of licence both ending when Tilney reached the seditious final scenes. But the prima facie evidence of the manuscript suggests the second scenario is correct. Tilney's directive cannot be interpreted as provisional approval, but neither can it be assumed, without further speculation, as anything other than an official record of his decision at the point of returning the manuscript to the company. He was, then, offering a way forward in making the play allowable for performance, though a difficult one. His objections focused on the insurrection episode in which Shakespeare became involved as a reviser.

Tilney's OT mark-up shows signs of increasing agitation with the material, starting out with small-scale amendments in Scene 1, crossing out individual lines, though he soon employed a more economical vertical marginal stroke, realizing the entire scene involved religious hostilities. Unrest between London's citizen class and continental Protestant exiles in the city had been a major problem in the 1590s, which may have been his main concern. Scene 2, the Mayor's sessions, in which More tricks the pompous Justice Suresby to get the petty felon, Lifter, off a death sentence, is untouched. Scene 3, in which the events of Scene 1 are discussed at Court, features certain marks for deletion, specific annotation—'Englishe' replaced by 'man', and 'straunger' and 'ffrencheman' by the more noncommittal 'Lombard'— and the directive 'mend this' against the first speech. Scenes 4 and 5, on fol. 4b, where the rioting starts, are again signalled entirely for deletion, replaced by Addition II B/C. Some lines are marked for deletion in Scene 7 where a rebel ringleader, Lincoln, is hanged despite More's previous promises of the King's mercy, though the scene mostly deals with the aftermath, and is orthodox in its treatment of royal authority. Tilney's final input comes at Scene 10 (OT fol. 17b), lines 80–104, where More, in defiance of the permanently offstage King, refuses to sign the Oath of Succession—not explicitly named as such—and resigns his post. The Oath recognized the legitimacy of Henry's heirs, More's refusal to acknowledge it essentially undermining Elizabeth's legitimacy as queen. The passage had to go, Tilney marking it for deletion and adding the crisp directive 'all alt[e]r' in the right margin.

Why he stopped annotating thereafter is unclear. We might assume the play had by that point become so unallowable that he just gave up on it, though the absence of mark-up and his clear directive at the beginning of the manuscript in broad terms presupposes his acceptance of the material. Chettle is the only dramatist involved in revising the later portion of the play, though why he ignored Tilney's Scene 10 directive is equally mysterious. He may have felt the matter of Henry's divorce was a Tudor problem that receded with James's succession, or hoped it had, the scale of rewriting required to the play's latter section seeming otherwise too prohibitive.[19] His Addition I reworking of two OT speeches in Scene 13 seems prompted by some of Munday's lines, generically critical of royal power:

> As for the prince, in all his sweet-gorged maw,
> And his rank flesh that sinfully renews
> The noon's excess in the night's dangerous surfeits.
>
> (OT3, 21–3)

But as Greg suggested, a 70-line revision seems like overkill. Why not just cut the three lines? Chettle also marks for omission parts of his own rewrite that court similar danger, getting needlessly tangled in further complications. It is also a heavy-handedly sentimental and repetitive re-rendering of the original moment. Munday's overall dramatization of More's downfall is the main meat of the play and a highly skilful piece of writing in itself, and it is easily forgotten that Shakespeare's main contribution is just a part-scene in More's initial rise. Curiously, the major revision to Addition IV, seemingly prompted by the aesthetic concern of reconstructing bitty episodes, has nothing to do with censorship. At the head of the heavily crossed-out OT Scene 8, Chettle writes 'this must be newe written', and Dekker subtly reworks the material, conflating Munday's Erasmus material with a scene in which More argues with Faulkner, the Bishop of Winchester's secretary's unruly servant. Chettle's most direct attempt to engage Tilney's comments is a reworking of deleted material from Scene 5, changing one of the OT's more seditious scenes of the prentice rioters inciting assault to noblemen decrying it. Yet he does nothing to 'mend' the Scene 3 material Tilney singled out dealing with the 'dangerous times' (3.3) those characters discuss there. Much of Chettle's work, then, was extraneous, and Hand C took charge of the second phase of revision, knowing Tilney's objections needed more serious attention. Simple redaction would not work, as without the section, the play's narrative action is effectively gutted, the only real option being to retain and rework. C took charge of the logistical preparation of the documents, and there is evidence of coordinated effort, Heywood, of all the contributing Worcester's/Queen Anne's dramatists, the most closely connected to Shakespeare's authorial involvement.

As Appendix 1 illustrates, Shakespeare and Heywood seem to have worked on revisions to the Addition II section at the same time, albeit separately, with Hand C shuttling pages between them as they worked. After C had transcribed Chettle's Addition II material onto 7b, he gave Heywood the page, along with fol. 5 and its original treatment of Scene 4, to supply his revision on 7a. Shakespeare's vagueness on details in his section—most famously his failure to give More an entrance direction, on the apparent misapprehension he was already onstage—probably means he had not seen C's clarifications to the revised staging at the foot of 7b, the page still with Heywood.[20] Shakespeare and Heywood may also have discussed the creation of the clown who appears in both their sections, probably at Heywood's instigation, a specialist in clown characters, using comedy to further soften the depiction of rebellion.[21] The character seems to have been developed from a hint of the silent onstage presence of George Betts' brother, Ralph, in the OT's Scenes 1 and 7 (1.92–3, 7.125). Heywood writes 'Clown' in his 7a speech-prefixes, after Hand C's help joining the dots in his stage direction on 7b, perhaps suggesting C communicated the plan to Shakespeare when he delivered the next page of OT along with a blank sheet for his reworking. C later alters some funny lines in Shakespeare's section assigned 'other' to 'Clown Betts', strengthening the sense of their collaboration as separate but coordinated.[22] But while Heywood's is the comic tonal contribution and Shakespeare's the moral relativist, the manuscript offers clues that theirs were the two most interdependent sections within the overall project of revision.

Despite scribal transcription, it is also clear that the opening Messenger's speech in Addition V is Heywood's from its duplication in the Addition VI material (fol.16) in his hand. And More's speech that follows seems to be Shakespeare's, with contributions by Heywood to further aid theatrical coherence.[23] Heywood's Addition VI is a moment of purely idiosyncratic comedy, working to link the play-within-the-play to the developing main plot, and adding purposeful characterization to More in accordance with Shakespeare's project of expansion. Heywood, then, helped bed Shakespeare's work into the overall revision, working mainly with C, who transcribed and pasted in the speeches Shakespeare wrote on a separate leaf, perhaps at Heywood's behest. Heywood's Add. II/fol. 7 contribution is essentially a transcription of Munday's original scene, with some added interjections for the Clown, to whom he gives further lines in the latter part of Scene 7, a comic tonal adjustment of limited power to a short portion of the Ill May Day material. It was clearly on Shakespeare's contribution, presumably brokered by Heywood, that the company's hopes rested.

Whether Tilney's original objection was to the depiction of insurrection or religious hostilities, Shakespeare covers both in the insistence on obedience and order he gives to More in his lengthy, impassioned plea for toleration. Shakespeare was probably sought for his particular ability to walk the line in dramatizing political disorder. He and Marlowe had skilfully depicted authority overcoming rebellion in a way that still challenges both in *2 Henry VI's* Cade episode, and several features of the Hand D section recall *Julius Caesar*, superficially in the phrase 'friends, masters, countrymen', but more significantly in More's handling of the volatile, vacillating crowd. The push-and-pull of dramatic modulation in setting a leading actor against a restless group energy against which he must work, imploring, and by degrees winning, silence through rhetorically arresting oration is a strikingly common tactic between the two plays. More synthesizes the disarming charisma, oratorical power, and inscrutable aura of Antony as he gets the hostile mob to decide, seemingly of its own volition, to let him speak. They both cheer for and reject Surrey and Shrewsbury in lines 24–55, to the point that even their leader, Lincoln, becomes dismayed with them: 'A plague on them, they will not hold their peace. The devil cannot rule them' (Add. II D, 53–4). Except, of course, that someone can:

> ALL   Peace, peace!
> MORE   Look what you do offend you cry upon,
>   That is, the peace. Not one of you here present,
>   Had there such fellows lived when you were babes
>   That could have topped the peace as now you would,
>   The peace wherein you have till now grown up
>   Had been ta'en from you, and the bloody times
>   Could not have brought you to the state of men.
>   Alas, poor things! What is it you have got
>   Although we grant you get the thing you seek?
> BETTS   Marry, the removing of the strangers, which
>   cannot choose but much advantage the poor
>   handicrafts of the city.
> MORE   Grant them removed, and grant that this your noise
>   Hath chid down all the majesty of England.
>   Imagine that you see the wretched strangers,
>   Their babies at their backs, with their poor luggage,
>   Plodding to th' ports and coasts for transportation,
>   And that you sit as kings in your desires,
>   Authority quite silenced by your brawl,
>   And you in ruff of your opinions clothed.
>   What had you got? I'll tell you: you had taught
>   How insolence and strong hand should prevail,
>   How order should be quelled. And by this pattern
>   Not one of you should live an agèd man;
>   For other ruffians, as their fancies wrought,
>   With selfsame hand, self reasons, and self right,
>   Would shark on you, and men, like ravenous fishes
>   Would feed on one another.
>
>   (Add. II D, 60–87)

The insistence on justice and mercy Shakespeare gives More shows an effort to avoid polemic, though he, among the revisers, balances most productively the need for censorial appeasement and purposeful, compelling, risk-taking drama. It is an arresting passage in a style seen nowhere else in the play, as individuated as an authorial stint by its startling idiolect as its distinctive handwriting. Its extended enargeia conjures a series of stark mental images, a detailed, moving description of the strangers' predicament, forcing the rioters to see it afresh and to be emotionally affected and changed by it. While the message differs radically from Antony's incitement to riot, the understanding that emotional directives are key to affective human response is powerfully shared. We get a picture of More as someone deeply attuned to, and concerned with, the arbitrariness of justice, fortune, and happiness in human life. As the play progresses, these issues resurface in More's discussion of his own good fortune, following his knighthood and appointment to the Privy Council in Addition III. Yet it is also shot through with characteristically Shakespearean ethical ambiguity, the ideological insistence on the theme of obedience greatly destabilized by the context Munday had established in his original Scene 1. That the heavily censored opening was intended for inclusion in the revised version is suggested by its presence in the manuscript prefacing the reworked riot scenes. There is nothing to suggest that Shakespeare saw the rest of the play—all he ostensibly knew was that revision had been called for, and that his job was to rework the pages he had been given. But while he may not have seen it, he would have needed to consult with Hand C and Heywood over the writing of Addition V at least, and may have asked about things in the wider plot he could work with and against. If he did know of Scene 1, his More then becomes a cold pragmatist, 'at once aware of the inequities and injustices in his social world and compelled to find ways to quiet objections to them'.[24] The bullying 'strangers', De Barde and Cavaler, Munday depicted there bear little resemblance to the desperate refugees Shakespeare's More describes.

The crowd-control scene as Shakespeare rewrites it is the most dramatically absorbing episode of the first part of the play, and he augments its importance for More's rise in the Addition III soliloquy, copied out by Hand C, reflecting on the fickleness of worldly power and fortune:

> MORE   It is in heaven that I am thus and thus,
>   And that which we profanely term our fortunes
>   Is the provision of the power above,

> Fitted and shaped just to that strength of nature
> Which we are born with. Good God, good God,
> That I from such an humble bench of birth
> Should step as 'twere up to my country's head,
> And give the law on't there. I, in my father's life,
> To take prerogative and tithe of knees
> From elder kinsmen, and him bind by my place
> To give the smooth and dexter way to me
> That owe it him by nature: sure these things,
> Not physicked by respect, might turn our blood
> To much corruption. But, More, the more thou hast
> Either of honour, office, wealth and calling,
> Which might accite thee to embrace and hug them,
> The more do thou in serpents' natures think them,
> Fear their gay skins with thought of their sharp state,
> And let this be thy maxim: to be great
> Is, when the thread of heyday is once spun,
> A bottom great wound up, greatly undone.

>   (Add. III, 1–21)

Both this and Addition V's short soliloquy—the only ones in the play—are also, as Jowett points out, 'key points of transition in the episodic middle scenes'.[25] They enhance our sense of More as a character, as well as of the play's transitional skill, linking episodes in which More meets and plays a trick on Erasmus, performs extemporarily in a play, and deals correctively with serving men of various stripes. They also serve the practical function of buying time for the company to double where pressure is put on cast size.[26] The use of soliloquy alters the play's structural dynamics quite significantly, introducing a more focused sensibility, Shakespeare's characteristic instinct to dramatize particular experience over systemic conflict something the revisers surely knew would help with the censor. It is possible that the only context Shakespeare had for his Addition II revision was the portion of Original Text he was to rework.[27] We can assume that Munday's now-missing original leaf was marked for deletion; indeed, the first two lines of fol. 10a after it show Tilney's original marks. It is possible none of the revisers—Chettle perhaps excepted—saw the whole manuscript or knew the gravity and specificity of Tilney's original annotations.[28] And yet all Shakespeare's contributions, though isolated, show deep engagement with the play, and with its protagonist in particular.

Shakespeare was, according to Taylor, drawn to 'abnormally interesting' male characters; indeed, he gives More 93 of II D's 152 lines. Without his revisions, certainly before the latter part of the play narrating More's tragic fate, the role is surprisingly wanting, the Lifter, Faulkner, and *Marriage of Wit and Wisdom* episodes not enough on their own to establish either dramatic character or a tonal prefiguration of what is to ensue. And a scene inserted by Shakespeare into the 1600 first quarto edition (Q1) of *2 Henry IV* during printing—3.1, the so-called 'insomnia' scene—makes an interesting analogue. There is no critical consensus on whether it, along with several other passages added into the Folio text, indicates censorship or authorially guided revision. The changes look backwards at the narrative trajectory of the sequence around Richard II's overthrow, and forwards to the uncertain way of civil dissension, all ending at 4.1, after which the text becomes politically 'safe' again.[29] Q1 was apparently set from authorial papers, which, having been transcribed and possibly expanded for a licensed theatrical promptbook later used as Folio copy, were no longer needed by the company. 3.1 feels logically like part of Shakespeare's original design, Taylor and Jowett suggesting it was a late-stage addition in the process of initial composition.[30] It is patterned in almost exactly the same way as the main portion of II D, after the latter's 50 or so lines of crowd-voiced preamble. Both are extremely strong set pieces built around a series of lengthy speeches, offering a depth of complexity to the male title character otherwise unavailable. In 3.1, Shakespeare economically joins private trauma to national catastrophe in tying Henry's sleepless sorrows to the gathering storm of rebellion in the north, exposing his inner self more nakedly than anywhere else in the two parts:

> Wilt thou upon the high and giddy mast
> Seal up the ship-boy's eyes, and rock his brains
> In cradle of the rude imperious surge,
> And in the visitation of the winds,
> Who take the ruffian billows by the top,
> Curling their monstrous heads, and hanging them
> With deafing clamour in the slippery clouds,

That, with the hurly, death itself awakes?
Canst thou, O partial sleep, give thy repose
To the wet sea-boy in an hour so rude,
And in the calmest and most stillest night,
With all appliances and means to boot,
Deny it to a king? Then happy low, lie down.
Uneasy lies the head that wears a crown.   (3.1.18–31)

Both in prosodic texture and in atmosphere it is a striking inter-vention. The sick king, through the imagined ship-boy on his mast, figures unnumbered subjects going about their difficult daily lives somewhere out 'there', beyond the confines of his Westminster bedchamber, a historiographical strategy doing much to align different parts of the play. *Part 2*'s emphasis is frequently on little lives passing through nature, private festivity, seasonal change, the agricultural calendar, bodily decay—a channel of time separated from the providential flow of 'history' that no other treatment of this narrative engages. But in dramatizing such experience too fastidiously, Shakespeare had almost forgotten to put it in robust dialogue with the narrative source and historical record against which it runs. There is also a structural mismanagement uncharacteristic of Shakespeare without 3.1, with two lengthy comic subplot episodes (2.4 and 3.2) going one into the other in an over-long departure from the play's main action. Its inclusion mirrors the scenic form of *Part 1*, which likewise has a charged central episode in which the King privately dreads his enemies' uprising, and has the added practical benefit of bringing the character onstage sooner. Henry's dying advice for his son to seek foreign wars to 'waste the memory of the former days' (4.3.344) if the body politic, as sick as his body natural, is to be healed, comes in the only other scene in which he appears. The added 3.1 acts as a fulcrum, lifting much imaginative and narrative weight and recalibrating the play's dramaturgical balance. Like II D, it achieves this by heavily foregrounding its titular subject, doing much to humanize and complicate them.

To judge by II D's—assumed here to be Shakespeare's—50 lines per side, the 103 lines of 3.1 are likely to have been confined to a single leaf, and probably to aid insertion into the manuscript (see Figure 3). The compositor was either initially confused about placement, or failed to discover it until typesetting and printing for the scenes

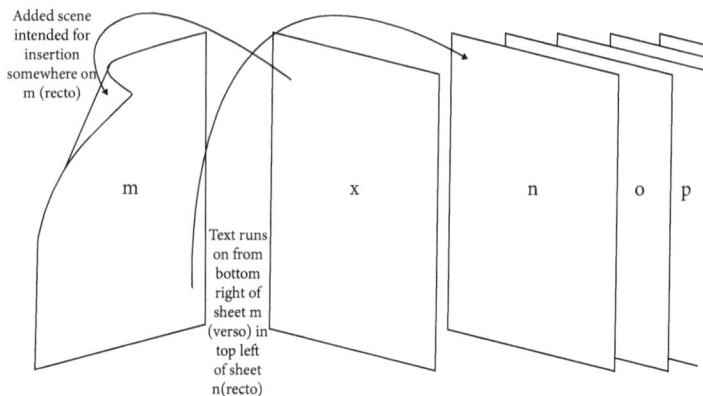

Figure 3 Conjectural reconstruction of a portion of the foul papers of *2 Henry IV*. Figure 22 of *The Oxford Shakespeare: A Textual Companion* (1987), edited by Stanley Wells and Gary Taylor with John Jowett and William Montgomery. Used with the permission of Oxford University Press.

around it were finished.[31] Two states of Q exist, some copies containing the scene (Qb), and some not (Qa). Partway through printing, then, and certainly after sheet E had been printed and sheet F had been set, the printer discovered the added scene or at least figured out where it was supposed to go, inferable, as Taylor and Jowett suggest, in part from its place on the continuum of the rebellion plot. If it was a revision of censored material, the compositor may have had to work around heavy crossings-out of the kind we see throughout the *More* manuscript—making the original material illegible and it impossible to tell that the extra page was a replacement—perhaps even missing among the mess a mark for its insertion. Or, if legibility was not at issue, he may have seen a mark but not realized what it meant until it became obvious that the material should have been set by now.

For the tricky job of inserting the scene, half of sheet E was removed, with leaves E1 and 2 retained, and a whole new sheet, E3-6, added to accommodate it. The new sheet also housed the calculated number of lines from adjoining scenes needed to be reset around 3.1, with 3.2.102 which ends the new E6ᵛ joining up seamlessly with 3.2.103 *et seq.* that had originally begun sheet F. Shakespeare wrote scenes of vastly varying lengths throughout his playwriting career, and may have thought in terms of single sheets, and sides, of paper as equating to structural units of time onstage, and of plays being apportionable in composition in this way. The principle that scenic form in playwriting is piecemeal as well as sequential and agglomerate—discrete units of action able to be slotted in, out, or together—functions well for post hoc revisions, and, analogously, authorial shares in planned collaborative projects. But a finished play sets stricter limits on what can be (re)inserted, either in printing or in conforming to the parameters of conditionally licensed material. The 150 lines of Shakespeare's *More* addition take up one and a half leaves, or three sides of paper, compared to Munday's OT pages of 75 lines per side, suggesting he was replacing material like-for-like in length and subject matter.

The *More* revisers all seem to have worked by sheets, Shakespeare's two leaves (fols. 8 and 9) one example, Heywood's fol. 7 and 16 another, the others being the lost sheet on which Dekker wrote his original Add. IV; the one on which Hand C transcribed it (fols. 12 and 13); and Chettle's fol. 6 and its lost other half, on which he drafted his Add. II contribution. There seems also to have been another on which Shakespeare and Heywood drafted Adds. III and V, and from which Hand C cut out their paste-down transcriptions. II D seems to be a first draft, its largely uncorrected state showing Shakespeare as a writer of extraordinary fluency in composition. Certain non-stylistic features—the extreme sloppiness of the orthography and calligraphy, the almost total absence of punctuation, placeholder entrance directions and speech-prefixes which Hand C attempts to correct—have been taken to indicate hasty composition, or disconnect from the wider processes of collaborative revision on the play. Yet the idea of Shakespearean unconcern when writing for others is undermined by the vagaries of speech-prefix assignation and stage direction we see in sole-authored texts set from authorial papers such as Q1 *2 Henry IV*, where Doll Tearsheet, for example, is given variously as 'Tere'., 'Teresh'., 'Doll/Dol', 'Dorothy', 'Doro'. and 'Whoore'.[32] Hand

D shows a pre-theatrical and purely authorial moment, the pragmatics of staging subordinated to the immediate job in hand.[33] Shakespeare was not indifferent, or lazy, or lost in the genius of invention, but rather aware, as an experienced professional dramatist, that his contribution was part of a process. He leaves space on the page for the playhouse annotator to clarify logistical details, in a similar way, as will be seen, to his collaborative approach to *Timon*. Hand C had the difficult job of piecing the play together with the finished contributions of all the revising dramatists, necessitating some minimal alteration in preparing the text. A point was clearly reached where he was no longer able to access Shakespeare's help as we see him rework a part of Hand D on the misperception that correction is needed (square brackets show authorial deletions, and strikethrough/bold C's attempted correction):

> wash your foule mynds w^t teares and those same hands
> that yo^u lyke rebells lyft against the peace
> lift vp for peace, and your vnreuerent knees
> [that] make them your feet to kneele to be forgyven
> ~~is safer warrs, then euer you can make~~
> ~~in in to yor obedienc~~
> ~~whose discipline is ryot, why euen yor~~ [~~warrs~~] ~~hurly~~
> **tell me but this**
> ~~cannot peeed but by obedienc~~ what rebell captaine

The physical evidence of the manuscript clarifies the error (see Figure 4). C becomes confused by the syntax, failing to grasp that terminal punctuation is implied after 'feet' in the fourth line, the problem exacerbated by Shakespeare's relineation through an interpolated phrase ('Whose discipline is riot./In, in, to your obedience! Why, even your hurly/). He attempts some deletion and functional rewriting, replacing multiple lines of carefully constructed verse— including Shakespeare's alteration of 'wars' to 'hurly', a word that enriches the sonic and imagistic effect of the poetry's detailing, also used in 3.1 of *2 Henry IV*—with a short, generic phrase. The precision of the few authorial micro-revisions in the passage is consistent with Shakespeare's discernment in many substantive changes seen in printed versions of his plays. The fussiness with which he could revisit words over time is seen in comparing Q2 and F *Hamlet*, *King Lear*, or *Othello*, for example, while the kind of *currente calamo* revisions seen

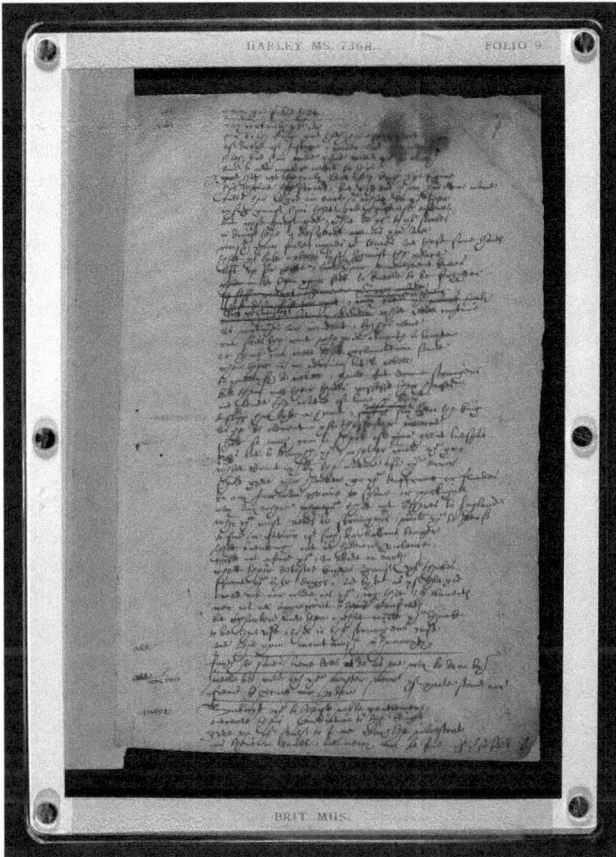

Figure 4 *Sir Thomas More*, MS. Harley 7368, fol. 9a. One of three manuscript pages making up Shakespeare's revision/addition to the play, the only extant dramatic writing in his hand. By permission of The British Library.

here—made in the act of foul-paper composition—are observable in texts printed from authorial papers, like Q2 *Romeo and Juliet* and Q1 *Love's Labour's Lost*. Yet despite the presence of the kind of granular revisions Shakespeare was likely to make, and the fact that the passage so clearly stands out—Jonathan Bate seeing 'Shakespeare's unique poetic intensity' in the language, and in the 'linguistic device of grammatical "conversion'" that abounds in it—perceptions remain of the scene as un-Shakespearean, or not substantially distinct from the verbal texture of much of the rest of the play.[34] A Shakespeare who is there and not quite there. We might observe, though, that Shakespeare's job was precisely to revise Munday's work, and while we can never know what that work looked like, we *can* see the original material around it, including Munday's version of what Chettle and Heywood would revise in Addition II. To judge by that, Shakespeare's Add. II contribution, like the 3.1 insertion in *2 Henry IV*, manages radical tonal reworking within the bounds of a 'finished' work.

Hand D makes visible a form of collaborative contribution hypothetically reconstructed by attribution study in *1 Henry VI*, *Edward III*, and *The Spanish Tragedy*. And until more recent arguments about Shakespeare's revision of an unknown author's work in *Edward III*, of Marlovian passages in *2* and *3 Henry VI*, and of Kyd's work in *The Spanish Tragedy* Addition 5 (which retains a few of the original lines in its expansive, transformative treatment), revision of others' material was something we had thought he otherwise never did. It is also in combining these old and new bibliographic and stylometric arguments across *The Spanish Tragedy* and *Sir Thomas More* that we can hypothesize close Shakespearean cooperation with Heywood across two projects in his sole-authorship dominated middle phase. Both give us a Shakespeare willing to rework others' plays, and to work closely with others to do so, even down to bits and pieces of added writing; levels of small-scale investment, unique within his dramatic canon, changing our sense of him as an unwilling or apathetic collaborator in the main part of his career.

Middleton: Collaboration and Adaptation

From early 1604, Shakespeare returned to sole-authorship for a stint that saw him finish *Measure for Measure*, and write *Othello*, *All's Well that Ends Well*, and *King Lear*. But in early 1606, he returned to full collaboration for the first time since the early 1590s. The precise dating of *Timon of Athens*, written with Thomas Middleton, has major implications for the way we understand co-authorship's impact on Shakespeare's mid–late career. If placed in late 1605–early 1606, as the

Oxford and New Oxford editions have it, then it participates in, even inaugurates, a heavily concentrated phase of tragic writing for Shakespeare, during which Middleton also wrote *The Revenger's Tragedy*. If early 1607, following Wiggins, that year becomes a turning point for Shakespeare, a decisive move back to co-authorship that would shape his artistic predispositions for the remainder of his professional career.

In this latter timeline, Shakespeare co-writes *Timon* and *Pericles*, leading, respectively, to *Coriolanus*—like *Timon* a classical tragedy of misanthropy—and the late romances, generically affined to *Pericles*. Roger Holdsworth, though, suggests the former, his chronology ordering *Lear*, *A Yorkshire Tragedy*, *Timon*, *Revenger's*, and *Macbeth* between October 1605 and July 1606.[35] Plague closed the theatres from 5 October to 15 December 1605, towards which much of the *Lear* dating evidence points.[36] When it was eventually performed, Middleton, immediately influenced by it, wrote *A Yorkshire Tragedy* into January 1606, and collaborated with Shakespeare on *Timon* in February–March, moving straight on to *Revenger's* which he finished in May. Shakespeare then wrote *Macbeth* solus in June–July, leaving him the rest of the year—another long plague closure—for *Antony and Cleopatra*.[37] *Timon* is also consistent with a Shakespearean working trajectory over a three-year period in its source usage. Plutarch's Life of Marcus Antonius contains the story of Timon, which Shakespeare encountered while beginning research for *Antony and Cleopatra*. Traces of Plutarch's Antony are also found in *Macbeth*, while the Life of Alcibiades is paired with Coriolanus, about whom Shakespeare wrote in 1608. Though the character Ventidius appears in both Middleton and Shakespeare scenes in *Timon*, Shakespeare's researches make him the likelier source of the Plutarchan name. It re-surfaces in *Antony and Cleopatra*, and Middleton often opted for generic names anyway, as is evident in his work on Scenes 5–11, and throughout *A Yorkshire Tragedy*.

But it is to *King Lear*, not *Antony and Cleopatra*, that *Timon* demonstrates the most striking imaginative response. Both plays start with profligates, ever but slenderly having known either themselves or the flatterers they hold dear; both chart the disintegration of self-governance, of age and hierarchy, and the faithlessness of close confidantes. Timon's fury, self-exiled and semi-naked in the wilderness, strongly recalls Lear's refusal of the human bonds by which he stands humiliated. *Lear* speaks many times about basic comforts—love, food, clothing, shelter, warmth—developing them alongside a series of images evoking a multiplicity of ways of feeling and sensing the world, all ideas that dominate *Timon*'s worldview. It is also particularly interested in nature—no other Shakespeare play uses the word as frequently—serving variously to articulate humanity, the passions, filial duty, obligation, kindred, bodily comfort, sanity, self-governance, human personality, health, bodily capacity for sensory experience, essential being, living things, natural affection, feeling, vital powers, flesh, the natural world. Growth and progeny are developed in parallel imagery around eggs and fertility, and Shakespeare's part in *Timon* seems relatedly interested in roots; both as nourishment and as symbolic of what should be harmonious fixity in a biosphere torn up by greed (the same earth yields gold). *Timon*, in other words, has a strong relative priority to *Lear* in the interests Shakespeare manifests. And yet it is also characteristically Middletonian.

The trio of satirical comedies Middleton wrote for the Children of Paul's 1604–5, covering, variously, litigation and debt (*Michaelmas Term*), marriage as commerce (*A Trick to Catch the Old One*), and greed and deception (*A Mad World, My Masters*), all present a debased social contract reduced to credit and debt. These are intrinsic features of Middleton's art for the eighteen months leading into *Timon*, and help explain the intellectual and thematic fissures so perplexing to generations of readers considering *Timon* as solely Shakespearean. It is city comedy meets classical tragedy, ostensibly as much a departure for Middleton, the slick young writer of urban comedy, as for Shakespeare, the lyrical poet from an older generation, the two meeting somewhere in the middle of each other's interests. Yet Shakespeare's 'problem' comedies invest in the same commercial milieu as Middleton's satirical writing from 1602 to 1605, *Measure for Measure* a disguised-duke play that may have inspired Middleton's *The Phoenix* (1604). After *Measure*, the King's Men moved hard in the direction of tragedy, another innovation Shakespeare led, and if anything Middleton had to change the most in this pairing. Or if, as part of his professional role, Shakespeare was inducting a younger writer into a house style, there is also a sense that their writerly personalities were worth exploiting to make *Timon* the thing it is, both in stylistic multivocality and plurality of vision.

An alternative history has seen Shakespeare in midlife crisis, out of fashion, and in need of a younger writer to rehabilitate his ailing career.[38] Another has him blooding a young playwright, who had written one short drama for the company, into more ambitious work for them. Like *More*'s, *Timon*'s early performance record is a blank, but unlike it and its rich manuscript evidence, we have only one printed text by which we can seek to determine *Timon*'s authorship. Bibliographic analysis suggests it was not even intended for inclusion in the 1623 Folio at first—perhaps in itself an indication of co-authorship—but was brought in apparently as a stopgap to solve publishers' issues with copyright over *Troilus and Cressida*.[39] The authorial shares are remarkably clear: Shakespeare is present mainly in the latter half, though also begins the play in semi-abstract, emblematic vein, the Poet and Painter characters recalling his *Spanish Tragedy* additions, while the caustic Apemantus also strongly evokes figures like Thersites and the Fool. Jowett observes Shakespeare's verse is densely metaphorical, an accessory to Timon's mental disintegration, while Middleton handles the grittier, worldlier depiction of civic corruption, greed, and debt in a sparer, more direct register:

> TITUS' SERVANT   I'll show you how t'observe a strange
> event.
> Your lord sends now for money.
> HORTENSIUS' SERVANT   Most true, he does.
> TITUS' SERVANT   And he wears jewels now of Timon's
> gift,
> For which I wait for money.
> HORTENSIUS' SERVANT   It is against my heart.
> LUCILIUS' SERVANT   Mark, how strange it shows.
> Timon in this should pay more than he owes,
> And e'en as if your lord should wear rich jewels
> And send for money for 'em.
> HORTENSIUS' SERVANT   I'm weary of this charge, the
> gods can witness.
> I know my lord hath spent of Timon's wealth,
> And now ingratitude makes it worse than stealth.

(3.4.19–29)

Parallels between Middleton's section and the source pamphlet for *A Yorkshire Tragedy* have also been noted, as has a linkage of the imagery of sexual disease to money in *A Yorkshire Tragedy* with the unnatural lusts of *Timon*'s sociology.⁴⁰ If Middleton writes the community, though, Shakespeare handles the tragic subject:

> TIMON   O blessèd breeding sun, draw from the earth
> Rotten humidity; below thy sister's orb
> Infect the air. Twinned brothers of one womb,
> Whose procreation, residence, and birth
> Scarce is dividant, touch them with several fortunes,
> The greater scorns the lesser. Not nature,
> To whom all sores lay siege, can bear great fortune,
> But by contempt of nature . . .
> There's nothing level in our cursèd natures
> But direct villainy. Therefore be abhorred
> All feasts, societies, and throngs of men.
> His semblable, yea, himself, Timon disdains.
> Destruction fang mankind. Earth, yield me roots.
>
> (5.1.1–8, 19–23)

Shakespeare's contributions have been described as 'disconnected fragments' which he left Middleton to merge.⁴¹ The play's relative unpopularity has even led to the idea of Shakespeare leaning on extraneous material from research for a future play, and leftover themes from his last one, for an unenthusiastic pairing within one of his greatest runs of individual creativity. But his combined share is both sizeable (972 lines to Middleton's 1195) and attentive, and certainly one he did not need to supply for any finacial incentive. Either Shakespeare started the play and let a proven, prodigious talent with the company finish it off, or he wanted to work with Middleton, whose organizing role in the venture may even suggest his instigation.

Middleton would go on to adapt *Macbeth*, *Measure*, *All's Well*, and probably *Titus*, after Shakespeare's death, perhaps feeling uniquely qualified to do so.⁴² This has been argued through attribution study, though ideas about the extent of his reworkings remain unsettled.⁴³ Material apparently added to the start of 1.2 in *Measure*, in which Lucio talks with two gentlemen, is rife with Middletonian stylistic and linguistic markers. We also see a duplication, with lines 1–67 (up to 'I am custom-shrunk') by Middleton, and the eight lines after it, 'How now . . . with maid by him', Shakespeare's original scene opening, intended as a cancel but set in type by the Folio compositors, adduced by both needless repeated exposition about Claudio's arrest, and confusion about it in Mistress Overdone's lines. She announces it, and seems ignorant of it a moment later. But it is a reference to the King of Hungary and the Palatinate wars, which had not begun when Shakespeare died, and which demonstrably found reportage in 1620–1 in the London corantos that grew around the European conflict, that seem to confirm later adaptation. Vienna, stewed in corruption in the play, was the seat of Emperor Ferdinand II—Middleton probably changed location from Italy to cement the Thirty Years War link—and Jowett notes how an anti-Catholic militancy creeps into Middleton's other work around this time, permeating his 1624 play *A Game at Chess*.[44] Other Middletonian interpolations include 2.1's meditation on justice and corruption for Escalus and some lines amplifying the sense of moral squalor for the clown, Pompey, who is also given a comic monologue to the same effect in 4.3.

Act intervals betray post-1608 revival, when the company acquired the indoor Blackfriars playhouse and began as a matter of course to mix outdoor and indoor performance, where candles needed trimming between acts. But a conspicuously solitary song, 'Take oh take those lips away', borrowed from *Rollo, Duke of Normandy* or *The Bloody Brother* (1617–20), pushes the date later still.[45] It opens Act 4, with the Duke's 'O place and greatness' and 'He who the sword of heaven will bear' soliloquies transposed, and a brief passage of dialogue added, to lock it into the dramatic action. The main motive was the development of Mariana's character, used by Shakespeare as a convenient plot mechanism, and by Isabella and the Duke as a convenient sexual substitute. The moment as Middleton re-envisions it also provides the only respite from the claustrophobic triangulation of court, brothel, and prison, and makes Mariana the play's most decisive voice in seeking for something over and above retributive justice, perhaps contrarily to what we might expect about Middletonian cynicism versus Shakespearean forgiveness.

Song is likewise a key marker of adaptation in *Macbeth*, with two— 'come away' and 'black spirits'—imported from Middleton's 1616 play, *The Witch*. The first appears in the otherwise Middletonian

'Hecate' scene (3.5), where iambic tetrameter—conspicuously unlike the topsy-turvydom of Shakespeare's trochaic variety—and dialogic rationalism gives the audience a mode for understanding the witches as characters with motive that Shakespeare strenuously avoids. The King's company had acquired a consort of musicians with the Blackfriars from its use by the royal children's companies, and the 'other three witches' mentioned in the Folio stage direction at 4.1.38.1 were probably the boy actors-cum-choristers used as spirits in 3.5. Taylor argued that Middleton's 'major adaptation was to transform into witches the three characters . . . identified as "weïrd sisters"' by Shakespeare, even suggesting Middleton's presence in the play's famous opening scene. In this reconstruction, Middleton adds the cryptic 'Greymalkin' (cat) and 'Paddock' (toad) references to witches' 'familiars', agents that nonetheless chime with Shakespearean ideas about natural/supernatural border-crossing throughout the play. Taylor further argues the infamous directive to '**hover through** the fog and filthy air' at 1.1.10 is a Middletonian change anticipating a series of staging effects—flats, moving properties, pulley 'flying' effects—planned for the revival and the technical affordances of the indoor Blackfriars, associated with music and the kinds of romance aesthetic so popular by the time of the adaptation. *The Tempest*'s masque of Ceres is a useful analogue. While the plays all moved between the Blackfriars and the outdoor Globe post-1608, the revival aesthetic still seems more in line with elite—therefore indoor—audience taste. Ambiguity also persists about the play's brevity reflecting either taut Shakespearean economy or ruthless Middletonian gutting.

Middleton lends *All's Well* a darker tone, deepening the cynicism with which war and sexuality are conflated, stripping the former of its moral imperatives, 'the French lords go[ing] to war not for ideological reasons but for cardiovascular exercise' only.[46] The added 'virginity' dialogue in 1.1 might also, as Taylor suggests, be seen either as 'an infusion of materialist realism and psychological complexity, or . . . a debasement that contradicts Shakespeare's original conception, disrupting this scene and haunting all Helen's behaviour throughout the play'.[47] Middleton's hand in *Titus* is more contested, largely because it is acknowledged that if he is present, he is trying very hard to sound like an early 1590s' version of Shakespeare, though his 'selective and semiotic' imitation of Shakespeare has been seen as unapt to prevent his own 'systemic and cellular' identity showing through in the language.[48] The fly-killing episode of 3.2 he supplies deepens the theme of madness, working as a compelling metacommentary on Aaron's lines at 5.1.141–2 in Shakespeare's original text.

Though revealing nothing about Shakespeare's approach to collaboration, Middleton's adaptations reveal different authorial processes, enabling entirely different questions and understandings of dramatic co-authorship in the period. Shakespeare's work with Middleton on *Timon*, his one definite mid-career collaboration, seems quite distant, and in places—like some of his revisions and micro-collaborations on *The Spanish Tragedy* and *Sir Thomas More*—relatively bitty. But he clearly saw something in Middleton's work that he liked, and Middleton's overall part in shaping the Shakespeare canon makes theirs a particularly significant pairing. Middleton did for Shakespeare what Shakespeare had done for Kyd in his *Spanish Tragedy* revisions, productively disrupting Shakespeare's canonical wholeness in ways that are unique and important to identify.

Shakespeare: 1607–8, 1612–13

Beginnings: George Wilkins

Pericles is not a particularly 'late' play—it was written 1607–8, six years before Shakespeare stopped writing—but embodies all we conventionally associate with Shakespearean lateness. The Victorian critic, Edward Dowden, saw Shakespeare entering a phase of 'serene wisdom', though Gordon McMullan reminds us that lateness in any authorial canon is as much about ideological construct as historical fact.[1] Dowden was the first to apply the term 'romance' to *The Winter's Tale, Cymbeline*, and *The Tempest*, written solely by Shakespeare 1609–11. His classification was led by medieval literature, where generic motifs ultimately founded in classical epic settled in the English tradition, and the co-authored *Pericles*, which he ignored, fits the template closely. It has the wandering knight winning the hand of the virtuous princess through combat, storms, great loss, trial, and disaster, all redeemed through wondrous and improbable interventions. It also resembles a cruder kind of Elizabethan drama, harking back to the late 1580s–early 1590s and plays like *Mucedorus* (*c*.1591), which Shakespeare's company had revived *c*.1605. That Dowden doesn't mention *Pericles* attests to its lengthy exile from critical favour and canonical acceptance—a lost child weathering centuries of neglect until, somewhat fancifully and romantically, it is restored through likeness to its father. The relation of the troubling 'author/ity' of fathers over progeny in the plot to paternalistic metaphors attaching to the play's authorship has not gone unnoticed.[2] Masten's distaste for attribution is held in the paradox that shared authorship in the play could not

Shakespeare and Collaborative Writing. Will Sharpe, Oxford University Press. © Will Sharpe (2023).
DOI: 10.1093/oso/9780198819639.003.0006

be described without singular authority being conferred on each of its two dads.

Pericles is the only Shakespeare play that survives only in a bad transmission. The 1609 quarto text shows frequent mislineation, repeated confusion of verse and prose, and much verbal repetition, leading to the tentative conclusion of memorially reconstructed underlying copy, probably by the Lychorida/Marina boy actor—perhaps apprenticed to the actor who played Gower, from whom he got the choric speeches—and another hired actor, who possibly played a fisherman, the Pandar, and other small parts. This has been disputed, but not entirely rejected, with bad scribal work another possibility.³ It was printed in two different print shops by different sets of compositors, but neither the underlying manuscript nor printing errors can adequately explain the stylistic divergences seen between Scenes 1–11 and 12–28. Irregularities in verse pervade the second half, albeit the poetic imagery is strong, clear, and powerfully affective, with the opposite true of the first half. There the versification is regular and 'unsubtle', while the imagery, 'when not commonplace, hovers between complexity and confusion'.⁴ Theories put forward to explain the difference of the first two acts are either that they are of an earlier Shakespearean draft; that Shakespeare wrote them with Gower's stylistic tonality in mind; that they are symptomatic of the reported means by which the 1609 quarto was assembled; or that they are by someone else.⁵ When the play's editors in the New Cambridge series say they 'don't really care who wrote *Pericles*', theirs is an objection to what they see as a boring question displacing critical appreciation of the play.⁶ MacDonald Jackson, on the other hand, asserts the question of *Pericles*' authorship as 'a significant fact of dramatic history and of Shakespeare's career'.⁷

The play is now understood to be co-authored by Shakespeare, who wrote Scenes 12–28/Acts 3–5, and George Wilkins, a disreputable and occasional dramatist who wrote Scenes 1–11/Acts 1–2, and one other sole-authored play, *The Miseries of Enforced Marriage* (1606), for the King's Men. He also co-wrote *The Travels of the Three English Brothers* (1606) with John Day and William Rowley for Queen Anne's, another play dealing with adventures across the Mediterranean world in a romance context, albeit in a contemporary setting. Wilkins was a nasty character, stated to have 'outrageously beaten one Judith Walton and stamped upon her so that she was carried home in a chair'.[8] He seems to have abused relationships and protocols in his writing work, directly plagiarizing parts of Lawrence Twine's *Pattern of Painful Adventures* (1594)—a reworking of Book 8 of John Gower's *Confessio Amantis* telling the story of Apollonius of Tyre, and part of his researches for *Pericles*—for his own novella, *The Painful Adventures of Pericles, Prince of Tyre* (1608). He likewise plagiarized a prior translation of *The History of Justine* for his own 1606 retelling, and seems to have exploited the success of *The Miseries of Enforced Marriage* by selling his authorial papers illicitly to a publisher. It was this last transgression that possibly got him fired from writing *Pericles*.

Shakespeare's share was written either in the latter part of 1607, or into early 1608, as, perhaps, was Wilkins' (we don't know how long the *Miseries* scandal took to take effect). It was definitely before 20 May 1608, when Edward Blount, one of the First Folio's publishers, entered his rights in *Pericles,* along with *Antony and Cleopatra*, in the Stationers' Register.[9] Blount's failure to publish has caused confusion, interpreted variously as a 'blocking entry' on behalf of Shakespeare's company, to stop others publishing it, or as Blount's attempt at publication which the company subsequently blocked.[10] If the former, it may have been protection against Wilkins, with whom the King's Men had no further dealings. Wilkins' sense of ownership of the story is likely reflected in his cashing in on it the following year with *Painful Adventures*, part-plagiarized not only from Twine, but also from the play, even describing itself on its title page as 'the true history of the play of *Pericles*'. *Pericles*, though, found its way into print by other surreptitious means, published in 1609 by Henry Gosson, and attributed to Shakespeare only.

Wilkins' dismissal, if it happened, may explain the absence of his name, which had appeared on the title page of the 1607 *Miseries* imprint, a scandal that had seemingly ended his playwriting career. Yet while *Pericles'* title page information may reflect active dissociation from Wilkins, it may simply be that Gosson, as a stationer emphasizing selling points, felt he was not a dramatist readers would care much about, even if they knew he had written some of the play. The 1600s had already seen *Thomas Lord Cromwell, A Yorkshire Tragedy, The London Prodigal,* and *The Puritan* all falsely attributed to Shakespeare in print, a subspecies of a wider drive across the decade to supply readers with his authoriality, seemingly in spite of his company's wishes.[11] *Pericles* was even for a long time lumped in with these spurious attributions. The King's Men seem to have cut off the supply of new Shakespeare plays to the presses at around the time they opened the Globe in 1599, taking a similar stance on all their assets going forward judging by the paucity of their extant repertory outside the Jonson (1616), Shakespeare (1623), and Beaumont and Fletcher (1647) Folios.[12] Only *Hamlet, Troilus, Lear*, and *Pericles* of all Shakespeare's post-1599 plays appeared in quarto during his lifetime; *Othello* appeared in 1622, a year before the Folio, though it and the others are all characterized by major textual puzzles that all in some way relate to the idea of authorization. Richard Preiss suggests both *Pericles* and Q1 *Lear*, a wholly Shakespearean authorial text, were published spuriously to help feed the Shakespeare market, perhaps in part accounting for the revision of *Lear* Shakespeare undertook around 1610.[13] Even if Wilkins' name had been hot in 1607, then, Shakespeare's was hotter in 1609.

That Wilkins wrote the prose novella to which *Pericles* has a clear commercial relationship makes it likely the play began with him. Twine's *Pattern* had been republished in 1607, a chance encounter with which most likely gave Wilkins a source for a new play that he started writing alone. He may have completed the first two acts for piecemeal payment, or been cashed out of them when his relationship with the company ended. *Painful Adventures* is structured in accord with *Pericles*' entrances, exits, and cues, and its prose is often metrical, as though channeling verse drama, showing strong verbal similarities with equivalent passages in Acts 1–2, though recalling the poetry of Acts 3–5 much less precisely. Wilkins evidently saw *Pericles* performed, and his sensory memory of it is strong, reconstructing its stage spectacle in his narrative, and agreeing in many details with it 'against all other versions of the story'.[14] He elaborates on the music Pericles performs at Simonides' banquet and its effects, and speaks of Lychorida bringing the baby on deck during the storm, a necessity of mimetic stage action that would more rationally involve Pericles going below in diegetic storytelling. Two acts may always have been his agreed contribution, though the NOS suggests limited linguistic evidence for his involvement in the Act 4 brothel scenes, meaning he either returned to work with Shakespeare on them, or more likely that Shakespeare reworked some material Wilkins had drafted.[15] But *Pericles* was probably begun by Wilkins for the company, and finished off by Shakespeare as de facto house dramatist, rather than a planned collaboration.

Wilkins' section is confected with rhyming couplets, within and between speeches, which Shakespeare's—apart from Gower, scene endings, the letter in Thaisa's coffin, and Diana's speech—otherwise eschews. The following passage shows this, as well as the evenness of Wilkins' verse compared with Shakespeare's, quoted on pp. 112–13:

> Sharp physic is the last. But O, you powers
> That gives heav'n countless eyes to view men's acts,
> Why cloud they not their sights perpetually
> If this be true which makes me pale to read it?
> Fair glass of light, I loved you, and could still
> Were not this glorious casket stored with ill.
> But I must tell you now my thoughts revolt,
> For he's no man on whom perfections wait
> That, knowing sin within, will touch the gate.
> (2.73–81)

Other formulaic Wilkinsian techniques in the first 11 scenes, identified by Jackson in his landmark study of the play's authorship, include a marked liking for the 'not/but' rhetorical construction:

> Which by my knowledge found, the sinful father
> Seemed **not** to strike, **but** smooth. (3.77–8)
> Decrease **not, but** grow faster than the years (3.85)

a tendency to repeat a word in a line for rhetorical effect, and an unusual favouring of the construction 'the which':

> To beat us **down**, *the which* are **down** already (5.67)

and a characteristic elision of the relative pronoun:

> Antioch, farewell! For wisdom sees, **those men**
>   (those men **who**)
> Blush not in actions blacker than the night (2.135–6)

Thou speak'st like **him's** (him who is) untutored to repeat.
Who makes the fairest show means most deceit. (5.73–4)

Gower, as chorus, is one of Wilkins' chief dramatic bequests, along with the Helicanus material in Scene 2, the Fishermen's dialogue in Scene 7, and Cleon and Dionyza's despairing at their failures of civil governance in Scene 5. Wilkins presents the play as a handed-down tale from the beginning, adopting the tetrameter and medieval lexis of its source, even resurrecting its author as a character. He uses Gower as a link to an older form of narration, less a psychological study than a poetic fable, the pointed archaism of the language something the dumbshows and deities further emphasize:

> To sing a song that old was sung,
> From ashes ancient Gower is come;
> Assuming man's infirmities,
> To glad your ear, and please your eyes.
> It hath been sung at festivals,
> On ember-eves and holy-ales;
> And lords and ladies in their lives
> Have read it for restoratives.   (1.1–8)

Although they did not collaborate directly, Shakespeare engages deeply and carefully with the writing Wilkins had left, carrying the medieval register over in his section, 'y-slakèd', 'eche', and 'y-ravishèd' all used in the first Gower chorus to open Act 3. Gower's was the best-known version of the Apollonius story, though Wilkins has his Gower acknowledge the longer heritage in a kind of meta-invocation—'I tell you what mine authors say'—suggesting all precursory authors as collaborators of sorts. Shakespeare shows himself an extremely conscientious co-author, taking pains to match in his approach to syntax and vocabulary the fairy-tale simplicity of Wilkins' style. This may just have been a careful attempt to balance his share with what Wilkins had left in order to make a coherent product of it, but the stylistic and narrative template are affordances Shakespeare exploits to effect a wondrous poignancy, unique in his canon. The play does change very definitely when Shakespeare takes over, caesurae and pause patterns migrating towards the middle of lines, and ideas running on in a more exploratory approach to poetic syntax than anything seen in the first two acts:

> Thou god of this great vast rebuke these surges,
> Which wash both heaven and hell; and thou that hast
> Upon the winds command, bind them in brass,
> Having called them from the deep. O still
> Thy deafening, dreadful thunders; gently quench
> Thy nimble, sulphurous flashes!—O, ho, Lychorida!
> How does my queen?—Thou stormest venomously.
> Wilt thou spit all thyself? The seaman's whistle
> Is as a whisper in the ears of death,
> Unheard.   (13.1–10)

Jackson's powerful account of the shift shows the play moving beyond what has been earthbound and limited; here the God Neptune is immediately summoned, the 'nouning' of the adjective 'vast' working economically to suggest a sea both expansive and liminal, the idea of the surges which wash both heaven and hell conjuring the huge peaks and troughs of the waves surrounding the 'ship' that is now the stage. It is in this storm that Pericles' wife, Thaisa, seemingly dies in childbirth. Shakespeare employs only subtly enhanced lexical imagery in the tender directness of Pericles' farewell, locking the two authorial styles together, even as he summons elemental depths of emotionality—augmented with the pointed and repeated use of stage spectacle—to give the drama dimension that has till now seemed beyond its purview:

> A terrible childbed hast thou had, my dear,
> No light, no fire. Th'unfriendly elements
> Forgot thee utterly, nor have I time
> To give thee hallowed to thy grave, but straight
> Must cast thee, scarcely coffined, in the ooze,
> Where, for a monument upon thy bones
> And aye-remaining lamps, the belching whale
> And humming water must o'erwhelm thy corpse,
> Lying with simple shells.   (13.55–63)

Other stylistic and prosodic features work to suggest Shakespearean authorship. Jackson adjudged the metrics of Acts 3–5 to be entirely characteristic of Shakespeare's verse *c.*1607, and markedly different from the metrical forms of Acts 1–2.[16] Patterns of research seem telling too: Pericles may derive from Sidney's *Arcadia*, which Shakespeare had used for *Lear*'s Gloucester subplot, or from Plutarch, which Shakespeare used extensively between 1606 and 1608, whose life of Pericles additionally names Cleon and Lysimachus. Shakespeare also introduces Marina ('of the sea'), turning what looks, in the first two acts, like a protagonist-led Mediterranean picaresque into the emblematic father–daughter-driven romance of his later work. The allegorical naming of heroines is a key feature of Shakespeare's three sole-authored late plays (Perdita, 'the lost one'; Innogen, 'innocence'; and Miranda, 'admirable'). Yet Marina embodies and emblematizes a key Wilkinsian component, which Shakespeare thematizes from the start of his contribution. In Wilkins' portion, the sea carries Pericles on his voyages, takes him home from Antioch to Tarsus, and washes him up on the shores of Pentapolis, where he finds and falls in love with Thaisa. In Shakespeare's it is the place where Marina is born, and where Thaisa 'dies'; it receives her body, delivers her to recovery, and aids the pirates who kidnap Marina to save her unwittingly from death. And it is the force that brings the drifting Pericles, at last, to Mytilene, and the child he thought dead:

> I am great with woe, and shall deliver weeping.
> My dearest wife was like this maid, and such a one
> My daughter might have been. My queen's square brows,
> Her stature to an inch, as wand-like straight,
> As silver-voiced, her eyes as jewel-like
> And cased as richly, in pace another Juno;
> Who starves the ears she feeds, and makes them hungry
> The more she gives them speech.   (25.95–102)

The hauntingly direct, emotive register of the verse, so necessary to the structural approach to story, allows Shakespeare to effect a reunion scene yoking an almost-broken frailty to a potent, regenerative vision through the sparest of poetic effects, yet guided integrally by Wilkins' work. While Shakespeare's focus is perhaps more characteristically on the personal experience of suffering and emotion, and Wilkins' on ideas of kingship and rule, interlinking themes carry across the authorial shares. Wilkins explores tyranny—inviting parallels of situation with Antiochus and Pericles as rulers—and incest, which Shakespeare responsively picks up on in contrasting the father–daughter relations of Pericles and Marina. The depiction of sex trafficking shows the real-world costs of border-crossing displacement typical of the diasporic romance plots in which *Pericles* trades, and Shakespeare has Lysimachus, the Governor of Mytilene, frequent the brothel to which Marina is sold, where he tries to rape her, before converting at her strong entreaties, and, somewhat troublingly, marrying her at the end. Wilkins makes Cleon the hubristic architect of disastrous famine in his city, Tarsus, and Shakespeare makes a would-be murderer of his wife, Dionyza, though they—like Antiochus and his daughter—are killed by the gods for their corruption and failure of civil rule. And while Wilkins conjures the gods apostrophically, Shakespeare gives them presence, makes them stage effects and overseers of the characters' fates, in Cerimon's god-like powers, in the music of the spheres, and in the figure of Diana, goddess of chastity.

Wilkins instigated a major shift in Shakespeare's work, fuelling a tremendously productive run of sole authorship in the romance vein, just as Middleton had helped drive another of the more extraordinary phases of his creativity. Admittedly, this neat generic narrative is interrupted by *Coriolanus* in 1608, and the revisions to *King Lear* c.1610, but Shakespeare's tendency was always to dissolve dramatic boundaries in any case. *Twelfth Night*, a late-Elizabethan festive comedy, foreshadowed, in the death and corrosive regret that haunt it, the darkening of his early Jacobean vision while anticipating the magical reunions of his late one. Conversely, *The Comedy of Errors*, a much earlier play that trades in slapstick frivolity, which used for its ending the same source as *Pericles*, paints the Mediterranean as a vast, hostile terrain making lost, lonely exiles of parents and children. Shakespeare had also dealt with improbable fantasy, even deities, on stage before, but in *Pericles* he seems to ask a different sort of imaginative engagement from audiences. In late Shakespeare, storms can be weathered, boats brought finally to safe harbour, and lost children can come home. *King Lear*'s protagonists were dashed against the rocks, but in *Pericles* Shakespeare re-imagines as he re-enacts, working, at last, the longed-for restitution he had so stringently denied audiences in his earlier tragedy (though characteristically Shakespearean difficulty breaks through the faux naivety, both plays seeing the male, paternal experience of suffering overbear the rightful centrality of the female child's). A new dramaturgy defined the final solo plays of Shakespeare's career, a development beyond collaboration, yet despite the singularities of his innovation he did not get there alone. He was, at the outset, gifted the beginnings of another man's play, and exploited the opportunities of being shown something new.

Endings: John Fletcher

Though *Pericles* underpins his late romance, Shakespeare must also have been influenced by the appearance and immediate success of *Philaster* (1609), co-written for his company by up-and-coming prodigy, John Fletcher, and Francis Beaumont. It ushered in a vogue for a more modern style of romance, building on Fletcher's *The Faithful Shepherdess* (1608), which had laid out the generic term by which an early modern audience might have better understood such plays: 'tragicomedy'.[17] Fletcher followed *Philaster* with *The Woman's Prize* (1610), a sequel to *The Taming of the Shrew* again for Shakespeare's company, with whom he and Beaumont enjoyed a bumper year together in 1611–12 with *A King and No King*, *The Maid's Tragedy*, and *The Captain* in rapid succession. Beaumont stopped writing for the public stage mid-1612. His final dramatic work was *The Masque of the Inner Temple*, in early 1613, after which he married the heiress Ursula Isley, a life choice often seen as prompting his voluntary retirement from writing, though the debilitating stroke he suffered several months later probably forced an involuntary one. *The Two Noble Kinsmen* (late 1613) includes a Morris dance taken from Beaumont's masque. While some interplay between the King's Men's masque entertainment and their Blackfriars repertory was well established by then, including in Shakespeare's sole-authored plays, this likely reflects Fletcher's affectionate tribute to his erstwhile partner, the masque originally having been written for performance by gentlemen of the Inns of Court.[18] Fletcher, over the eighteen months that followed Beaumont's final bow to the theatres, turned to a writing partner in Shakespeare, collaborating on the final three plays of Shakespeare's career. And it is difficult to know which of the two was the company's main authorial brand by then.

We also do not know the instigator of this creative relationship. It began in the second half of 1612 with *Cardenio*, a play never printed, and surviving only partially through Lewis Theobald's 1727 adaptation, *Double Falsehood*. Of Fletcher's ten plays to that date, only *The Faithful Shepherdess* and *The Woman's Prize* were sole authored, the remaining eight co-written with Beaumont. Fletcher contributed five plays in the tragicomic vein to Shakespeare's company—including *A King and No King*—all in collaboration, and it is perhaps as part of this trajectory that we might best understand the characteristics of his Shakespeare collaborations, different as they are from either *Pericles* or Shakespeare's solo romances. Raphael Lyne has remarked on Fletcher's responsiveness to Shakespeare's work in his own plays as 'creative commentaries', and *Kinsmen* is filled with homage to the moods and motifs of *A Midsummer Night's Dream*, *Hamlet*, the Sonnets, and *Macbeth*, among others.[19] *Cardenio* is perhaps too buried in Theobald's adaptation to tell, though *All Is True* might well be Fletcher, having already appropriated *Shrew* for a sequel, wanting to work with Shakespeare on a new kind of history play. It features a song, which, albeit written by Fletcher, shows much imaginative and tonal affinity with the dramaturgy of Shakespeare's sole-authored romances, as does the dream vision episode, with its quasi-divine, ceremonial dumbshow.

And yet their collaborations are almost like a mini-canon within the Shakespeare canon, more redolent overall of Fletcher's mode of romance, while bearing distinctive hallmarks of Shakespeare's earlier interests in his sections.[20] *Cardenio*—which draws on Cervantes' *Don Quixote*, a source Shakespeare had never used before—appears to have been a comedy of deception in love very similar to *The Two Gentlemen of Verona* in a number of respects of plotting, resolved in a way that recalls early Shakespearean comedy more strongly than late romance. *All Is True* sees Shakespeare return to the history play for the first time since the 1590s, while in *Kinsmen* he goes back to Chaucer's 'Knight's Tale' for a love-rival comedy he last exploited in *A Midsummer Night's Dream*. Yet *Pericles* had drawn thematically and dramaturgically on much earlier romance, and *The Winter's Tale* had adapted work by

Robert Greene, the transformation of 'mouldy tales' a self-conscious, deliberate component of Shakespeare's late drive at originality:

From this perspective Shakespeare is Fletcher's competitor, as well as collaborator, alert to the new directions the younger man is taking, but resistantly finding his own distinctive line in a process of generic recuperation and revision.[21]

But both Fletcher and Shakespeare brought rich innovations in their collaborations to a genre whose revival and refiguring was led by the King's Men. Fletcher was the first to bring tragicomedy—collaboratively at that—into another company's repertory through *The Honest Man's Fortune* (1613). Although a politicized approach to genteel drama was not exclusively the preserve of the King's company's Blackfriars' repertory—the plays also graced the Globe—the more elite Blackfriars' audience nonetheless did not favour the style and action of plays like *Pericles*, with *Cardenio*, *All Is True*, and *Kinsmen* written with their spectatorship first in mind. Still, more exclusive audiences were no guarantee of success. *All Is True* was apparently first performed in 1613 at the Globe, and seen there by a noble patron, Sir Henry Wotton, who, in a letter of 2 July, suggests the play was new and that its chief theatrical innovation was an expensive ceremonial grandeur that came to feel decidedly cheap:

The Kings Players had a new Play, called *All is true*, representing some principall pieces of the raign of Henry 8. which was set forth with many extraordinary circumstances of Pomp and Majesty, even to the matting of the stage; the Knights of the Order, with their Georges and Garter, the Guards with their embroidered Coats, and the like: sufficient in truth within a while to make greatness very familiar, if not ridiculous.

This grandeur was, indeed, fatal to the Globe theatre, which burned down as a result of cannon fire before a ceremonial entrance in 1.4, a disaster that Wotton's letter records in some detail. His account of one potential victim being saved with beer poured onto his burning breeches is a famously vivid anecdote. The play was printed ten years later in the Folio, where it was given the title 'King HENRY the Eight' and positioned, according to the chronology of historical events, as the last play in the Histories section. Chronologically, it is the latest play preserved in the Folio, and the only Fletcher collaboration to be included. It was apparently of interest to the Folio editors only as a history play, the genre in which it sought to make Shakespeare pre-eminent. A mysterious delay in the acquisition of copy for typesetting may reflect Fletcher, an important asset to the company by 1623, not wanting his collaborative work included in a volume attributed to Shakespeare alone, though there is no indication he had any power to do this.[22] That *Cardenio* and *Kinsmen* were excluded is no confirmation, and possibly determined by repertory as much as collaboration—*Kinsmen*'s 1634 quarto is based on prompt copy containing mid-1620s' theatrical annotation.[23] There is no need, in other words, to read the Folio's treatment of the Fletcher–Shakespeare canon as a black mark against collaboration in general, or a way by which we might infer the popularity of their work together.

Their mode of collaboration seems quite separate, and there may even have been significant distance between the two authors on at least one of the plays if, as many suppose, Shakespeare had returned to Stratford. His brother, Richard, died there in February 1613, and the Globe theatre burned down on 29 June that year, either one of these events perhaps finally prompting a move home. If the former, then *All Is True* was certainly a remote collaboration. We do not know the circumstances of *Cardenio*'s composition in 1612, though it was apparently written half-and-half, while *All Is True* and *Kinsmen* are more mixed together in authorial stints by scenic unit (see Appendix 1).[24] *Kinsmen* has been thought of as the most distant collaboration, the authorial shares distinguishable by varying metrical scansion, and, to a lesser degree, the spelling of the name 'Pirithous', trisyllabic in Shakespeare following North's Plutarch, and tetrasyllabic in Fletcher following Chaucer.[25] Lois Potter also notes the play's sharp 'separation of main plot and subplot and its large number of soliloquies' as 'designed to facilitate collaboration' at a remove.[26] Act 5 shows a more complex intermixing of scenes, either suggesting proximate collaboration at that stage or increased confidence in working apart.

We can say that all three of the collaborations between Fletcher and Shakespeare are exceptionally well planned, perhaps further reflecting contingency for working at a far remove from one another, or perhaps just Fletcher's habitual mode of collaboration. Indeed, the patterns of authorial stint in *All Is True* and *Kinsmen* look markedly similar to *Philaster*'s, all plays almost exactly 60–40 in Fletcher's favour, with the same kinds of scenic division common to both pairs of writers:

Beaumont: 1.2, 2.1, 2.3–4.1–8, 3.1–2, 4.3–6, 5.1–3.117, 5.5
Fletcher: 1.1, 2.2, 2.4.9–190, 4.1–2, 5.3.118–92, 5.4

The Fletcher–Shakespeare patterns do not necessarily suggest remote collaboration, then, being virtually indistinct from at least one Beaumont and Fletcher method.[27] *All Is True* has a co-authored scene, started by Shakespeare and finished by Fletcher, and it is notable that the early texts of both *The Woman Hater* and *Kinsmen* have scene divisions at points where the stage is not cleared, and where stylometry indicates change of authorship.[28] Scribal confusion at authorial stints in different hands, and possibly on different pages of the underlying copy is the likeliest explanation for this, in what are nonetheless carefully coordinated handovers between the authors. But the increasing flexibility across their three collaborations may suggest Shakespeare needed time to get used to Fletcher as a writing partner. All relationships, no matter how productive, take work.

Source use in *All Is True* seems consistent with remote collaboration. Fletcher worked from John Speed's *Theatre of the Empire of Great Britain* (1611) and Shakespeare his favoured Holinshed's *Chronicles* (1577, rev. 1587) for their various approaches to the main plot. Fletcher also, in a kind of meta-collaboration, reworked material from his and Beaumont's *Maid's Tragedy* (1611) into *All Is True*'s comic rioting episode of 5.3, while for 1.2, Shakespeare seems to have drawn on the anonymous King's Men play, *Thomas Lord Cromwell* (1600, published 1602), a so-called apocryphal work, attributed to 'W.S'. in early editions. Other borrowings have been noted from John Foxe's *Acts and Monuments* (1563, repr. 1610), and perhaps John Stow's *Annals of England* (1592). The commixture of chronicle and dramatic sources behind the play has contributed to an editorial and interpretative disjuncture, apropos its different titles; between its status as a narrative based on historical material and as a more emblematic dramatic reimagining that calls attention to its own semi-fictional status, which perhaps speaks most strongly of all of the 'distance' between Shakespeare and Fletcher.

As the picture of Shakespeare as collaborator—and indeed secondary collaborator—on the play gathers strength, though, the question of its title arguably gains clarity. We cannot be certain that original audiences did not know it as *Henry VIII, or All Is True*, much like the play printed in the Folio as *Twelfth Night, or What You Will*. *All Is True* has made awkward sense as the title of a Shakespearean history play to generations of critics, but to conceive of it tonally, formally, theatrically, generically, even chronologically as more allied to Fletcherian romance may help align its titular identity with its theatrical origins. It may also have been influenced, in the form of its title as well as its subject matter, by the other, equally cautious, dramatization of events from Henry VIII's life, Samuel Rowley's *When You See Me You Know Me* (1604), reissued, and possibly revived, in 1613. Walter Cohen, conversely, suggests the valorizing *Henry VIII* may be Fletcher's revision, pushing the 'more Protestant outlook' of his scenes in the play, with the original *All Is True* a reflection of Shakespeare's more 'uncommitted treatment of religious controversy'.[29] It would also reflect Shakespeare's tendency elsewhere to use proverbial titles: *Love's Labour's Lost*, *Much Ado about Nothing*, *Measure for Measure*, *All's Well that Ends Well*, and the aforementioned subtitle, *What You Will*. Whether the monarchic title was promoted by Fletcher or, as is more likely, the Folio editors, there is no reason to doubt *All Is True* as characteristically Shakespearean in outlook.

Its negotiations with 'truth' as a lexical item (see the Prologue in particular), a titular identity, a supposed approach to the adaptation of source material, and the presentation of complex and controversial historical personages—which Annabel Patterson has discussed as an inherent tension between the impetus to present a versified chronicle versus a complex 'meditation on the effects of the Reformation in England'—have been reflected in many editorial and attributional discussions.[30] Equally, critics have proposed the Folio's title as an alternative hermeneutic framework through which to understand the play, or at least that the two titles evidence authorial discontinuity in the treatment of religion, history, and dramatic representation. In turn, the expectation that the biographical 'truth' of each author's religious convictions would receive face-value representation in a fictionalized reimagining, a complex work of art, has been as frequently dismissed as a shrinking of authorial agency. Truth is explored most obviously and most literally in Katherine's speech in defence of herself, strongly recalling Hermione's trial in *The Winter's Tale*:

> Sir, call to mind
> That I have been your wife in this obedience
> Upward of twenty years, and have been blest
> With many children by you. If in the course
> And process of this time you can report—
> And prove it too—against mine honour aught,
> My bond to wedlock, or my love and duty
> Against your sacred person, in God's name,
> Turn me away, and let the foul'st contempt
> Shut door upon me, and so give me up
> To the sharp'st kind of justice.   (*All Is True*, 2.4.32–42)

Both women, incidentally, invoke their fathers as idealized arbitrators, perhaps reinforcing the links Masten noted between ideas of paternity and authenticity. If the play shares anything with *Pericles*, it is most strongly felt in the romance trope of fortune's rise and fall, and of faith, and faithfulness, as the guiding light, Katherine epitomizing this even if her truth is not rewarded in life. She is the Catholic monarch making way for Anne Boleyn, and, therefore, the Protestant Reformation, and the play's emotional heart, while Anne is a small role and far less romanticized character. While the play aims at a greater sophistication than *Pericles*, and more ostensible political neutrality than Jacobean comedy or early Shakespearean history, it is still surprisingly cynical about the mechanisms of courtly power. Yet it chooses, ultimately, to focus on the corrupt ambition for which its second-largest role, Wolsey, takes the fall:

> Farewell, a long farewell, to all my greatness!
> This is the state of man. Today he puts forth
> The tender leaves of hopes; tomorrow blossoms,
> And bears his blushing honours thick upon him;
> The third day comes a frost, a killing frost,
> And, when he thinks, good easy man, full surely
> His greatness is a-ripening, nips his root,
> And then he falls, as I do.   (*All Is True*, 3.2.354–61)

The play shares the same monarch with *Sir Thomas More* —an off-stage presence only in the latter, though *All Is True*'s largest speaking role—and both find workaround ways to present him without controversy. Portmanteau structures aid avoidance of the more obvious arc of Henry's life story and the tragic collateral waste of those close to him. Both also employ the tactic of foregrounding one of his famous chancellors as a focal point, albeit More's martyrdom is in clear contrast with Wolsey's downfall as a topic to worry the censor. If *Henry VIII* is the play's homogenizing First Folio 'histories' name, *All Is True* destabilizes historical narrative with ambiguously opposing claims either to rigid veracity ('hand on heart, this is true') or amorphous permissiveness ('everything is true, and anything goes'). The play absorbs fractal and conflicting visions of historical events, persons, and reputations; it divines and effectively stages the transference of power from the Tudor to the Stuart dynasty—James is figured as 'A pattern to all princes' even while the infant Elizabeth is exalted—a difficult reconciliation achieved through an agile fidelity to both. And all done through an accommodation of the coincidences and divergences in a collaborative enterprise between two very different creative artists. Even without the surviving documentary evidence, the competing transformations the play attempts have been plausibly held as integral to its original title.

The largely intuitive divisions of *All Is True*'s two styles have been borne out by more forensic approaches. William Montgomery in the 1986 Oxford Shakespeare relied chiefly on Cyrus Hoy's assessment of the authorial shares, at the time the most up-to-date and comprehensive stylometric analysis of the play.[31] Hoy was more conservative than James Spedding and Samuel Hickson, who, in 1850, were the first to suggest Fletcher's co-authorship of the play giving much of the material they assigned to Fletcher back to Shakespeare, though allowing that Fletcher may have 'touched up' some or all of it. Shakespeare's principal stylistic fingerprint in the play, beyond lexical preferences, is a marked predilection for run-on verse, reflecting what is termed by Russ McDonald as 'divagatory syntax'. It displays an unusually pronounced blend of fluidity—the sinews of the verse stretching conspicuously across line-endings and beginnings—and a syntactical and ideational idiosyncrasy, pushing beyond even the radical experiments of his late sole-authored work. Although *Cardenio* is lost to us, *Double Falsehood*'s supposed Shakespearean portion is the most heavily adapted, suggesting the arduous style of his contributions to *All Is True* and *Kinsmen* might have similarly characterized the writing there.[32] While Shakespeare was the more minor partner in his contribution to their collaborations, he makes his parts in them opportunities to experiment with hybridizing form and genre. His writing with Fletcher is perhaps the most authorially distinct of all his collaborative pairings. If *Pericles* used imagistic and syntactical sparsity, Shakespeare's language in *Kinsmen* and *All Is True* can be awkward, hyper-extended, unusually elliptical and knotty, containing as it does many feminine endings, with crabbed, difficult, and inverted stress patterns, something many feel he carried to extremes, as in this example:

> Then you lost
> The view of earthly glory. Men might say
> Till this time pomp was single, but now married
> To one above itself. Each following day
> Became the next day's master, till the last
> Made former wonders its . . . The two kings,
> Equal in lustre, were now best, now worst,
> As presence did present them. Him in eye
> Still him in praise, and being present both,
> 'Twas said they saw but one, and no discerner
> Durst wag his tongue in censure.
> (*All Is True*, 1.1.13–18, 28–33)

And in this, a 16-line sentence in which syntax, sense, and metre balk at resolution:

> Honoured Hippolyta,
> Most dreaded Amazonian, that hast slain
> The scythe-tusked boar, that with thy arm, as strong
> As it is white, wast near to make the male
> To thy sex captive, but that this thy lord—
> Born to uphold creation in that honour
> First nature styled it in—shrunk thee into
> The bound thou wast o'erflowing, at once subduing
> Thy force and thy affection; soldieress,
> That equally canst poise sternness with pity,

> Whom now I know hast much more power on him
> Than ever he had on thee, who ow'st his strength,
> And his love too, who is a servant for
> The tenor of thy speech; dear glass of ladies,
> Bid him that we, whom flaming war doth scorch,
> Under the shadow of his sword may cool us.
>   (*The Two Noble Kinsmen*, 1.1.77–92)

Collaboration is often seen, in aim and execution, as an intricate, inextricably blended process, but here the marked shifts seem almost to want to signal authorial boundaries, even while working ostensibly to a common aim. Stanley Wells has suggested a 'growing distaste for the demands of popular theatre' evident in these last works with Fletcher, Shakespeare's writing almost wilfully dysfunctional.[33] Fletcher's share, especially in *Kinsmen*, has drawn praise as the more coherent and dramatically compelling of the two, yet the show-stealing part of the Jailer's Daughter is a complex co-creation, which the dramatists expanded from a hint in Chaucer. It is reminiscent, across both authorial stints, of earlier Shakespearean tragic motifs of madness, Ophelia especially, and distinctively embedded in the play's dramatic and generic modes.

Shakespeare ends on collaboration, and seems a particularly willing co-author in his late work. His *Pericles* contribution adopts Wilkins' direct, pared-back register to powerful dramatic and imaginative effect, while the Shakespearean sections of *All Is True* and *Kinsmen* strongly conform to the thematic, structural, and tonal patterns of Fletcherian romance. Yet he also crafts some of his most adventurous, highly individuated poetic syntax in these plays, his writing with Fletcher, radically experimental in idea and language use, changing again our understanding of the ever-shifting contours of his style and influences. And *Kinsmen* notably breaks the mould of providential romance with its sombre conclusion, in which lip-service only is paid to the equanimity and restorative justice of the gods, a world away from *Pericles*:

> The gods have been most equal . . .
>   . . . O you heavenly charmers,
> What things you make of us! For what we lack
> We laugh, for what we have, are sorry; still

> Are children in some kind. Let us be thankful
> For that which is, and with you leave dispute
> That are above our question. Let's go off,
> And bear us like the time.   (5.6.114, 130–6)

Kinsmen, like *Pericles*, is classically set and based on a famous medieval source. The inventory of Henry Condell's widow Elizabeth's library lists a copy of Chaucer's Works, suggesting possible ownership by the company, and availability for use by either dramatist.[34] As already noted in this chapter, Shakespeare had last used 'The Knight's Tale' for *A Midsummer Night's Dream* in 1595, and before *Pericles*' use of *Confessio Amantis*—an ancient Greek tale in which a hero wanders the world to find what is lost, restored through chance and divine intervention—it had served as influence for *The Comedy of Errors* back in 1594. But if his late writing is in any way rethinking his early, it is perhaps most seen in the interests—as in *Two Gentlemen*, *Love's Labour's Lost*, even *The Winter's Tale*—in difficult male friendships, and in pairings. Palamon and Arcite, Valentine and Proteus, Leontes and Polixenes, Mercury and Apollo, Spring and Winter. Comparing Shakespeare's last dramatic words, speaking emptily as they do of harmony with the gods, Mars and Venus, to some of the first words he wrote in the early collaboration *Titus Andronicus*—'Madam, though Venus govern your desires, / Saturn is dominator over mine'—there is a definite sense of reciprocity, of going back to the beginning. But there is also a common idea of division, with no sense of easy reconcilement.

Coda

In linguistics tests on the supposed Shakespearean portion of *Pericles*, the strongest affinities are not only with Shakespeare's sole-authored late plays, but also with the tragedies in which he began significantly experimenting with syntactical form and structure: *Macbeth* and *Antony and Cleopatra*. The groundwork for his abstruse versifying with Fletcher is seen here, as he looked for more complex ways of figuring psychological process through form. *The Winter's Tale* contains some of the most striking examples, especially in the strange, fractured speeches given to Leontes. Their tense effect is compounded by the kind of structuring seen in Shakespeare's tauter tragedies, the narrative building sequentially with a purposeful, even claustropho-bic intensity. But comfort is near at hand. 'Thou met'st with things dying, I with things newborn' (3.3.99) says the Old Shepherd to his son, and, with Time's speech, the second half ushers in a languid, expansive dramaturgy, heavy with darkly comic prose. The centre-piece of this Mercurial extravaganza, the so-called 'sheep-shearing' scene, in its meandering Arcadian rhythms and near 900-line length utilizes a scenic form Shakespeare had not used since *Love's Labour's Lost*, perhaps Shakespeare's first assertion of sole-authorship as the Chamberlain's poet–dramatist.

John Jowett has suggested that the mysterious epigram at the end of the 1598 quarto text—'The words of Mercury are harsh after the songs of Apollo'—alludes, in a fleeting and ambiguous fashion, to his old quarrel with Robert Greene.[35] Shakespeare was reasserting a position first advanced in *Venus and Adonis*, where the title page had quoted Ovid's *Amores* for its motto: *'Vilia miretur vulgus: mihi flavus Apollo / Pocula Castalia plena ministret aqua'* ('Let what is cheap excite the marvel of the crowd; for me may golden Apollo minister full cups from the Castalian fount'), aligning the work with the classical poet, and implying artistic consanguinity. The epigram, Jowett argues, was, as discussed at the end of Chapter 3, part of a stance against the cheaper, flashier end of print culture that was finding its strongest expression in the early 1590s through Greene and others. Greene was a journalistic powerhouse in the late 1580s–early 1590s, whose dis-solute lifestyle led to his premature death in September 1592. Both his sensational living, and the sensationalist style in which he doc-umented his semi-fictionalized accounts of it, made him a highly desirable, albeit short-term, commodity. As Thomas Nashe said of him: 'Glad was that printer that might be so blest to pay him dear for the very dregs of his wit'.[36] Greene churned out a number of plays and an even larger number of pamphlets, many on 'coney catching'—ribald descriptions of lowlife criminality in the city, and of Greene's association with various 'copesmates' and cozeners. But he also wrote the prose novella *Pandosto, or The Triumph of Time* (1588), on which Shakespeare based *The Winter's Tale*.

The first couplet of the pedlar's pack song, sung by the rogue, Autolycus—*Lawn as white as driven snow, / Cypress black as e'er was crow* (4.4.219–20)—as he enters about a third of the way into the play's longest scene, contains the imagery Ovid associates with the mythical Autolycus, child of Mercury, in Book 11 of the *Metamorphoses*:

> Now when she full her time had gone, she bare by
>   Mercury
> A son that hight Autolycus, who proved a wily pie,
> And such a fellow as in theft and filching had no peer.
> He was his father's own son right: he could men's eyes so
>   blear,
> As for to make the black things white, and white things
>   black appear.
>   (*Metamorphoses*, 11:322–26; tr. Golding 1567)

Autolycus is the embodiment of the Ovidian, and, by extension, as he now appears as a human character personated on a stage by an actor, the Shakespearean shape-shifter, living by deception, theft, confidence tricks, and disguises. Mercury was the mythical messenger of the gods, associated with eloquence and sophistry, and Shakespeare's Autolycus lives by convincing the simple-minded that black is white, that his trinkets are valuable, and his tall-tale ballads true. Ballad-selling was one way of luring in willing dupes, with a showman exciting the marvel of the crowd while his accomplice went round the distracted throng cutting their purses, as Greene himself describes.[37] Ovid's Autolycus had a twin, Philammon, the child of Apollo, who inherited his father's gift for music; and when we first see Autolycus in the play, displaying the characteristics both of his twin and of himself in singing a ballad, mixing the high and the low, we have a fusion of the Mercurial and the Apollonian, and perhaps an indication that we are working towards a state of reconciliation between the two.

Mercury was the inventor of the lyre, and without his gift of invention there could be no Apollonian music. Apollo lends his spirit to the high tragedy of the first half of the play, and his actual words to the trial of Hermione, pronouncing her innocence and Perdita's legitimacy. Mercury, the liar and thief, comes into the ascendancy for a large portion of the post-Time second half pulling the wool over the audience's eyes with comedy when tragedy had clearly been expected. If *The Winter's Tale* is governed by Apollo and Mercury, one of the main links between their two worlds is the idea of print. In Apollo's, it is a legitimizing, validating force, something trust-worthy, irrefutable, bound up with human genetics, and with nature itself. As Paulina says to the mistrusting Leontes of his newborn daughter:

> Behold, my lords,
> Although the print be little, the whole matter
> And copy of the father—eye, nose, lip,
> The trick of's frown, his forehead, nay, the valley,
> The pretty dimples of his chin and cheek, his smiles,
> The very mould and frame of hand, nail, finger.
> (2.3.97–102)

Reiterating what Leontes has already spoken doubtfully of, saying to Mamillius:

> Why, that's my bawcock. What? Hast smutched thy nose?
> They say it is a copy out of mine.   (1.2.123–4)

Possibly as part of his increasingly frenetic gynophobia in this scene, he is quick to undermine the notion of print by associating it with women, making it therefore something fickle and untrustworthy:

> Yet they say we are
> Almost as like as eggs. Women say so,
> That will say anything.   (1.2.131–3)

And, indeed, Mopsa, a simple shepherdess, is the chief advocate of Autolycus' false prints, saying 'I love a ballad in print, a-life, for then we are sure they are true' (4.4.258–9). By the fifth act, though, the female proves to be the validating force behind print, and thereby behind what can be trusted, the conveyor of art through reproduction. Looking upon the face of his long-estranged friend's son, Leontes says:

> Your mother was most true to wedlock, Prince,
> For she did print your royal father off,
> Conceiving you.   (5.1.123–5)

Print and the written word authorize in Sicilia; they can convey or carry the imprint and the copy of art, just as the statue, the conflation of art and nature that restores all at the end of the play, is supposedly a copy of the natural original. Apollo, absent in bodily form, is a distant voice who communicates only briefly through ink and paper, leaving the realms of art and nature to contend with one another. The artwork itself is all, and the need for the creator's voice to intervene, minimal. But they have an entirely different function in the Bohemia of Autolycus. There, print is just print: inked pieces of paper, sheets, materiality, words and not songs, unsuccessful art unable to compete with life for precedence. Autolycus shares his name with the mythical son of Mercury, under whose influence he was 'littered'. He is both ballad seller and stealer of sheets drying on lines, just as sheets of inked paper were left to hang in printing houses, marking him out as a literary thief as well as a promoter of bad art. Greene was not only an actual thief, but a shameless plagiarist, his work containing many paraphrased borrowings from earlier works, passed off as his own observations of the London scene. It is not the medium itself that is being attacked, but a cheap, stolen, imitative version of it.

No early modern writer editorializes less than Shakespeare. He seems to have known—as Ovid knew in ancient Rome—that the process of mythic self-creation depends upon the sustained portrayal of a playful yet eternally elusive figure at the margins of the all-important work of art. And no other writer captured Shakespeare's imagination more forcefully than Ovid. Moreover, as Shakespeare greedily encountered the *Metamorphoses* as a schoolboy, the spirit of metamorphosis itself, of shape-shifting, integral as it is to the art of theatrical drama, left an indelible imprint on his imagination, finding vivid expression in his later life as a dramatist. With *The Winter's Tale*, Shakespeare seems to be inverting patterns to meld Ovid and Greene, his Apollo and Mercury, together, in a feat of adaptation displaying playful, masterful, deeply imaginative approaches to intellectual collaboration and precursory authorship; a kind of metamorphic transformation of source material.

Shakespeare's tale radically reshapes Greene's, aligning the racy pamphlet more harmoniously and skilfully with Ovid by reversing place: in Greene, Pandosto (Leontes in Shakespeare) is the King of

Bohemia, the likelier winter court, and Egistus (Polixenes) of the sun-
drenched Sicily, ripe for pastoral. In Shakespeare, Sicily and Ovid
enter Bohemia, land of Mercury, of Autolycus—of whom there is no
equivalent in Greene—through Perdita's link to the myth of Proserpina at 4.4.113–29. Proserpina was raped while gathering wild flowers
in a Sicilian meadow by Dis—as he is called in Golding's translation of Ovid, from which Shakespeare worked—and taken to the
underworld.[38] Grieving, Ceres, goddess of the earth and Proserpina's
mother, begged Jupiter, Dis's brother, for her release. He allowed
it on condition that Proserpina had eaten nothing from the underworld, but she had, and in the compromise Jupiter proposed, was
fated to divide her time cyclically between Ceres and Dis: spring and
summer her time on earth, autumn and winter her return to the underworld. When Perdita, the lost one, 'returns' to the play after sixteen
years, she brings the summer and we leave Leontes' winter. Ovidian
transformation has already been invoked through Florizel's:

> Jupiter
> Became a bull, and bellowed; the green Neptune
> A ram, and bleated; and the fire-robed god,
> Golden Apollo, a poor humble swain,
> As I seem now. Their transformations
> Were never for a piece of beauty rarer
> (4.4.27–32)

One of the things that must have struck Shakespeare about Ovid's
writing was the medium in which he encountered it: a book printed
within his lifetime, in what to Ovid would have been a state unborn
and accent yet unknown. Ovid provided Shakespeare with proof of,
and a model for, literary survival, and Shakespeare is continually alive
to writing as equating to lasting fame, a constant preoccupation of
the Sonnets, for example. Immortality through verse is often intimately tied to immortality through procreation, the passing of one's
own beauty onto something else, the genetic inking of a blank sheet.
It is only through a being's ability to reproduce itself that survival is
likely, yet art will always win out; the newborn will eventually die,
while art is forever, not subject to weathering or change, therefore
better than nature in design.

Yet we see Shakespeare re-engage this Renaissance topos in *The Winter's Tale* as a way of trying, at last, to make peace between the worlds: between Apollo and Mercury, art and nature. The argument is being rehashed through the redemptive, forgiving mode of romance, albeit that the virtuosity of the play, as well as the wry wit underscoring it, are strong reminders that this is a choice rather than a necessity. The image of grafting, in the conversation between Perdita and the disguised Polixenes, grafts the metaphorical onto the literal in figuring art as a by-product of nature. In reply to his asking why she does not agree with it, she says:

> For I have heard it said
> There is an art which in their piedness shares
> With great creating nature.   (4.4.86–8)

To which he replies:

> Say there be;
> Yet nature is made better by no mean
> But nature makes that mean: so, over that art
> Which you say adds to nature, is an art
> That nature makes. You see, sweet maid, we marry
> A gentler scion to the wildest stock,
> And make conceive a bark of baser kind
> By bud of nobler race: this is an art
> Which does mend nature, change it rather, but
> The art itself is nature.   (4.4.88–97)

The 'art' she speaks of is horticultural grafting, which she equates with the unnaturalness of cosmetics. Polixenes' argument is that one makes the other; that that which the created creates, though an improvement, is nonetheless drawn from the raw materials it inherited. Art improves on nature, but nature facilitates art, and in this 'mankind is not a usurper of nature but a collaborator'.[39] Just as the deities Ceres and Dis between them mark summer and winter, as Perdita embodies a link between their two worlds, effecting the change between both, the brothers Apollo and Mercury are present in Florizel and Autolycus: high and low art, Greene and Ovid, the printed word and the natural world all grafted together, and in each case we cannot have one without the other. Hermione's body in statue form is both natural original and artwork, both creator and created. The play's moment of Apollonian recreation, it transpires, could not have been possible without the intervention of Mercurial deception, just as the play's most memorable stage image could not be possible without a synergy of the real and the artful, the magical, the deceptive. If magic is illusion, a sort of artful confidence trick, then the play finds a way to validate it as that which makes the familiar patterns of nature and art new, unexpected, redemptive. We see it in Leontes' words as he embraces his 'resurrected' wife for the first time in sixteen years:

> O, she's warm!
> If this be magic, let it be an art
> Lawful as eating.   (5.3.109–11)

Shakespeare's art, his process, had arguably never found such self-conscious expression in anything he had written before, and this stripping bare would surely not be happening were the design not to create something totally new. Shakespeare is here like Ovid, and like Ovid's Pygmalion, who carved a statue so lifelike that he fell in love with it, and, with a little help from Venus, breathed literal life into it with a kiss; like the Renaissance artist, Giulio Romano, the only contemporary artist ever named by Shakespeare, a miracle worker creating living form from inanimate raw materials. But the Apollonian music that governs Shakespeare's high tragedy cannot effect this change on its own. The truth is that it needs Mercury's words to convince us that black is white. And in the merge Shakespeare effects a series of astonishing transformations, inspired by a tale in Ovid that is itself something of a reversal—women in Ovid are usually turned *into* statues, birds, trees, animals, not the other way around. From the prose medium of Greene's novella, to the artificial shaping, the excelling nature of theatrical performance, turning both lurid tragedy and arch satire into something magical and forgiving, Hermione, after her time in the underworld, turns death into life, winter into spring, tragedy into comedy, and disbelief into wonder. The result is just a lie, of course, an elaborate hoax, a winter's tale; but the redemptive, emotive power enabled by the combining of distinct talents, influences, even rivalries, is transformative and real.

Shakespeare and Greene never collaborated so far as we know, though may have been indirectly connected around *Locrine* (see next chapter). The *Groatsworth*, Greene's final and posthumously published work, marks Shakespeare out as an enemy usurper within a group of individual talents. When Shakespeare wrote *The Winter's Tale*, they were long gone. The changes by 1610—to poetic style, repertory, genre, personnel, company management, patronage, monarchical rule, social order, even, perhaps most pointedly, to Shakespeare's individual status—would have been unimaginable to Greene. Yet the *Groatsworth* may have driven Shakespeare to a form of authorial self-assertion he might not otherwise have attempted as aggressively without it.[40] *Venus and Adonis* is partly explicable as a high-end literary publication for a high-end patron, the Earl of Southampton, during a particularly virulent outbreak of plague. Yet the precise arrangements of the enterprise as a whole, and the quarto's Ovidian paratext in particular, seem, beyond formulaic homage, to have been cut from a form of hostile interchange in the medium of print, away from, though ultimately about, the dynamic collaborative energies of the theatre, supposedly lending Shakespeare reflected and unmerited success.

Mercury and the upstart crow connote theft, hinting, on one level, at the practices of collaboration Shakespeare was accelerating in the commercial theatres. *Venus*, on the other hand, asserts a move back towards individual, literary authorship, Renaissance ideas of poetic art on the classical model dominated by sole authorship.[41] But a committed return to collaboration in Shakespeare's late works, and a career-long commitment to commercial drama, suggest a long rethinking, and, perhaps, part resolution of those tensions. While it would almost certainly be false to say that Shakespeare could not have done what he did without the spur—antagonistic or artistic—of Greene's influence, it simply *was* a part of the reality he inhabited, and of the writer that he became. His return to it after such a long career without it seems to betray an awareness that it was no less formative, or at least no less real, than the work of the ancient poets to whose high achievements he aspired. Even in working against for so long, Shakespeare was somehow working with, and even before the period of unbroken collaborative authorship that defined his career's end, he seemed to recognize the inescapability, and the great value, of that fact. In a play so recognized and lauded as Shakespeare's alone, collaboration—its synergies, its hermeneutics, its processes, its obligations, its inspirations, its debts—can be felt everywhere.

6

Page

Prestige

In late 1616, Shakespeare's erstwhile King's Men stablemate, Ben Jonson, asserted himself as sole author of the writing bound within a prestige folio edition of 'Workes'. Though not the first printed collection of plays to that date—William Alexander's *Monarchic Tragedies* of 1604 seems to hold that distinction, though Tara L. Lyons has suggested Richard Jones's 1590 publication of *1* and *2 Tamburlaine* together is an earlier paradigm—it was certainly the grandest.[1] Drama had never before appeared in the folio format, usually reserved for Bibles and the kind of scholarly tomes Shakespeare used as sources. It was an image of dramatic authoriality that Shakespeare—who had died in April that year—would not have recognized in his lifetime, and one so important to Jonson that he had had to omit several collaboratively written plays in order to present it authentically. While most of the book's design features—the ornate engraving of a classical, triumphal arch, the prominent typesetting of Jonson's name in cursive italics beneath the even more prominent, capitalized title—were down to the printer, William Stansby, Jonson was heavily involved in the revision and preparation of its contents. The central, isolated part of a Latin motto, 'locum teneant' ('keeping the place of') on the volume's title page (Figure 5), beneath an image of the 'theatrum', explicitly suggests the literary object standing in for different conditions of commercial authorial creation. But the volume misrepresents those conditions, and Jonson's part in them, in a number of ways.

Shakespeare and Collaborative Writing. Will Sharpe, Oxford University Press. © Will Sharpe (2023).
DOI: 10.1093/oso/9780198819639.003.0007

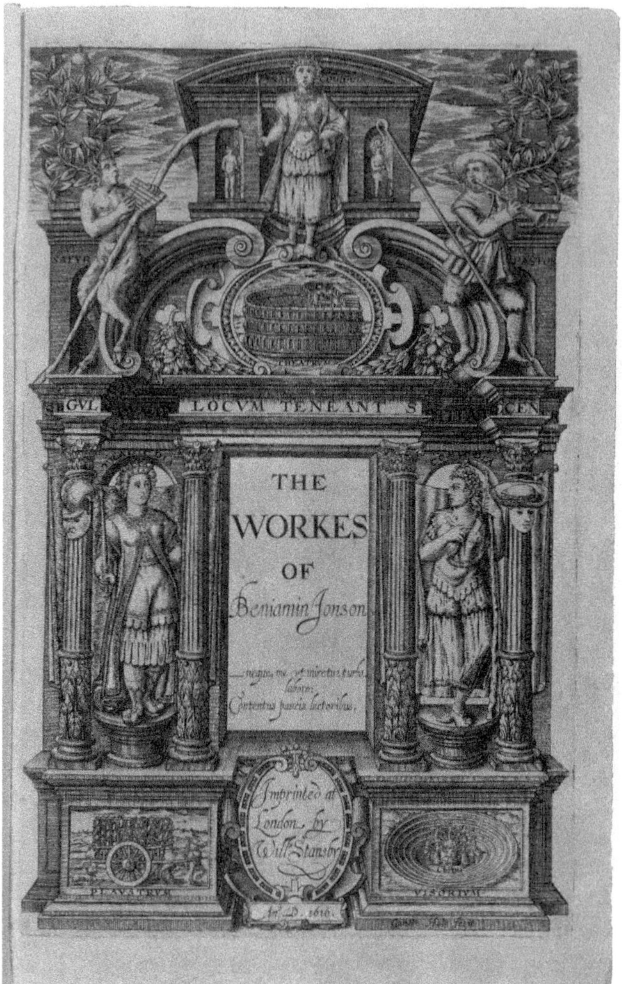

Figure 5 Title page of Ben Jonson's *Works*, F1 (1616), STC 14751, sig. ¶-2, used by permission of The Folger Shakespeare Library under a CC-BY-SA 4.0.

It omits his early collaborations for Henslowe, *Hot Anger Soon Cold*, *Page of Plymouth*, and *Robert II, King of Scots*, as well as *The Isle of Dogs* and *Eastward Ho!*, both of which had landed him in trouble with the authorities. Jonson had also replaced material by 'a second pen' in

Sejanus, as he notes in the epistle to the 1605 quarto, used as copy for the Folio, which also leaves out *The Case Is Altered*, a play sometimes suspected to have been at least revised by another author if not collaboratively written with them. It does include several court masques, stately entertainments created in another kind of collaboration with the architect and designer, Inigo Jones. Jones designed extraordinary sets and costumes that overshadowed—sometimes literally—the sycophantic drama Jonson produced in that medium. It is clear from surviving documentation that this working relationship, although effective, was not easy or friendly. But in print, Jones's achievements, and the collaborative enterprise they represented, were all but swept from view. They were of necessity recreated in Jonson's descriptive language, though only a couple name Jones at all, in fleeting fashion, and he is not mentioned in any of the volume's prefatory material. Jonson's Folio is one of the first commercial expressions of a 'complete works', and its model of proprietary single authorship is a product of the author's own curatorial control.

Seven years later, a similar statement was made on Shakespeare's behalf. Jonson's Folio was undoubtedly the paradigm for the presentation of Shakespeare as sole author of the writing in a prestige edition preserving work by George Peele, Thomas Middleton, John Fletcher, Thomas Nashe, Christopher Marlowe, and at least one other anonymous playwright. It was an image so important to the Folio's editors and publishers that they needed to efface the other dramatists' contributions in order to present it as authentic. They also omitted several other plays in which Shakespeare was involved as either collaborator or reviser. Some they did include—*1 Henry VI*, *Timon of Athens*, and *All Is True; or Henry VIII*—were being printed for the first time, while some had appeared before in cheap editions, all silent on collaboration, even on the matter of Shakespeare's authorship. *Titus* and *Contention* were published in quarto in 1594, and *Richard Duke of York* in octavo the following year, the latter two becoming *Part 2* and *3* of *Henry VI*, and presented as solely Shakespearean. *Part 1* was a play Shakespeare had slightly adapted, just as Middleton had done with *Titus Andronicus*, *Macbeth*, *Measure for Measure*, and *All's Well That Ends Well*. Though a reasonably prolific figure in bookshops as a writer of civic entertainments and pageants especially, Middleton had only four attributed plays in print by 1623: two sole-authored works for boy companies in *Your Five Gallants* and *A Trick to Catch the Old One*, and two adult-professional collaborations in *The Roaring Girl* and *A Fair Quarrel*, his biggest, and most notorious hit, *A Game at Chess*, not written until the following year.[2] Nonetheless, the Folio seems to have no more reason, or desire, to make space for him alongside Shakespeare than it does for Fletcher, also still alive and working for the King's Men at the time of its publication.

Whether the theatrical audiences of Middleton's adaptations understood and received them as diachronic collaborations between a celebrated dead dramatist and a celebrated living one is something we cannot know. If they did, the Folio's project of attributing them in their entirety to Shakespeare seems to raise difficult questions about the relationships between commercial drama and the book trade. As with Jonson's Folio, the primacy of the single-author idea required active dissociation from the theatrical practices of collaboration that had helped bring some of the works it contained into being. Our image of Shakespeare as author may be more lastingly defined by what the Folio—the most influential of all early imprints of Shakespeare—conceals than by what it reveals. One of the main ways authorial collaboration is visible to us is in the advertising paratexts of the printed plays that survive. And with the exception of one quarto, single-play publication, at which this chapter will arrive, Shakespeare was presented exclusively and often falsely as a sole-author in early print. But the Folio is entirely compatible with how dramatic 'works' volumes marketed themselves for the thirty years after Jonson's set the paradigm, with collaboration an undesirable association for 'complete' authorial canons.[3] John Marston's *Works* of 1633 excluded all of his collaboratively written plays—*The Malcontent*, *Eastward Ho!*, *Histriomastix*, and *The Insatiate Countess*—though like Shakespeare's that was not an authorial decision; Marston had quit the stage around 1606–8 to become a priest, distancing himself from the image of playwright thereafter.

In 1647, though, the King's Men's other great authorial brand, Beaumont and Fletcher, were celebrated in the first prestige folio edition of plays to cast its image of authoriality falsely, in the case of a third of the volume's content, *around* collaboration. Although the same textual object as Jonson's—a prestige theatrical complete works—it signified radically differently to book buyers in the much-changed social and political worlds of its Civil-War publication moment, five years after the official closure of the theatres. It was 'keeping the place of' the stage in a far more pointed and literal way, asserting the old world of performance and royal patronage as one of conviviality, partnership, friendship, and mutually beneficial and harmonious relationships in life and work, actively evoking collaboration as the symbol of past theatrical glories. Humphrey Moseley—the volume's publisher, along with Humphrey Robinson—aimed it ideologically at a gentlemanly, and therefore royalist, market. For over thirty years he was as interested in the political as the commercial value of his wares, and recognized as the main promoter of a Royalist aesthetic throughout the austere Protectorate through prolific publication of specifically literary forms. Drama, inextricably associated with royal patronage, became elevated to the level of poetry, which Moseley also printed, and his work aided the rise in perception of plays coming from authors rather than theatre companies.[4] This was mainly intended to draw those who still remembered the old plays of the old stages to take up reading as a fashionable pursuit in its own right, even a preferred substitute for the stage.[5] He still had a business to run.

Moseley does distinguish between, and suggests the volume contains, plays Beaumont and Fletcher had written both 'jointly' and 'severally' (individually). But the book is a false image of their collaborative relationship. The two only ever collaborated on eight plays, between *c.*1606 and 1612. Of the thirty-five works the Folio contains—thirty-three plays, one masque, and one four-act interlude—only three feature Beaumont at all: two plays in collaboration with Fletcher, and a masque he wrote alone.[6] The majority of its contents were written either by Fletcher solus, or in collaboration with writers not named or implied in its main marketing strategies. Fletcher lived for nine years after Beaumont's death, and became a far more prolific author and collaborator. Of the fifty-three plays in which he had a hand, eighteen were written solus—eleven preserved in the Folio—and thirty-five in collaboration. The other twenty Folio plays, then, are collaborations, their main co-author, Philip Massinger, completely uncredited in the volume.[7] Massinger was a prolific collaborator—with fourteen, possibly fifteen, of his collaborations preserved in the Folio—though his print reputation belies this almost entirely. All thirteen of his sole-authored plays in quarto were attributed unambiguously to him alone on their title pages. Of his seven co-authored plays in quarto, only four name him: two in full, one by his initials only, and one presenting the play as his alone in another denial of his co-authorship.[8] The 1656 imprint of *The Old Law*, notoriously implicated in misattribution as will be discussed, also incorrectly names him as a co-author. He may have tried to dissociate himself from the practice, both as a reflection of his upward social mobility and the negative associations attaching to collaboration by then. His heavy involvement with the printing of *The Roman Actor* (1626), which he called 'my Minerva', seems a statement on his persona as a commercial sole-author, and it is likely a combination of this, and the strong prior association of Beaumont and Fletcher together, that kept him such a hidden co-author among book-buyers, despite being one of the most printed.

John Webster spoke of 'the no less worthy composures of the both worthily excellent Master Beaumont and Master Fletcher' in his address to readers of *The White Devil* as far back as 1612. The Folio is a posthumous commemoration, concerned with promoting their co-authorship exclusively, but none of their collaborations in quarto were in the Folio, which Moseley himself acknowledges in his address to readers, mainly because the rights were held by the stationers that had printed them. They were added to the 1679 Second Folio entitled *Fifty Comedies and Tragedies*, published by John Martyn, Henry Herringman, and Richard Marriot, set in all cases from quarto copy. *The Woman Hater* was their first true collaboration published in quarto, in 1607, with no authorial information. *Cupid's Revenge* (c.1607), their second play together, appeared while Beaumont was still alive, in 1615, attributed solely to Fletcher. *The Scornful Lady* was the first to credit both, in its 1616 first imprint, meaning their collaborative associations in print, if anything, strengthened after Beaumont's death. *A King and No King* (1611) followed in 1619, attributed to both, and from then they became an established pairing. The three 1620s' imprints of their 1609 play, *Philaster, or Love Lies a-Bleeding* (1620, 1622, 1628), the reprints of *Scornful Lady* and *King* in 1625, as well as the 1630 reprint of *Cupid's Revenge*, all named both. Most identified them as 'gentlemen', and some set their names inside ornate brackets, as the 1634 quarto of *The Two Noble Kinsmen* does to Fletcher and Shakespeare.[9] The fact of their collaboration went from something 'promiscuous', to use Jowett's term, haphazard, an incidental reality of theatrical authorship, to something monogamous, stable, deliberate, and purposeful through its framing in quarto publication, something the Folio was so keen to exploit, and Massinger so keen to avoid for himself.[10] Here collaboration moved effortlessly from its theatrical origins to a literary, even bibliographic milieu, the authorial pairing bound visually together by typographical means symbolizing the realities of their working relationship.

Perhaps unexpectedly, then, it was the ephemeral end of the market that drew their relationship most authentically, and the prestige that falsified it the most. Both mispresented Shakespeare. The work of Peele's, Middleton's, Nashe's, Fletcher's, and Marlowe's preserved in the Folio was presented, and for a long time accepted, as Shakespeare's alone. And no cheap imprint acknowledged his collaborative work until *Kinsmen*. Neither of the two-part *Contention* plays, *Titus*, nor *Pericles* did; neither did *Arden of Faversham* nor *Edward III*, *Pericles* the only one of those to acknowledge authorship at all. Thomas Pavier, who published *A Yorkshire Tragedy* as Shakespeare's in 1608, reissued it in a 1619 collection of quartos, printed by William Jaggard, one of the Folio's publishers. Alongside a handful of solo Shakespeare plays printed previously by other stationers, reprinted anew without licence, it gave certain collaborative ones, including *Pericles*, the *Contention* plays, and *Sir John Oldcastle* (1600)—an Admiral's play by Munday, Drayton, Wilson, and Hathway—explicitly to Shakespeare alone. The collection seems also to have once included Jaggard's 1617 imprint of Heywood's *A Woman Killed with Kindness*.[11] The *Oldcastle* attribution was evidently an attempt to cash in on the runaway success of *Henry IV Part 1*, Pavier hoping book buyers would accept, or at least not question, the fudge. Shakespeare was the only playwright to have works misattributed to him on title pages during his lifetime, further suggesting his name was commercial hot property, which cheap and prestige imprints alike were keen, either falsely or legitimately, to exploit.[12] But it was a property marketed entirely on his sole authorship.

Origins and Evolution

In order to better understand collaboration as a saleable commodity in early bookshops we must clearly look beyond Shakespeare. The first major playwrights of the post-Reformation period were sole authors. John Heywood's *Play of the Weather* appeared in print in late 1533, the year it was written, while other significant single-authored plays of the pre-professional era, Nicholas Udall's *Ralph Roister Dois-ter* (1552) and William Stevenson's *Gammer Gurton's Needle* (1553), were printed, as were most mid-Tudor plays, some years after their earliest performances.[13] Entertainments for royal entries had long been produced collaboratively, such as Anne Boleyn's of 1533, and her daughter Elizabeth's of 1559, but these involved different authors supplying verses, rather than multiple writers dividing responsibility for a single work. Dramatic collaboration first entered the English theatres, and the arena of the book trade, in the early 1560s through pre-professional academic drama, and *Gorboduc* (1562) represents a series of firsts. It was not only the first drama in English to employ the medium of blank verse, but also the first collaboratively written play to be advertised as such on the title page of its 1565 first imprint, comparatively soon after it was written. It was performed by the Gentlemen of the Inner Temple, and written by two of its members, the collaborative enterprise evidenced with a high degree of specificity on the quarto's title page: 'whereof three Actes were wrytten by *Thomas Nortone*, and the two laste by *Thomas Sackuyle*'.

It was an exclusive piece of drama that none but the Queen—again according to the title page—and law students would have seen. Norton was a lawyer, and Sackville, 1st Earl of Dorset, a statesman who was to serve as Lord High Treasurer under both Elizabeth and James. The play was reprinted twice (the first time without their names), but Q1's parsing of authorship seems insistent on individual contribution. The milieu in general was deeply concerned with the display and acknowledgement of authorial talent and input, a far cry from the often uncredited, commercially pragmatic labour associated with later professional dramatic collaboration. But it was the first form of collaborative drama to enter the book trade. Prior to *Gorboduc*, translation, not straightforwardly separable from authorship, was the vehicle for another kind of joint writing; and Jasper Heywood's translations of Seneca, between 1559 and 1581, which *Gorboduc*'s authors used, represent the first major 'collaboration' between the living and the dead in printed commercial drama in England.

Other early surviving exemplars are often manuscript works of 'closet' drama, serving mainly to mark intellectual achievement, such as Jane Lumley's *Iphigenia* (1555?, translating Euripides), though numerous printed examples also exist from the 1570s to the 1590s,

most notably *Cornelia* (1594) and *Antonius* (1592), translations of
Robert Garnier out of French by no lesser figures than Thomas Kyd
and Mary Herbert (née Sidney), Countess of Pembroke, respectively.
Brian Vickers has skilfully shown how Kyd's deliberate amendments
'enlarged the emotional scope of the original', transforming rather
than simply interpreting.[14] While the play—trading in the kind of
static Senecan sententiae that had become unpopular by the 1590s,
ironically because of the innovations of writers like Kyd—seems
never to have been performed, Kyd could nonetheless write for the
stage if he wanted to. Sidney could not, though her distinctly original
Antonius, and the companion piece she commissioned of her protégé,
Samuel Daniel, *The Tragedy of Cleopatra* (1594), undoubtedly influenced Shakespeare's *Antony and Cleopatra*. Still, translation found its
way more directly onto the public stages, and even right up until the
1650s we see playwrights named alongside classical writers on title
pages, as in the 1651 imprint of Thomas Randolph's university play
Hey for Honesty, Down With Knavery (1627), which credits Randolph
with translating Aristophanes' *Plutus*, though in reality he heavily
reworked it.

A century earlier, the Inns of Court drama, *Jocasta* (1566), described
on its 1573 title page as having been 'written in Greke by *Euripides*, translated and digested into Acte by George Gascoygne, and
Francis Kinwelmershe of Grayes Inne', brought collaboration, translation, and performance together. Gascoigne was not a professional
playwright, but an early Elizabethan poet and translator of some
significance—most notable for *A Hundred Sundry Flowers* (1573)—
whose dramatic work was written for a courtly audience. His sections
feature scene divisions, lacking in his co-author's work, that show,
at least, different conceptions of the formal signalling of dramatic
structure among the two writers. Martin Wiggins adds Christopher
Yelverton as the author of the play's epilogue, gives Gascoigne Acts 2,
3, and 5, and Kinwelmersh 1 and 4. Yelverton reappears as a deviser
of dumbshows in *The Misfortunes of Arthur* (1588), a play performed
by gentlemen of Gray's Inn at Greenwich Palace in February that
year. The octavo is unusually precise in its paratexts about the nature
and distribution of authorship, down to contributors of individual
speeches, even acknowledging how the collaborative ecology of performance changed the play: '*here set downe . . . as it was presented,*

excepting certaine wordes and lines, where some of the Actors either helped
their memories by brief omission: or fitted their acting by some alteration'.

Tancred and Gismund, or *Gismond of Salerne* (1568) came from the
same Inn as *Gorboduc*, as the 1591 quarto attests:

COMPILED BY THE GENtlemen of the Inner Temple, . . . *Newly reuiued*
and polished according to the decorum *of these daies. By* R[obert]. W[ilmot].

It also names Roderick Stafford, Henry Noel, the unknown 'G. Al'.,
Christopher Hatton, and Robert Wilmot as the respective authors of
the five acts, a hangover from the early days of private theatre. Most
professional plays of the early 1590s were not even credited to authors,
and certainly not by specific breakdown. Wilmot's revisions, turning
the play's rhyming quatrains into blank verse, follow stylistic 'decorum' as defined by Marlowe and Kyd in the late 1580s, and their
massive popularizing of the medium. Yet though *Gorboduc*'s blank-
verse innovation was their model, they had also rejected the Senecan
topoi in which it traded, with its heavy focus on debate over action.
And *Locrine* (1591) is a play that, through adaptation, bridges the
divide between the static, aphoristic Inns of Court fare and the kind
of combat and clowning exclusively germane to the public stage of
the mid-1590s. A manuscript note in the hand of George Buc, later
the Master of the Revels, on a surviving copy of the play's sole 1595
imprint notes:

> Char. Tilney wrote< a>
> Tragedy of this mattr <w^{ch}>
> hee named Estrild: <& w^{ch}>
> I think is this. it was l<ost?>
> by his death. & now s<ome?>
> fellow hath published <it.>
> I made dūbe shewes for it.
> w^{ch}I yet haue. G. B<.>[15]

Locrine, then, appears to be a diachronic collaboration; *Estrild*
(1585), minus Buc's dumbshows, adapted by an early 1590s' dramatist
who may or may not have been Robert Greene.[16] It is also written
in a combination of blank verse and prose, another way it crosses
over from private to popular appeal. Buc is keen to credit Charles

Tilney—brother of Edmund, Buc's predecessor in office—as the play's orginal author, and himself as supplier of its dumbshows, common to academic drama. Buc had entered the Middle Temple in 1585, and we see in his note a fastidiousness about who did what characteristic of gentleman authors. But *Locrine*'s title page reflects how far professional-era theatrical writing had moved away from gentlemanly collaboration in seeming to want to give the play to a single author, and cryptically at that. It states the text is '[n]ewly set foorth, ouerseene and corrected, By *W.S.*'. Any possible implication of Shakespeare's authorship here is veiled in ambiguity, as is the precise role of newly setting forth, overseeing, and correcting, so we cannot know if his single authorship specifically, or even the idea of authorship more generally, is being promoted here. And in the early days of the professional stage at least, the truly prestige names attached to printed plays were the noble patrons of the companies for which they were written. It is hard, then, to use print to gauge the public perception of collaboration in the theatre industry, especially as authorial information in printed playbooks is so scarce before the late 1590s.

Robert Wilson, the main theatrical author of the 1580s after Lyly and Peele, always went by R.W. on title pages, while Lyly was never mentioned at all on six of the eight plays—*Endymion, Campaspe, Sappho and Phao, Gallathea, Midas,* and *Mother Bombie*—published during, and shortly after, the time he spent working as a dramatist for children's companies *c.*1583–91.[17] Though often considered a 'private', and therefore more courtly, dramatist, Lyly's authorship in print is nonetheless consistent with the pattern of title-page attributions across the 1580s–early 90s for the public drama. But in 1594 a clutch of seven plays was published—*A Looking-Glass for London and England, Friar Bacon and Friar Bungay, The Wounds of Civil War, The Cobbler's Prophecy, Dido, Queen of Carthage, Edward II,* and *The Massacre at Paris*—all written 1588–93, and all naming for the first time, unambiguously and in full, authors from the public theatres. Two of these authors, Robert Greene and Christopher Marlowe, were already dead; and two of their plays, *Looking-Glass* and *Dido*, were, unlike all other printed drama since the Inns of Court days, including the plays to which Shakespeare is attached in his early career, advertised as collaborations.

Looking-Glass says 'Made by *Thomas Lodge* Gentleman, and *Robert Greene. In Artibus Magister*', also attributed to both in the 1594 Stationers' Register entry. Greene's infamous reputation as an author in print in his lifetime had been made solely through non-dramatic works. This was, then, perhaps surprisingly, the first play of his to be printed, even more so in that it establishes him as a dramatic co-author. Perhaps even more oddly, it and *Dido* are the only instances of title-page attribution to multiple dramatic authors of the 1590s, collaboration in printed drama disappearing from view after this for another decade. Of the 26 extant professional collaborative plays printed from Shakespeare's career beginnings to his death, fewer than half advertise co-authorship:[18]

Arden of Faversham (1592)
Titus Andronicus (1594)
Dido, Queen of Carthage (1594)
A Looking Glass for London and England (1594)
First Part of the Contention (1594)
Locrine (1595)
Richard Duke of York (1595)
Edward III (1596)
1 Sir John Oldcastle (1600)
Death of Huntingdon (1601)
Patient Grissel (1603)
The Malcontent* (1604)
Doctor Faustus (A) (1604)
1 The Honest Whore (1604)
Eastward Ho! (1605)
Northward Ho! (1607)
Sir Thomas Wyatt (1607)
Westward Ho! (1607)
The Woman Hater (1607)
The Travels of the Three English Brothers (1607)
The Dumb Knight (1608)
Pericles (1609)
The Roaring Girl (1611)
The Insatiate Countess (1613)[19]
Cupid's Revenge (1615)
The Scornful Lady (1616)
Doctor Faustus (B) (1616)*
*revision rather than collaboration

Others either acknowledge only one of the play's authors (as with *Pericles*) or are silent on authorship altogether (as with *Titus*). External evidence, then, can be deficient, even deliberately misleading, as with the false ascriptions to Shakespeare of plays such as *The London Prodigal* and *A Yorkshire Tragedy*.[20] But collaboration, judging by the extant printed drama, did not really become acknowledged and sold as a practice until the 1600s, and even then took time to gain any real traction. Webster was the first to achieve any kind of consistency for associations with co-authorship, named first as adapter of *The Malcontent* in the 1604 second imprint, then as co-author with Dekker on the title pages of *Northward Ho!*, *Sir Thomas Wyatt*, and *Westward Ho!*, all printed in 1607. The 1605 quarto of Chapman, Jonson, and Marston's *Eastward Ho!* names them on its title page, though several co-authored plays printed that decade efface collaboration on theirs: *1 Sir John Oldcastle* (1600), *The Death of Robert, Earl of Huntingdon* (1601), and *Patient Grissel* (1603), are the only extant collaborative plays printed at this time from Henslowe's companies, all without attribution of any kind, the diary being our only source of information.

We do not know how Henslowe's late 1590s' authors were perceived and received as collaborative writers by theatregoers, but the extant print record suggests they had little or no commercial value as names or partnerships in themselves. The 1600 *Oldcastle* quarto was ascribed to the Admiral's company on its title page, as was the 1619 reprint (falsely dated to 1600), which gave the play to Shakespeare. The 1659 imprint of *The Blind Beggar of Bethnal Green* (1600), the only other Henslowe collaborative play to survive, and not printed until nearly sixty years after it was written, either ignores, or is ignorant of, Henry Chettle's co-authorship in attributing it solely to John Day. Dekker and Middleton's *1 The Honest Whore* (1604), for Prince Henry's, was attributed solely to Dekker (as was their 1610 play *The Bloody Banquet*), while *Pericles* (1609), as we have seen, dropped George Wilkins' name to give the play to Shakespeare alone. The 1607 quarto of *The Travels of the Three English Brothers* has no attribution, though its preliminaries exist in two states: one lacking a dedication, and one with, signed by its authors John Day, William Rowley, and Wilkins.

The more consistent advertising of Beaumont and Fletcher as a duo on title pages helped establish collaborative authorship, or at least *their* collaborative authorship, as an attractive category of play marketing in quarto by the 1620s. Fletcher's *Wit without Money*

(1614, printed 1639) was even falsely attributed to both him and Beaumont. But other collaborative plays involving Fletcher went unacknowledged, *The Elder Brother* (1618, printed 1637), which he wrote with Massinger, for example, bearing only Fletcher's name, and *A Very Woman* (1623?, 1655) ascribed to Massinger alone, though Massinger may be a special case as already discussed. Shirley's revisions to Fletcher's *The Night-Walker* (1615, 1640) were unattributed, while the 1653 title page of *The Spanish Gypsy* (1623) omits Ford and Dekker's contributions, naming Middleton and Rowley only. Middleton and Rowley, in fact, became the other significant authorial duo to be marketed consistently as such. The respective 1617 and 1620 imprints of *A Fair Quarrel* (1615–16) and their masque, *The World Tossed at Tennis* (1620), named them as authors, as did the 1653 first printings of *The Changeling* (1622) and *The Spanish Gypsy* (1623). Their period of work together, incidentally, is when Middleton is likeliest to have adapted the four Shakespeare plays in which his hand has been detected. The other attributed collaborative plays in print up to 1660 are:

> *The Maid's Tragedy* (written 1610–11, first printed 1619, first printed with authorial attribution 1630)—'Written by *Francis Beaumont*, and *Iohn Fletcher* Gentlemen.', King's Men at the Blackfriars
>
> *The Virgin Martyr* (written 1620, printed 1622)—'Written by *Phillip Messenger* and *Thomas Decker*.', King's Revels at the Red Bull
>
> *Herod and Antipater* (written c.1619–22, printed 1622)—'*Written by* {GERVASE MARKHAM, *And* WILLIAM SAMPSON.} *Gentlemen*.', King's Revels at the Red Bull
>
> *The Fatal Dowry* (1617–19, printed 1632)— '*P. M. and N. F.*' (Massinger and Field), King's Men at the Blackfriars
>
> *The Late Lancashire Witches* (written, performed, and printed 1634)— 'WRITTEN, By THOM. HEYWOOD, AND RICHARD BROOME.', King's Men at the Globe
>
> *Chabot, Admiral of France* (written by Chapman 1611–12, revised by Shirley 1635, printed 1639)—'Written by {*George Chapman*, | and | *James Shirly*.', Lady Elizabeth's Men in 1612, Queen Henrietta Maria's 1639
>
> *Fortune by Land and Sea* (1609, printed 1655)—'WRITTEN BY {*THO. HAYWOOD. AND WILLIAM ROWLY*.', Queen Anne's at Red Bull

The Old Law, or A New Way to Please You (1618, printed 1656)—'By {*Phil. Massinger.* | *Tho. Middleton.* | *William Rowley.*', Prince Charles's at the Cockpit (?)

The Sun's Darling (1624, printed 1656)—'Written by {*John Foard* and *Tho. Decker*} Gent.', Lady Elizabeth's at the Cockpit

The Witch of Edmonton (1621, printed 1658)—'By divers well-esteemed Poets; *William Rowley, Thomas Dekker, John Ford*, &c.', Prince Charles's at the Cockpit[21]

The 1656 quarto of *The Old Law*, which Middleton and Rowley wrote with Heywood, published by Edward Archer, was notorious for containing Archer's 'Exact and perfect CATALOGUE of all the PLAIES that were ever printed'. The list, some 622 plays long, attempted in many cases to attribute authorship.[22] Q1's title page, though wrong on the detail of Massinger's involvement, admits the play's collaborative authorship. But the catalogue is wrong more often than not, both in simple misattribution—including many to Shakespeare—and in almost never allowing collaboration.[23] Its major exception is for Beaumont and Fletcher, though it follows neither their quarto nor Folio canons systematically, leaving out some Folio plays altogether; attributing some to Fletcher alone—including *Bonduca* (correctly), and *The Captain* (one of the two genuine Beaumont and Fletcher collaborations)—and variously omitting and misattributing certain of their quarto collaborations. It gives *A King and No King* solely to Fletcher, and *The Two Noble Kinsmen*, in contradiction of the play's sole imprint, entirely to Shakespeare.

Archer's list came some fourteen years after the theatres had closed, and four before the Restoration saw them reopen in radically new guises. Women would act and write professionally, links with royal patronage and public performance solidify, and sole-authorship dominate. But in his almost wholesale denial of collaboration, Archer goes against, if not the principles, then the practical realities of the working theatres Shakespeare had known. In the early days, any legal or commercial rights a dramatist had in a play were all but removed in the act of selling it to a company. Money, or advertising for revivals, might prompt those companies to sell plays to stationers who in turn exploited whatever was popular about them. Authorship typically had less purchase than those things—a company, a royal performance, a beloved character, salacious plot details—we often see these adorning title pages. But as theatrical authorship became more visible in print, we must consider that a playbook advertising joint authors meant that the same information had been available to, and an exciting prospect for, the theatre audiences that had seen it, and one of the very things driving its commodity value for whichever stationer was venturing to publish it. Especially as theatrical authors like Greene and Nashe had attained a level of celebrity as nondramatic authors in the marketplace of print. Sometimes authorship is confined to the material circumstances of a play's composition, and sometimes it serves as a key imaginative component of its reception.

Tiffany Stern has argued playbills informed title pages, and that theatre audiences may have had the same information as potential book-buyers.[24] How and why this began to happen is not entirely clear. Francis Meres and Robert Allott, in *Palladis Tamia* and *England's Parnassus* respectively, seem to have been highly influential in popularizing dramatic authorship as an idea, and specific authors as commodities. The 1598 quarto of *Love's Labour's Lost* marked Shakespeare's first appearance on a title-page, the same year Meres praised him as the best English dramatic author, and Thomas Dekker, much anthologized in Allott's 1600 publication, began to appear as both sole and co-author consistently thereafter, while not at all before.[25] Stern has also shown that title pages were hung in public places, taking the same form, and serving the same advertising function, as playbills. Was the book trade creating, or cashing in on, different popular ways of understanding and taxonomizing theatrical and creative authorship? Who wrote title pages, and to what extent can we trust their declarations of collaborative authorship? And what about co-authored plays that do not advertise the fact? How we interpret title-page attributions in the period, and why they change over time, are questions lacking easy answers. But the diverse agents and circumstances involved in the transmission of texts from theatrical to print markets—across many years and radically shifting economic and cultural priorities—means collaboration comes in and out of focus in thoroughly unsystematic ways, a problem intensified by the partial nature of the extant record.

Shakespeare

In 1634 the stationer John Waterson made Shakespearean collaboration visible to book buyers, and thereby to posterity, for the first time.
His edition of *The Two Noble Kinsmen*, published when Shakespeare
had been dead for nearly twenty years, and Fletcher nearly ten, is the
first printed document to name, and correctly identify, Shakespeare
as a collaborative author. The play was entered into the Stationers'
Register on 8 April 1634, and printed later that year, its title page
claiming that it was:

> Presented at the Blackfriers
> by the Kings Maiesties servants,
>   with great applause:
>
> Written by the memorable Worthies
>   of their time;
>   {M^r. John Fletcher, and}
>   {M^r. William Shakespeare.} Gent.

Waterson had published other plays in quarto leading up to *Kinsmen*, most famously Webster's *The Duchess of Malfi* in 1623—the
same year as the First Folio, that most definitive statement in print
of Shakespeare as sole author—and two by Philip Massinger, all of
which named their authors on the title pages. He also published
two by William Davenant that did not. After *Kinsmen*, he published
Fletcher and Massinger's *The Elder Brother*, attributing it solely to
Fletcher, which, as we have seen, is not unusual where Massinger is
concerned. Fletcher as co-author though, had, with his most famous
writing partner, Francis Beaumont, become a highly saleable commodity in the cheaper end of the book market, possibly helping
explain *Kinsmen*'s title-page advertising, complete with the orna-
mental parentheses so often deployed to bind Fletcher to Beaumont
(Figure 6). Waterson borrows, undoubtedly, from the advertising
paradigms and print popularity of their collaborative pairing, and it
is particularly notable that Shakespeare is being drawn into this collaborative model only two years after the Second Folio's restatement
of him as an exclusively sole author. It is also interesting that it was an
entirely unsuccessful venture.[26] As Chapter 3 discussed, this was not

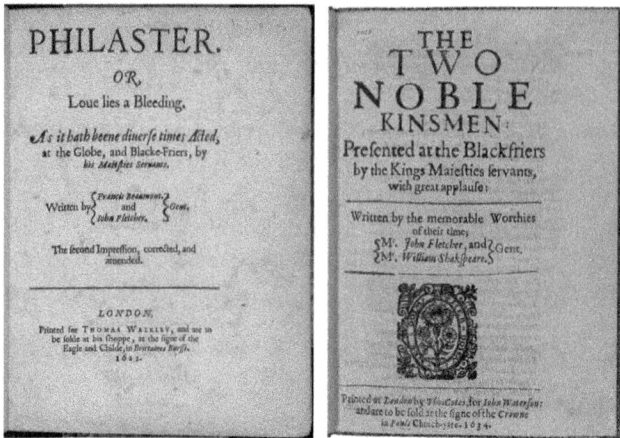

Figures 6a and 6b Title pages of *Philaster*, Q2 (1622), STC 1682 sig. A1r, and *The Two Noble Kinsmen*, Q1 (1634), STC 11075, sig. A1r, used by permission of The Folger Shakespeare Library under a CC-BY-SA 4.0.

all about authorship: *Arden*, *Titus*, *Contention*, *Richard Duke of York*, and *Edward III* all enjoyed decent reprint rates despite having no named connection to Shakespeare. The collaborative *Pericles* named Shakespeare alone, and outsold the solo-authored *Hamlet*, which also did, so it is more likely a judgement on the quality of the play than a statement about Shakespearean authorship affecting book-buying figures. But while Shakespeare the named collaborator did not sell to *them*, Waterson's book is of enormous value to us.

Following the terms of Stern's analysis of the popular ways of marketing drama on playbills and title pages—not all of which were ever guaranteed to appear—Waterson gives us theatre, company, and authors, in that order. It is clearly a commercial decision to supply all this information, and again there seems a desire to sell the prestige of the past, the authors described as 'the memorable worthies of their age'. Unlike the Beaumont and Fletcher Folio, though, the authorial attribution Waterson's cheaper imprint supplies is entirely accurate. In this, it breaks the mould established by the many imprints of collaborative Shakespeare plays to that date, including those in

the Shakespeare First Folio, a prestige edition insisting—in its paratexts, in its engraving, in its cataloguing and named attributions—
on Shakespeare's single authorship. Given Shakespeare's reputation
today, the order in which Waterson orders Fletcher and Shakespeare's
names might seem surprising. It may simply be alphabetical, as were
all of Beaumont and Fletcher's title-page attributions, or may reflect
Fletcher's main contribution in the collaboration.[27] We cannot be
sure Waterson could have known this, though, there being continued
ambiguity about the underlying copy's status as holograph or scribal
transcript.[28] Or it may be commercial recognition of Fletcher's links
with collaboration in print, or the appeal of his style by that time.
William Davenant's *The Rivals* (1664), an adaptation of *Kinsmen*,
does not mention Shakespeare anywhere in its 1668 imprint, and is
based mainly on passages now attributed to Fletcher, the most popular playwright of the old theatres in the Restoration. But whatever
the reasons, after Waterson had shone a light on it for the first time,
Shakespearean collaboration all but disappeared from view in print.

Seven plays added to the second edition of the 1664 Third Shakespeare Folio, including the genuine Shakespeare collaboration, *Pericles*, were all treated as sole-authored. Philip Chetwinde, the volume's
publisher, was probably following the authority of their early quarto
title pages in this. The others, the apocryphal mainstays *Locrine*,
Sir John Oldcastle, *Thomas Lord Cromwell*, *The London Prodigal*, *A
Yorkshire Tragedy*, and *The Puritan Widow*, had all asserted—overtly,
or ambiguously—sole authorship by Shakespeare. While quarto
imprints of drama in general frequently advertised collaboration,
Shakespeare's sole authorship was a popular idea in print even in
his own lifetime. All these discrete phenomena have arguably led to
a conceptual blurring of lines between apocrypha and collaborative
drama, most notably exemplified in recent times by the RSC's *Collaborative Plays by Shakespeare and Others*. Nicholas Rowe, considered
the first editor of Shakespeare, included all seven of the Third Folio's
additions in his 1709 edition, though his successor, Alexander Pope,
banished them from his of 1725 as 'wretched plays' that 'cannot be
admitted as [Shakespeare's]'. At least two are genuine collaborations,
one involving Shakespeare, though in the Third Folio and onwards
into Rowe, they are all brought under the aegis of Shakespearean single authorship. Of them, only *Pericles* has been confirmed by modern

scholarship, though on the strength of it alone we see the limitations of the 1623 Folio as a text which can tell us the whole truth about Shakespeare's authorship.

The validity of all attributions to Shakespeare outside its canon would need to be settled—as would all other instances of Shakespeare's co-authored writing, *Kinsmen* included—with extreme difficulty and controversy, through stylistic and stylometric arguments that continue to this day. *Kinsmen*, omitted from the Third Folio, next appeared in print in the 1679 second Beaumont and Fletcher Folio, remaining a stable part of the Fletcher canon ever since. As a Shakespeare play, though, it has taken a lot longer to gain acceptance, not appearing in an edited complete works until 1841. W.W. Skeat's 1875 single edition was the first since Waterson's to attribute the play to both authors on its title page, Clifford Leech's of 1966 the first of the twentieth century to do so. This was partly because the play had been drawn into the orbit of C.F. Tucker Brooke's influential 1908 volume, *The Shakespeare Apocrypha*. It was not considered in the first two Arden series, Lois Potter's 1997 Arden 3 edition its first inclusion there. Malone in his 1780 *Supplement* to his 1778 edition included *Pericles*, which has remained part of the Shakespeare editorial tradition since, though not edited on the assumption of co-authorship until its appearance in G.L. Kittredge's impressive 1935 complete works, which also included *Kinsmen* as a Shakespeare–Fletcher collaboration. Wilkins's presence was not fully articulated, though, until the 1986 Oxford Shakespeare, the first complete Shakespeare edition to represent collaboration systematically.

Waterson's edition of *Kinsmen* is instructive in several ways about what we might imagine are the different expectations of early modern book-buyers and modern readers of Shakespeare. For one, it supplies no details of the division of labour between the two authors, information we might want a good edition to supply, or at least a question we might want it to address. Users of modern scholarly texts are the beneficiaries of types of bibliographic encoding around authoriality never before available to readers or interpreters of these plays, and the remainder of this chapter will consider modern editions of Shakespeare and what their various statements about collaborative authorship enable, or hinder, for readers.

Complete/Single

Nothing has done more to shape the popular perception of Shakespeare as a collaborative author than prestige volumes of his complete works. No single edition, let alone academic study, has had a comparable impact. They present canon, so linked to bigger ideas about Shakespeare and cultural value, in an intrinsically consolidated way, authorizing and popularizing the oldest claims with the vividness of novelty. They act as interface between esoteric scholarly argument and popular revelation, just as Shakespeare acts as interface between closed, ivory-tower academic culture, and familiar, beloved literary iconography. Their use as college textbooks gives them a large captive audience, and there is a pattern of media interest in banner releases of complete volumes—going back to the 1986 Oxford Shakespeare, but seen also in the two RSC volumes and the NOS—simply not there for other kinds of publication. As I began researching this book in early 2017, the *New Oxford Shakespeare* had just been published to a flurry of global press interest for its naming of Christopher Marlowe as Shakespeare's collaborator on the *Henry VI* plays. Again, this is an old claim, but the NOS's edition-as-monument symbolism, and the attendant marketing power of the Oxford brand, made it visible in ways not otherwise possible. The NOS was as characterized by attribution as the 1986 *Oxford Shakespeare* was by theatre, so perhaps the strangest thing about it was its continued marketing around the idea of Shakespeare solus. It was still 'Shakespeare', and still 'Oxford'; it was just 'new'.

But modern textual editing enfolds another form of collaboration as scholars compromise with publishers on an edition's orientation in the marketplace. Design teams might not worry how or why a cover would signal the presence of other writers, many of whom—Peele, Nashe, Wilkins, Fletcher—are unknown to most modern readers. An academic selling point may not be an actual selling point. The 2007 *Thomas Middleton: The Collected Works*, so far the only other hefty complete works of a Renaissance dramatist available in single-volume paperback, contains work by Dekker, Jonson, Rowley, Heywood, Webster, Ford, Munday, and Shakespeare, while the more specialist, expensive, multi-volume hardback *Collected Works of John Ford*

contains Dekker, Rowley, Middleton, Massinger, and Webster. Their
covers, though, tell a different story, seeking commercial clarity in
the figure of the single author. Complete works will be read alike by
scholars, students, giftshop-browsing playgoers, interested parties of
all kinds, most of whom are far likelier to buy for their bookshelf than
engage with academic turf wars, and concise messaging about authorship is, then as now, still the more marketable proposition. Yet the
practice, even the idea, of collaboration was not much valued or discussed before the work of the 1986 Oxford editors, and all of the above
volumes have helped transform our recognition and understanding of
it. In this they differ vastly from their early modern counterparts.

The 1986 Oxford's collaborative canon comprised *1 Henry VI*,
Timon, Pericles, All Is True, and *The Two Noble Kinsmen*. It printed the
Shakespeare-only passages from *Sir Thomas More*, named Middleton
as the adapter of *Macbeth*, namechecked him as probable adapter in
Measure for Measure, and discussed *Double Falsehood* undogmatically
as the possible descendant of a Shakespeare–Fletcher collaboration,
likely to have been called *Cardenio*. But no other play that stayed in—*2*
and *3 Henry VI, Titus*—or was left out—*Arden of Faversham, Edward
III*—was identified as a Shakespeare collaboration. The accompany-
ing *Textual Companion* discussed Peele's possible co-authorship of
Titus and Shakespeare's of *Edward III* in open-minded terms, with
co-authorship in *2* and *3 Henry VI* and *Shrew* acknowledged as possible. *Arden* was ruled out, and *The Spanish Tragedy* not discussed. The
2005 second edition, though, named Peele as collaborator in *Titus* and
Middleton as adapter in *Measure*, and offered full texts of *Edward III*
and *Sir Thomas More*—for the first time in a major complete works of
Shakespeare—illustrating well the shifting sands of editorial canons,
and how much the first edition had changed the landscape in the
intervening 19 years.

For single editions, though, single authorship has remained both
the editorial and commercial benchmark. Of the three major scholarly Shakespeare series, only Oxford and Arden name co-authors at
all, sometimes on title pages, and never on front covers. The New
Cambridge does not name them anywhere in the preliminaries, and
something of an anti-collaboration stance pervades the series in general, though it has been updating its introductory materials to take in
newer perspectives in recent years. Entries for the Oxford series began

being issued before the 1986 complete volume's publication. Eugene M. Waith's 1984 *Titus* disavowed collaboration, unlike his 1989 *Kinsmen*, and Jay L. Halio's 1999 *Henry VIII* seemed essentially to accept it, though he frequently couched the discussion in ambiguous terms, Fletcher's name not appearing on the title page as it did in Waith's *Kinsmen*. Arden 2 had not even included *Kinsmen*, and considered *Timon, Pericles,* and *Henry VIII* entirely Shakespearean, despite discussion of possible collaborative origins in the textual apparatus. All appeared in the Arden 3 series as collaborative plays. Jonathan Bate's 1995 *Titus* made a case for sole-Shakespearean authorship, though Bate, who has done much to acknowledge and popularize collaboration in the last decade, revised it in 2018, marking the first time the Arden imprint had acknowledged co-authorship in the play.

No single edition of the *Contention* plays has ever assumed collaboration. Roger Warren and Randall Martin both worked on the assumption of Shakespeare's sole authorship in their respective 2003 and 2001 Oxford editions of *Parts 2* and *3*, while John D. Cox and Eric Rasmussen's 2001 Arden 3 *Part 3* drew on the influential Foucauldian-inspired work of Masten and others around the socially constituted text. This meant the play could be discussed as conceptually collaborative but remain essentially 'by Shakespeare', emendation guided by the single-author rationale. The present writer will edit the play for the Arden 4 series as a Marlovian collaboration, and it will also be included in the forthcoming Oxford edition of Marlowe's works. There the edition will reflect, in its textual treatment and apparatus, a different authorial basis. Edward Burns' Arden 3 *Part 1* argued that 'Harry the Sixth, by Shakespeare, Nashe and others', would be plausible, if inelegant', justifying its ascription to Shakespeare alone as 'a necessary commercial fiction'—an open acknowledgment, in other words, that Shakespeare sells better.[29] Michael Taylor's Oxford edition noted that 'the word Shakespeare conceals problems and anomalies, not the least of which is the presence of other hands in the play's construction'.[30] Like Burns, he acknowledged co-authorship while naming, and editing on the basis of, Shakespeare's characteristic usages. It has only been through the attribution studies of the last 30 years that we have come to understand how *Part 1* differs in kind and provenance from the *Contention* plays, and begun to see the entire sequence differently in its collaborative shaping of Shakespeare's career beginnings, though the latter proposition remains controversial.

There is not scope here for a history of the editing of Shakespeare's collaborative plays. For a long time they were either accepted into editions' canons on the understanding they were wholly Shakespearean, or rejected as 'apocrypha', legitimate Shakespearean collaboration routinely swept into the dubia dust-pile. This has been as true of plays now considered stable entries—*Pericles, Kinsmen*—as of outliers like *Edward III*. Tucker Brooke's *Apocrypha* contained *Arden of Faversham, Edward III, Sir Thomas More*, and a century later all were included in the NOS's main Shakespeare canon. Arden put *Arden of Faversham* into its Early Modern Drama series, though released *Double Falsehood* under its Shakespeare banner in 2010, as it did *Sir Thomas More* the following year, and *Edward III* in 2017.[31] Such apparently simple acts of branding are also definitive statements about authorship. The 2013 RSC *Collaborative Plays by Shakespeare and Others*, to which the present writer contributed, contained them all. Other more securely canonical collaborations, *Titus, Timon, Pericles, Henry VIII*, and *Kinsmen* were gathered in the main 2007 Shakespeare volume. Some entries in *Collaborative Plays* were chosen for genuine Shakespearean co-authorship, and others for explicit early modern attribution to Shakespeare. The volume's title was an attempt to signify all this while avoiding the 'apocrypha' label, partly because of Tucker Brooke's iconic volume, and partly the baggage around the word's implications.[32] The edition came under fire for a failure to meet the promises apparently bound in its title, both in rationale for inclusion (why include any plays that Shakespeare did not write?) and exclusion (where are all the collaborative plays he *did* write?)[33] Like all editions, it was an imperfect compromise.

How far editors feel the burden of responsibility to bring everything sole- or co-authored by a writer under the aegis of an edition, and how they establish this, are questions at the heart of any given project. There are previous editions to consider, and the diminishing returns of editorial time and labour in preparing new texts of, in some cases, widely available plays. A variety of practical factors beyond authorship can also determine editions' approaches to canon. In complete works, for example, a single column of text may be more reader-friendly than double, but puts pressure on the number of plays the edition can include. Paper stock can help; the NOS and Norton Shakespeare—both of which used a single column—used very thin, low-weight paper, allowing more pages to be squeezed in.[34] Printing only those parts of a play by a particular author can help with space issues, as the NOS and Norton did with *Sir Thomas More*, but beyond the question of how having bits of text in isolation benefits readers, it is also a potentially confused statement on the nature of collaboration. Digital editing mitigates these issues, but raises new ones about limits, usefulness, and access. And defining canon is at once a pragmatic problem to be solved, and a thorny theoretical question, caught up in both real and abstract issues of value and its ramifications. On the one hand, there are apparently disinterested investigative aims around who wrote what; on the other, unease about an edition's symbolic power to shape ideas of canonicity and cultural status, and it may ultimately be difficult to get collaborating teams of editors to agree. Even supposedly empirical grounds are never entirely neutral, and the methodological can quickly bleed into the ideological, so editions must make decisions about their statements of authorship, and be aware of the judgements that might attach to them. The NOS was in many ways the culmination of attribution studies' growth in Shakespeare, and of a decades-long interest in collaboration. But it met with immediate resistance, its editors and contributors styled as new disintegrationists, showing just how live these issues of authorship remain.

Determining Collaboration

Editing Collaboration

An edition might choose to demote authorship, but can never completely neutralize or remove it. While we may identify other agents of transmission behind a text, authorship is the thing against which we discern them; it forms the rationale for the editor's assembly and critique of the text, is the benchmark for intervention in cases of error, and acts as our control in matters of emendation. Modern editing on the basis of authorship relies on attribution work, just as attribution relies on knowledge developed through editorial practice. Both have their roots in conservative New Bibliographic methods purporting the scientific analysis of texts, factual inquiry about points of textual origin, both in how the book came to exist in its material form, how its text was written, and how one influences the other. Even editions eschewing attribution involve a kind of it in compositorial and scribal identification, crucial to determining the nature of a text's underlying copy. And just as the editor intersects with the book historian, the stylometrist intersects with the editor, and the words in the book become tools for reconstructing the authorial text in another way—an author's likely usages no longer just standards in the correction of error, but 'markers' against the profiles of other authors. And if we recognize a play as collaborative, different authorial sections must then affect editing. It is no use emending Fletcher on the basis of Shakespeare's characteristic usage.

For collaborative drama, the benefits of editorial and book-historical knowledge in questions of attribution are clear. Several

Shakespeare and Collaborative Writing. Will Sharpe, Oxford University Press. © Will Sharpe (2023).
DOI: 10.1093/oso/9780198819639.003.0008

pieces of evidence, for example, point towards a scribal transcript of joint-authorial papers serving as copy for the Folio text of *All Is True*.[1] William Montgomery's work, chiefly looking at the spelling of 'has' with an apostrophe (ha's) and the extremely high incidence of round-bracket use, extended R.A. Foakes's analysis of contractions as non-authorial and non-compositorial features of the underlying copy, confirming Greg's suggestion that it was scribal.[2] Fredson Bowers also noted a range of spellings shared between the authorial stints of both writers that seemingly reflect scribal regularization, while A.C. Partridge identified certain grammatical preferences—auxiliary *do*, and *doth*, *hath*, and *them* for Shakespeare, and *'em* and *ye* for Fletcher, as well as *y'are* for *you're*, which appears ten times and only in Fletcher scenes—that survived transcription.[3] Foakes, who was keen to disavow Fletcher's hand, cautioned against absolute trust in these features as evidence of authorship, noting in particular Compositor B's tendency to alter *ye* to *you* in parts of *Troilus*, as well as discrepancies in verb forms between quarto and Folio *Lear* (*hath* and *doth* changed to *has* and *does*, with the reverse happening in *Othello*). Yet the evidence for scribal copying distinguishable from compositorial influence, and the survival of authorially differentiated features through transcription and typesetting, seem most likely to suggest scribal copying of a manuscript containing the hands of both authors. It is only in taking note of such careful, granular differentiation that stylometric arguments accrue real credibility.

Spelling as a marker of authorship is considered on a case-by-case basis, depending on the nature of the underlying manuscript as determined by textual scholarship. Compositorial spelling might vary for no apparent reason—spelling inconsistency within individuals is a common feature of both manuscript and print culture in the period—for the practical reason of justifying lines of type, or because different compositors are at work on the same page. Q1 *2 Henry IV* is considered authorial in part because of the recurrence of 'scilens' (silence), a spelling which only appears elsewhere in the professional drama in Hand D.[4] Another Hand D feature, shown to be unique in a large manuscript survey of over 250 different writers, is an open 'a' form with a horizontal spur at the back, easily confusable in secretary hand with a 'u/v', suggesting why in Q2 *Hamlet*, set from authorial manuscript, we get 'deale' for 'devle' and 'Gertrad' for 'Gertrud'. Hand D also has the spelling 'devle' (devil), found elsewhere only in a fifteenth-century religious play, two medieval poems, and the Folio text of *Henry V*.[5] Such knowledge of manuscript and print features works mutually to determine authorship in ways that affect both editing and attribution. While the Hand D section is short it can tell us a lot. But as its authorship remains contested, its use can be taken variously as either confirmation of Shakespeare, or confirmation bias.

Agents of transmission typically sought to avoid the kind of interference that might affect 'authorship', though scribes and compositors might, as they worked, alter characteristic authorial features. There is another potential layer in that not all texts were set from manuscript: compositors often worked from quarto copy—easier to read and cheaper to acquire than manuscript—when reprinting a play. We know the Folio syndicate used quarto copy in many cases, typically annotated with reference to theatrical manuscripts that Shakespeare's company lent for a limited time, to improve upon its forebear. But in typesetting, the text nonetheless absorbed a number of the transmissional contingencies of the previous imprint.[6] Printers typically 'improve' manuscript copy in setting initial capitals and regularizing punctuation and spelling, improving any printed copy in seeking to correct manifest errors, though many escaped notice. Joseph Moxon's 1683 handbook on printing, the first of its kind, provides a statement we can assume applied to the setting of Shakespeare's plays nearly a century earlier: that 'by the laws of printing, a compositor is strictly to follow his copy', though he allows a 'duty . . . to discern and amend [its] bad spelling and pointing'. But Don McKenzie explored the idea that punctuation, even typography, adds new meaning to a text, and considered the possible role such functionaries play in bringing texts through different phases of use as a kind of diachronic collaboration.[7] Punctuation—Hand D is almost entirely unpunctuated, probably typical of Shakespeare's manuscript—is understood as an un-systemized feature of printing-house practice in Shakespeare's time anyway.[8] Even modern editors must repunctuate as part of the difficult interpretive job of modernizing Shakespeare's dramatic syntax, but such alteration is still logically separable from primary authorship, and editorial knowledge aids our understanding of what collaboration is, and is not, as a process. The example of Q1 *2 Henry IV* shown in Chapter 4 illustrates well that reconstructing the process by which a text was assembled is as instructive about primary authorship as about secondary transmission.

The 1623 Folio text of *3 Henry VI*, as a different example, is about 1,000 lines longer than its smaller, cheaper counterpart, the 1595 octavo *Richard Duke of York*. Both texts, as Randall Martin suggested, share a common, and lost, point of origin in the manuscript someone tried to reconstruct in O, and that Shakespeare later reworked in F. While this has been the lasting orthodox position, F's text of the play has also been long suspected as not wholly Shakespearean. That O contains writing by people other than Shakespeare is clear. Many readings seem explicable only as some kind of disrupted transmission from an original, or as material adapted and/or imported from other sources—subtly altered passages lifted straight from Peele's *Battle of Alcazar*, for example—with some additional new lines in an unknown hand.[9] But the random distribution of O's unique material does not map onto what we might consider a typical authorial stint, and the plagiarized nature of some of it further suggests a dubious job of reconstruction for sale in print.[10] Neither revision, collaboration, nor regular agents of transmission—company scribes or printers— adequately explains the text. Though unattributed on its title page, O was used as copy for a reprint, Q3, part of Thomas Pavier's 1619 collection of Shakespeare plays, which explicitly claimed Shakespeare's sole authorship, as did F. F was set with very limited reference to Q3, which has a clear line of transmission from O through Q2. But the long-held report/revision dichotomy of a single-authored play has been significantly disturbed by recent work; O now looks like a memorial report, and F a revision, of an originally collaborative play. Apparently non-Shakespearean material common to both texts seems most likely to reflect regular collaboration, and a number of the lines unique to F look like Shakespearean revision of the text as preserved in O. If we accept F's passages attributed to Marlowe, then O does contain some of his writing, albeit reconstructed, even with some internally duplicated lines: 2.3.3–5 are seen again, lightly adapted, at 5.2.25–7.[11] Still, while we might edit O as an alternative version for its own intrinsic interest, it is not a reliable witness to an early version of the collaboration between Marlowe, Shakespeare, and another.

Perhaps surprisingly, no major commercial single-edition Shakespeare series has modelled co-authorship into its approach to a range of issues like emendation, lineation, stage directions, spelling, or forms of contractions. Eugene Waith's Oxford Shakespeare *Kinsmen* offered a general rationale for modernizing early texts that did not acknowledge co-authorship's effect on specific decisions. Potter's edition's introduction offered a breakdown of the authors' shares, doing far more than any single-text edition to that date to even acknowledge collaboration, let alone bring it into the discussion of editorial method. It identified multiple verse features, feminine endings in particular, as common to both Shakespeare and Fletcher *c.*1613, and framed press correction, punctuation, and manuscript in more purely bibliographic terms, distinguishing from 'the author' features likely to derive from theatrical and print-house personnel.[12] Attribution made implicit the understanding of which author was behind a given scene, though—undoubtedly affected by series guidelines—the edition did not make an explicit point of editing Fletcher scenes on the basis of his practices for copy-readings and emendation.

But some editions have found active, even 'messy', ways to signal co-authorship. The 2005 second edition complete Oxford Shakespeare edited *Sir Thomas More* in full, with authorial stints demarcated and attributed, manuscript annotations set in bold, and text marked for deletion by the censor underlined. The Arden 3 text, edited, like the 2005 Oxford, by John Jowett, also signalled authorial shares, with symbols employed for lacunae, limited conjectural reconstruction, and phases of revision and transmission. Gary Taylor's NOS treatment of *Cardenio*, stripping away all but the Shakespearean writing theoretically still visible in Theobald's adaptation, looked essentially like scattered remnants of verse on the page. Brean Hammond's Arden text, on the other hand, was an edition of *Double Falsehood*, with a long introductory discussion of authorship and textual genealogy. The Oxford Middleton included 'genetic' texts of *Macbeth* and *Measure for Measure*, aiming to show the conjectural process of Middletonian adaptation; bold text illustrated material Middleton added or moved, with, in the latter case, duplicate text in grey to show it in its original position. Gary Taylor made as much of a point of discussing authorship in the commentary to his treatment of *Macbeth* as Jeffrey Masten made of not discussing it in his edition of *An/The Old Law*. Both appeared in the same volume, which is one form of authorial organization, and chose differently inflected views of the workings of collaborative authorship, which is another. And in both cases the editor's approach was at odds with their early texts' statements about authorship; the Folio presented *Macbeth* as solely Shakespearean, while the *Old Law* quarto wrongly identified the play's collaborating authors.

Masten saw as 'old historicist' the authorship-led approach to editing, favouring newer 'models of "agency", "individuality", "style", corporate effort, contention, influence', which, he acknowledged, required 'the invention of new kinds of editorial apparatuses, criteria for and modes of emendation, etc.', which Suzanne Gossett critiqued for 'offering no methodological specifics'.[13] His approach was, though, somewhat borne out in his edition, preferring the text's framing in matrices of early modern reception and production, promoting the input of a host of non-authorial agents as a legitimate, and more historically appropriate, form of collaborative 'authorship'.[14] Apart from a short paragraph in the textual introduction, and a title-page attribution to Rowley, Middleton, and Heywood—both no doubt reflecting compromise with the volume's general editorship—authorial collaboration was buried within the *mise-en-page*. Masten offered a 'clean' text with a marginal commentary around the 'plurality' of word meanings for early audiences, along with a running collation grounding its minimal correction in ways emphasizing editorial history over authorship. Still, we might argue that although authorship here is consciously sidelined, relying on historical collation for emendation means it is still imported as a standard in the correction of error.

The fact of Shakespeare's collaborative authorship and the instances of notation typical of theatrical manuscripts in surviving texts of his work, in spite of their many possible transmission scenarios, position Shakespeare at work within the early professional theatres, and the practices of both textual criticism and stylometric analysis seek to recover and identify his authorship as a process within that context. But this is never an easy thing to do, and not always a welcome one, as the remainder of this chapter will suggest.

Stylometry and Attribution

The word 'stylometry' covers a series of fine-grained statistical approaches to literary language in order to measure, and thereby determine, authorship. Some basic examples include analyses of collocations, imagery, preferred oaths (swear words), prepositions, (relative) pronouns, modifiers, verb forms, function words, exotic vocabulary (lexical words), contractions, metrics, pause patterns, and other far more complex methods, to build profiles for individual authors through the characteristic linguistic and stylistic features of their writing.[15] A survey of even the Shakespeare-focused history of the field is too big to cover here, though works suggested in the Further Reading section offer extensive detail. Some of the major methods in Shakespeare studies today include Word Adjacency Networks (WAN), a technique that 'examines, by way of complex mathematical processes, how high-frequency (function) words are positioned in relation to one another—within texts by different authors'.[16] Principal Components Analysis (PCA)—a method of reducing the dimensionality of large data sets, which John Burrows pioneered as an attribution technique—is a way of processing and mapping the strongest factors among word counts employed in any particular test.[17] Rolling Stylometry refers to a set of methods whereby a text is broken up into partially overlapping, equal-sized blocks and analysed sequentially and independently according to particular search criteria—for example, Rolling Delta (RD) tests—to parse authorial signals in collaborative texts. More recently, 'entropy', a method borrowing its metaphor for communication from physics (the second law of thermodynamics), is used to map how much information there is in a communication, or rather the quantifiable reduction of uncertainty. Drawing on statistics, it charts the relative entropy between 'Markov chains' that represent authors' habits of placing each of around 100 function words in proximity to each other.[18] Beyond Chapter 3's more impressionistic observations about commonalities of imagery and language between the *Henry VI* plays and *Arden*, this was the main method by which Shakespeare's co-authorship in them was more plausibly advanced.[19]

Language 'tokens' can be tagged according, for example, to their status as Iota (least frequent words), Delta (most frequent words),

Zeta (recurring lexical words across texts), or n-grams (numerical clusters of words or collocations, such as bigrams, trigrams, tetragrams etc.). These can be used to produce lexical- and function-word profiles for authors, as well as more general appraisals of style, genre, sociolect, and idiolect. They have even been applied to early drama attribution to describe identity and influence, to understand the difference in stylistic profile between authors and the characters they voice, and even to know when co-authors are imitating one another.[20] The idea behind stylometry is that it processes literary language on a far more granular level than the naked eye could ever detect, and has been brought to bear in questions of Shakespeare's involvement in plays and poems both outside the traditional canon, and—as the NOS and the glut of reactions and counterarguments to it show—within it. Many claims have failed to achieve any scholarly traction, despite lengthy studies arguing Shakespeare's hand in, for example, *Edmond Ironside*, *Thomas of Woodstock*, and *The Birth of Merlin* in recent decades.[21] The major exception has been *Arden of Faversham*, the main focus of critical dispute between different factions of attributionists over a number of years, either as a play linked to Shakespeare or even as a collaboration.[22] Mainly about counting, stylometry is often seen as distinct from the humanist, interpretive approach of stylistics, reliant on more general appreciations of poetic technique, idiolect, and readily observable parallels between works. Stylometries are rooted in the kinds of corpus linguistics germane to English language departments, and are, and have been, integral to quantitative and computational linguistics for some time. But they have struggled in various ways for acceptance in literary circles. Opposition in general falls into three main kinds: rejection of the idea of attribution out of hand; rejection of the models, methods, or conclusions of particular attribution studies in favour of alternatives; and rejection of the paradigm of the biographical author in favour of different modes of describing text creation.

Arguably the most heated opposition to attribution methods has come from within the discipline itself, chiefly in the long-standing war of words between Brian Vickers and Gary Taylor. Vickers' branch of stylometry refutes both the efficacy and ethics of what it terms 'quantitative' textual analysis, favouring the application of anti-plagiarism software in order to find trigram matches—parallels between texts consisting of three words—mainly using the Literature Online (LION) database, performing collocation searches across thousands of texts to expand exponentially the range of negative check evidence. Practitioners of computational stylistics can, and do, he suggests, get away with claims most people lack the mathematical competence to refute, incompatible with the findings of more traditional attribution methods.[23] Vickers' 'literary' methods, which retain the meaning and context of language he argues as necessary to identify authorship, have been critiqued as vigorously by proponents of quantitative methods for their vulnerability to things like plagiarism, conscious or unconscious imitation, revision, or stylistic modification by one writer when working with another. Quantitative practitioners like Taylor and Craig do not in fact dispute the importance of literary analysis as a part of profiling, but still get caricatured as robotic number-crunchers. Whatever methods are used, if one practitioner avers an author's presence in a scene or play, and one refutes it, it naturally follows that someone is wrong. And if the second practitioner proposes an alternative candidate, it is possible for both to be wrong.

The often-bitter wrangling in attribution study betrays a moral divide at its heart in wanting to 'credit' writers for their work on the one hand (Taylor), and to 'protect' Shakespeare from association with inferior works on the other (Vickers). These are entrenched positions. The eminent Shakespeare scholar, E.K. Chambers, way back in 1924 labelled attempts to reassign parts of Shakespeare's plays to others as 'disintegration', a loaded word, redolent of ideological contest.[24] The New Oxford Shakespeare, along with its *Authorship Companion* volume, amounted to the biggest reappraisal of Shakespearean collaboration in a major edition. For many it represented exciting progress, though it provoked vehement resistance and counter-attribution arguments alike. William Proctor Williams saw its editorial board as blinkered by mutual reinforcement of each other's approaches and intellectual prejudices.[25] Vickers described a 'crisis' in which practitioners were damaging Shakespeare, in terms similar to the stand-off between the first wave of 'disintegrationists' and their opponents.[26] The verbal shock tactics were seemingly intended to draw opprobrium to the practice in general, though a turf war was also at hand, with Vickers preparing an edition of Thomas Kyd, to whom he attributes *Arden of Faversham* in its entirety. Kyd's canonical boundaries have represented probably the biggest schism of the past twenty years of Shakespearean authorship studies, until the NOS's *Henry VI* claims. Vickers has agreed with Taylor on Shakespeare's main canonical dramatic collaborations, his 2002 book *Shakespeare, Co-author* reconfirming several conclusions outlined in the 1987 *Textual Companion* to the original Oxford Shakespeare, though differences in methodological approach have provoked what are to many outside the discipline alienatingly hostile quarrels over a long period of time.

Eighteenth-century editors of Shakespeare can be considered the first to practise attribution on scholarly, as opposed to purely commercial, grounds, though methods refined beyond broad observation of stylistic and ideational parallels were not really seen until the nineteenth century, when Charles Bathurst, F.J. Furnivall, and F.G. Fleay developed metrical profiles for Shakespeare's verse as ways of testing authorship. The twentieth century had begun with New Bibliographers' assiduous examinations of the print and manuscript record, and with intense close readers like H. Dugdale Sykes and E.H.C. Oliphant, with whom Chambers clashed. Chambers also repudiated Fleay's efforts, seeking to 'protect' Shakespeare, though metrical tests were further developed to determine authorship, especially by Karl Wentersdorf.[27] More traditional studies of style and parallel accompanied the rise of hardcore statistical work, including those of Muriel St Clare Byrne, Kenneth Muir, Cyrus Hoy, Sam Schoenbaum, and David J. Lake.[28] MacDonald P. Jackson has undoubtedly been the leading figure of the last 50 years, whose methods and conclusions fed into the landmark 1986 Oxford Shakespeare, instrumental especially in shifting our understanding of *Pericles* as a collaboration, which he consolidated in 2003 with another major study. The field developed through the late 1980s into the '90s in the work of Marina Tarlinskaja, Thomas Merriam, Jayne Carroll, and Hugh Craig, and came to renewed prominence through Vickers' *Shakespeare, Co-author*. Attribution work before the 1990s had to be carried out manually—Jackson's *Middleton and Shakespeare* the prime example—though the development of computer software and online databases enabled it to be done far more quickly, and on a more comprehensive scale, than was ever before possible.

Attribution offers valuable perspectives on the different mechanisms by which we imagine collaboration to have functioned. It is ultimately how we assess the truth of early documentary claims for Shakespeare's authorship and co-authorship—*The London Prodigal*, *A Yorkshire Tragedy*, and *The Two Noble Kinsmen*, for instance—and how we locate Shakespearean collaboration within printed texts that are silent on the matter, such as *Edward III* and *Titus Andronicus*. The likeliest additions to the canon are in fact all works bearing no attribution to Shakespeare in their earliest textual states. It is how we see Fletcher finish a scene Shakespeare starts in *All Is True*, and vice versa in *Kinsmen*, plays, as Gordon McMullan points out, that are only available for other kinds of collaboration discussion because attribution has confirmed their co-authorship in the first place.[29] *Timon* shows a more finely blended co-authorship seeming to suggest even closer working, but actually reflects the opposite, Middleton acting variously as part-transcriber, reviser, and fragmentary contributor to sections at different parts of the play (2.2 and 5.1) that Shakespeare wrote alone. The fact that 'the interview arranged between Flavius and Ventidius in a passage written by Middleton [in 2.2] never materializes in Shakespeare's share of the play' further suggests distant collaboration, though consistent with synchronic work, and distinct from the diachronic Middletonian revision in parts of *Measure for Measure* after Shakespeare's death.[30] Texts often get revised, much as buildings get renovated, and attribution can help us understand those processes, albeit imperfectly. It cannot typically detect the kind of micro-contributions in a printed text that we can see in the *Sir Thomas More* manuscript, for example. Random 2,000-word samples for analysis—often employed to avoid assumptions about the level at which the collaboration breaks down in the text—would treat them as statistically insignificant in any case. But slightly larger sections with any distinguishing, quantifiable stylistic effects are typically assumed to reflect authorship, and can help us at least identify multiple authors at work on the same scene, even if we cannot always exactly demarcate what they did.

Taylor, addressing Middletonian adaptation/revision in *Macbeth*, called for the systematic use of every linguistic unit in a passage in a large number of collocation combinations, to combat the problem of textual additions tending to produce small sample sizes, and perform short-passage analysis effectively.[31] Advocating a greater sensitivity in close reading and a burden of responsibility to be shifted back onto human cognition, he, perhaps unexpectedly, showed a measured sense of the efficacy and efficiency with which computers produce meaningful conclusions about authorship. Taylor termed this work 'micro-attribution', which he also applied to *Arden of Faversham*, and performed what he called 'deep reading' on the fly scene in *Titus Andronicus* (it might be observed that attribution study originated through what is essentially close reading).[32] He drew ire from those who felt more computational support was needed, those who reject the mathematical analysis of style, and those who reject the attributions in question.[33] Stylometry has also been brought to bear on functions beyond the biographical author. Where repertory studies have asserted that playing companies themselves were the main determiners of plays' styles, driven by economics, audience, playhouse, personnel, genre, métier, Hugh Craig and Brett Greatley-Hirsch's data shows authorship still emerging as the strongest link between texts.[34] Siobhan Keenan has also pointed out that authors' distinctive styles can be seen across their writing for different companies, between which plays also often moved, while Roslyn L. Knutson has questioned whether authors' 'voices' are subsumed in, or creating, anything perceived as 'company style'.[35]

The governing principle of all methods is that few things individuate people more starkly than the way they employ language. This is an ancient principle; Shakespeare's contemporary, William Scott, noted that Cicero in his writing 'discerns as many differences in style as there are persons that write'.[36] At both mundane and more artificially complex levels, language is the most supple and precise instrument we have, both a shared system, foundational to the way we communicate lived experience, and a talent. It is why we discriminate in our appreciation of the way certain people speak or write, why we value phraseology, wit, or a verbal precision that not everyone can match; why Tweets go viral in virtual rounds of applause for feats of linguistic alchemy. But lexical showboating is at odds with the idea of the linguistic 'fingerprint'—one of the preferred metaphors in attribution studies—which dictates that patterns too minute or spread out to discern readily, even by authors themselves, are the most telling. In this, function word use (literally ifs, ands, and buts), of which authors are in less conscious control, is favoured, as lexical or content words can drag the data into genre- and play-specific contexts. But a fingerprint is a natural profile that is unique and unmistakable, while authorial data can never be quite so secure, no matter how refined the method. The metaphor further toils in that fingerprints can securely identify a person, but cannot account for the complexities of their personhood. Stylometry, to its detractors, seeks to exhaust the phenomenon of creative authorship through mechanical measurement positing that anything—the poetry of self-expression, the functions of the human brain—can be reduced to an algorithm.

Cognitive theory, which focuses on the brain's interaction with the external world, has been used to insist on Shakespeare's authoriality as something literally organic.[37] While man vs machine techno-scepticism is one kind of opposition to attribution study, another is a more theorized part of the STEM vs Humanities rift, inherently distrustful of any work purporting to 'solve' a text. The literary human-ities in general perceive truth as something constructed rather than intrinsic, a text's ramifications in culture far more important than its distillation to factual data and metadata. Even if something could be proven to be 'by Shakespeare', that fact in itself might be used to reconfigure any number of power dynamics around the institutional or cultural reception of him specifically, and of authors and author-ship more generally. Historicist methods aver that something either happened or it did not, while theoretical approaches worry about the significance of that. Stylometry seems to sell the stability of the empirical, the incontrovertible, order from chaos, truths held to be self-evident, a universally thankful readership, which its opponents see as a troubling move to quash interpretation. Further exception is taken to the idea of stylometry begging the question, cherry-picking data the computer supposedly harvests impartially. Edward Pechter worries that by putting the process beyond the reach of cognition, people can make it say and mean anything they want, and do so 'because [they] can'.[38] This, he suggests more radically, is why we now 'exaggerate the importance of collaboration'—because we create it artificially.

There is, then, an increasing resistance to, and scepticism around, computational studies as the dominant scholarly model for under-standing collaboration. The gut rejections are simple enough: that people and their creativity are so much more than statistics, and that with enough computers, time, and inclination anything can be made to sound like anyone. The digital humanities are most commonly acknowledged as a good thing around dissemination and access—high-resolution images of early books and manuscripts online, for example, or the xml coding that makes electronic editions more functional and responsive. In the field of computational stylistics, though, the digital affronts the human. But stylometry allows style as something human, bound in personhood—it merely insists that within it are constituent parts, mundane features, that are both individualizing and countable, and a more reliable guide than those effects that are subject to imitation. It is governed by style-based research questions in which the computer is used merely as a tool alongside literary interpretation of the poetic schema and surface textures of language, beyond its raw data. While computational number-crunching is quick in itself, the work overall is extremely labour-intensive in the use of multiple tests which must either be designed or refined, many of which prove fruitless, or too ambiguous to be telling. The stability and efficacy of any data is never guaranteed, which is why the use of control tests using texts of known authorship and the importance of convergent results are so vital, as Burrows highlights:

The introduction of statistical analysis into literary studies merely highlights an ancient truth: with internal evidence we form our conclusions on the balance of probability. And that balance tilts in our favour when several independent tests yield mutually corroborative outcomes at high levels of confidence. That is why we must keep trying out the tests in cases where the truth is known.[39]

Poetic language is characterized by artifice and innovation as writers experiment with their own style from work to work, even within works. The best practitioners are keenly aware of these factors, working assiduously to mitigate them, and the integrity and scepticism of the researcher should be assumed rather than not. There is the difficult job of establishing corpora, the recognition and negotiation of difficulties such as text sample size, corpus comparability, and transmission interference, which we know about from editing and book history (and tests are often carried out on unedited digitized transcriptions). There is the time involved in investigating different kinds of difference, some quantifiable and subject to degree-of-significance checks, others measures of distinctiveness correlating with style as a literary scholar might understand it. Marlowe's canon, for example, if it is as collaborative and/or adapted as it seems to be, offers significant challenges in establishing a clear authorial profile for subsequent comparisons. Ruth Lunney and Hugh Craig showed detailed awareness of this in their testing, as well as the differences between drama and non-dramatic prose in their profiling of Nashe to separate him from Marlowe.[40] Attribution is frequently criticized for Shakespeare-centrism, yet was largely developed through other writers—Hoy's pioneering work on Beaumont and Fletcher, and Jackson and Lake's early studies of Middleton's canon, for example. The same principles and methods have more recently been applied to other writers, as in the Middleton and Ford volumes already discussed, the Cambridge Aphra Behn edition, the profiling of George Wilkins as part of Jackson's *Pericles* study, and Darren Freebury-Jones's work on Greene, to name a select few.[41] And Shakespeare is profiled precisely for the ways in which his writing distinguishes him from others, so it is always working both ways, the techniques developed for recognizing Shakespeare always aiding our identification of non-Shakespeare. Parsing Shakespeare's contributions can be seen as a fetishized obsession with his sole-authorship, but might equally be motivated by the desire to better understand him as a working dramatist. In this, NOS attributionism arguably sought a place between radical author-scepticism and conservative author-centrism. It sought to disintegrate Shakespeare precisely in order to integrate him.

Against/With

Jeffrey Masten, as we have seen, has opposed attribution study. His advocacy for the 'authorlessness' of early plays, a textual polyphony that is a more historically appropriate version of what we might call anonymity, has been influential in shaping understanding of the difference between theatrical and literary authorship in particular.[42] Aaron Pratt, though, felt the fundamental question was 'whether attribution studies now misrepresents the conditions of authorship then', noting that we routinely 'find evidence of collaboration at virtually all stages of the writing process, but this evidence alone does not tell us how authorship worked within a culture and its various milieux'.[43] By conflating ideas of the process and reception of authorship, he argues, we are in danger of 'posit[ing] a collaborative mindset, both for authors and their audiences . . . under the guise of historicity'. David Nicol has characterized Masten's 'an extreme response' that 'effaces precisely the concept that . . . study of collaboration raises: the idea of *diversity* within the text'.[44] Masten's historicism—fixing play-texts in a specific environment and time in which authorship was dispersed and supposedly immaterial—is sharply at odds with stylometry's, which purports to be a material analysis of the practical outcomes of historical labour.

But stylometry's data, for its critics, goes beyond an observable relationship with language, cannot be processed by simple reading, and therefore lacks the factual bases to which it lays claim. Conversely, the rigorous theatre-historical work underpinning Masten's conclusions is critiqued as unhistorical for being read through modern theories of gender and sexuality. Who wrote a play is a theatre-history question when it helps identify the working patterns of particular dramatists, methods of play composition, repertories of different companies and their approaches to genre or commercial competition. But when does such investigation cease to be a neutral act with self-evident historiographical benefits, and become something that precludes other experiences and viewpoints in the present? Masten, indeed, has spoken of some ad hominem critiques of his work as latently homophobic. And here, if attribution is legitimately anti-collaborative in the way Masten figures it, is a far darker implication: that the single-author model, tied systemically to heteronormative, paternalistic values, sets exclusionary limits on what is discussed, and on who does the discussing. In the early modern theatres in which Shakespeare worked, dramatists were exclusively male, and exclusively white, which speaks to the most fundamental schism in authorship studies currently: are apparently simple facts about the past separable from their cultural legacies in the present? While opaque mathematics and an apparent return to pre-1960s' ideas of 'the author' has made modern stylometric attribution work unpopular and untrusted among other factions of the literary humanities—the latter seen, at best, as the unseemly fetishization of authorship—a more serious implication is of a canonicity perpetuating exclusion by the amplification and apparent glorification of dead, white, male voices. And of one in particular.

These issues, in the wake of the NOS's publication, came most conspicuously to a head in a 2017 blog post for the 'Before Shakespeare' project.[45] Borrowing Masten's ideas about paternity, it portrayed a toxic field, the preserve of senior, white, male academia, where petty squabbles serve to bury awkward questions of power and complicity. Attribution study became an unsuspecting focal point for a reappraisal of inequalities within the profession, seeming to make an already unpopular critical field dismissible on moral grounds. The piece, though selling its own vision of early modern collaborative authorship, was nonetheless influential in forcing these conversations to emerge. It was also a striking index of the protocols around social media in the academic community, which has not yet fully reckoned with the changing role it plays in the shaping of professional discourse. For those who feel marginalized by historicist work in general, and by attribution study in particular, for a host of perceived critical blind spots in the questions it asks—or, indeed, fails to ask, around gender, race, heteronormativity, ableism, class, seniority, and their attendant privileges—it is the potential for political co-option that is troubling, in ways that are perhaps beyond the aims envisaged by the particular investigator. This is in addition to what canonical construction means to us as continued readers and performers of these plays, especially where Shakespeare is involved.

B.K. Adams's work linking the terminology of 'fair/foul' so integral to the New Bibliography is an important case in point.[46] She takes the definition of 'fair', cognate with beauty in early modern writing, and with purity in early twentieth-century conceptions of Shakespeare's manuscripts, towards equality, and 'the inherent *unfair* structural barriers located in the field', a textual history of Shakespeare defined by systemic whiteness' privileged access to the archive others have been denied.[47] We cannot ask what collaborative writing *was*, then, without also asking for whom it *is*, as its study involves vast methodological, epistemological, even egalitarian difference. As Masten noted, 'feminist, queer, and critical-race scholarship has worked hard to ask substantial questions about writing, imitation, and identity, and to develop complex models, some of which it would benefit attribution studies to contemplate'.[48] There are, in Masten's scholarship, clear parallels with, and influences from New Historicism, which itself did not—in fact could not—harmonize with empirical accounts of history to build its arguments, rooted as it was in modern philosophical theories about networks of influence. Masten's is brave, necessary work, aimed more at provocation than practical solution, reminding us that critical thought is as much a component of human knowledge as hard data. It is poiesis, it is how ideas get made, and an ideal scenario sees the two interconnected. But bridges seem difficult to build, and there is perhaps a deep paradox in that scholars who analyse collaboration might do with being more collaborative in spirit.

Attribution study has undoubtedly advanced our understanding of how early drama, and Shakespeare, worked; it is how we know about most of Shakespeare's collaborative activity in the first place, and underpins all the arguments made about it in this book. It is how we know about different kinds of collaboration, how we are able to reform our understanding of its place in Shakespeare's career, and Shakespeare's own place in its development. But for its detractors, it is how it is practised—the perceived aggressive posturing, indifference to other methodologies, and apparent empiricism/theory binary it sets up—that is most off-putting, especially to those fundamentally uninterested in modelling collaboration or authorship in these ways. Other methodologies and ideas, some reviewed throughout this book, have done just as much to reshape our conceptions and understandings of Shakespeare and of the modes and means of artistic production in the early theatres and book trade; indeed, Adams shares Masten's hope that we will continue to look for answers in the 'spaces that exist' at the 'intersection of . . . subfields' as we progress.[49] Interest in, and understanding of, collaboration's significance, its practices, its prevalence, its varieties, has seen strident development. But there is much still to be done; work that will determine not just how we understand Shakespeare as a collaborative or a sole author, but how we—as scholars, students, practitioners, readers—continue to be able, and willing, to work together.

Attribution by Play

The following attributions, unless otherwise stated, are keyed to the New Oxford Shakespeare (2016–17). Appendix 2 of John Jowett's *Shakespeare and Text* volume in this series gives detailed information about the various imprints in which these plays first appeared.

Arden of Faversham (1590)

Written originally by Shakespeare in direct collaboration with at least one other dramatist for unknown company—possibly Strange's or the Admiral's—in or around 1590, with the following attribution:

> Unknown writer(s): Scenes 1–3, 10–18, Epilogue
> Shakespeare: Scenes 4–8
> Disputed: Scene 9

2 *Henry VI* (1591)

Written originally by Shakespeare in direct collaboration with Christopher Marlowe, and, probably, another dramatist for Pembroke's in the first half of 1591 (possibly begun in May). Originally called *The First Part of the Contention betwixt the Two Famous Houses of York and Lancaster*, it was revised by Shakespeare around May–June 1594 and eventually retitled *The Second Part of Henry the Sixth*. That version, printed in the 1623 Folio, has the following attribution:

> Marlowe: 1.1, 1.3, 1.4, 4.2.99–162, 4.3–10 (Scenes 1, 3, 4, 14.99–162, 15–22)
> Shakespeare: 3.1–4, 4.1, 4.2.1–98 (Scenes 9–14.98)
> Unknown writer(?) 1.2, 2.1–4, 5.1–5 (Scenes 2, 5–8, 23–7)

3 *Henry VI* (1591)

Written originally by Shakespeare in direct collaboration with Christopher Marlowe, and, probably, another dramatist for Pembroke's in the latter part of 1591. Originally called *The True Tragedy of Richard Duke of York*, it was revised by Shakespeare around May–June 1594 and eventually retitled *The Third Part of Henry the Sixth*. That version, printed in the 1623 Folio, has the following attribution:

Marlowe: 1.1–2, 2.3, 4.2–8, 5.2 (Scenes 1, 2, 7, 15–21, 24)
Shakespeare: 1.4, 2.1–2, 2.4–6, 3.1–2, 4.1, 5.1, 5.3–7 (Scenes 4–6, 8–12, 14, 23, 25–9)
Unknown writer(?) 1.3, 3.3, 4.9 (Scenes 3, 13, 22)

Titus Andronicus (1592)

Begun originally by George Peele, who wrote the first act and the beginning of the second for Pembroke's; turned over to Shakespeare for completion for unknown reasons, probably in winter/spring of late 1591–early 1592, with the following attribution:

Peele: 1.1, 2.1–2
Shakespeare: 2.3–4, 3.1, 4.1–4, 5.1–3

Edward III (1592–3?)

Written originally in direct collaboration by unknown dramatists—possibly including Marlowe—in, probably, the latter half of 1592, either for Strange's or Pembroke's, and revised by Shakespeare late 1593, possibly for Derby's, with the following attribution:

Unknown writer(s): 1.1, 1.2.1–89, 3.1–5, 4.1–3, 4.5–9, 5.1
Shakespeare: 1.2.90–627, 2.1, 4.4

1 *Henry VI* (1592/1594)

Written originally by Thomas Nashe in direct collaboration with Christopher Marlowe and at least one other dramatist for Strange's in early 1592, certainly by 3 March, its first recorded performance in Henslowe's Diary as 'Harry VI'. Adapted/revised/retitled for the Chamberlain's—along with *Parts 2* and *3*—around May–June 1594 by Shakespeare, who added:

'Temple Garden' scene, 2.4 (133 lines); two scenes dealing with Talbot's exploits in France, 4.2 (56 lines) and 4.5 (55 lines)

The Spanish Tragedy (1587/1599?)

Original text written by Thomas Kyd, perhaps for the Admiral's in 1587. Revised, in what was seemingly a coordinated project of adaptation between Shakespeare and Thomas Heywood, some time perhaps in early 1599, for the Chamberlain's:

> Heywood(?): Addition 1 (54 lines)
> Shakespeare: Addition 2 (11 lines), Addition 3 (47 lines), Addition 4 (160 lines), Addition 5 (49 lines)

Sir Thomas More (c.1600/1603–4)

Original text written by Anthony Munday, and, probably, Henry Chettle, most likely in 1600, and probably for Derby's.[1] Presented to, and refused by, the Master of the Revels, Edmund Tilney, that year. In *c.*1603–4, the playhouse functionary/scribe known to us as Hand C apparently offered the text first to Chettle, and subsequently to other dramatists for adaptation/revision, probably for Worcester's, with the following sequence of work:

STAGE 1: CHETTLE AND DEKKER

- Chettle annotates Original Text MS in section that Dekker will rewrite, writes Add. I and part of Add. II, revising the most violent scene in the play (prentice riot in which a senior city alderman is attacked)
- Dekker revises Scene 8 in Add. IV, fols. 12 and 13, replacing material found partially on 11b and 14a (the two leaves used to paste addition slips III and V onto), and at least one other leaf now lost

STAGE 2: HAND C, SHAKESPEARE, AND HEYWOOD

- Hand C transcribes Chettle's part of Add. II (Scene 5) on fol. 7b, leaving 7a blank for Heywood to copy his lightly revised/expanded Scene 4. The opening SD for Scene 4 is on previous leaf in OT, though C adds to it, and supplies opening/closing SDs for Scene 5, and an opening SD for Scene 6, containing clear directives for the benefit of both dramatists, at the head and foot respectively of fol. 7b. Heywood clearly had the page, along with fol. 5 (OT Scene 4), which he largely follows, when Shakespeare—whose speech prefixes suggest ignorance about who is on stage—was working on his part. Hand C transcribes Scene 8, probably to effect its integration into a new place more smoothly, though almost certainly also to clarify and unify Dekker's revisions, which took the form both of new sections added on new sheets of paper, and annotations to the OT. Speculatively, C may have added some linking lines here, e.g. 'How now, what's the matter?'

(8.47)—similar to his, 'Tell me but this' in Hand D—to join the various subsections

- Shakespeare and Heywood write Add. II (Scenes 4 and 6), and Heywood adds Clown parts to Scene 7. Shakespeare replaces at least a whole leaf, now lost, joining up with the OT at the beginning of fol. 10
- Shakespeare writes Add. III
- Shakespeare writes Add. V and Heywood revises it

STAGE 3: HAND C, HEYWOOD, AND DEKKER

- Hand C takes a smaller piece of paper, cuts it in half, transcribes Adds. III and V on the two halves, sticks them to deleted/replaced material on 11b and 14a. Deletions to Hand S here are by Chettle/Hand C(?), and are thus part of revision rather than censorship. Adds. III and V bookend Dekker's Add. IV (Scene 8)
- Heywood writes Add VI and Messenger speech at end that subsequently appears at beginning of Add. V, copied vertically into the margin of pasted slip by Hand C
- Messenger SD placed at end of Hand C's transcript of Scene 8 (Dekker), but is crossed out when Dekker adds another ending to the scene himself

Timon of Athens (1606)

Written in direct collaboration with Thomas Middleton for the King's in early 1606, with the following attribution:

Shakespeare: 1.1, 2.1, 4.1.33–92, 4.2, 4.3.1–29, 5.1.1–441, 522–742, 5.2–4 (Scenes 1, 3, 11.33–92, 12, 13.1–29, 14.1–441, 522–742, 15–17)
Middleton: 1.2, 3.1–6, 4.1.1–21, 93–101, 4.3.30–51, 5.1.442–521, and probably transcribed and added touches to Poet/Painter episode at ll. 522–629 (Scenes 2, 5–11.1–21, 93–101, 13.30–51, 14.442–521, 522–629?)
Inextricably mixed authorship: 2.2 (Scene 4)

Pericles (1607–8)

Begun originally by George Wilkins, who wrote the first two acts for the King's mid-late 1607, and turned over to Shakespeare for completion, probably because Wilkins was fired (see Chapter 5). NOS suggests the possibility of Wilkins's hand in the brothel scenes, with the following attribution:

Wilkins: Prologue, 1.1–4, 2.0–5 (Scenes 1–11)
Shakespeare: 3.0–4, 4.0–1, 4.3–4, 5.0–3, Epilogue (Scenes 12–18, 20–1, 24–8)
Possibly mixed authorship: 4.2, 4.5–6 (Scenes 19, 22–3)

Cardenio (1612)

Written in direct collaboration with John Fletcher for the King's in the second half of 1612. The play survives only partially through Lewis Theobald's 1727 adaptation, *Double Falsehood*, from which the following authorial shares are conjecturally reconstructed:

>   Shakespeare: 1.1–3, 2.1–4, 3.1–2
>   Fletcher: 3.3, 4.1–2, 5.1–2

All Is True; or Henry VIII (1613)

Written in direct collaboration with John Fletcher for the King's in the first half of 1613, probably late spring/early summer, with the following attribution:

>   Shakespeare: 1.1–2, 2.3–4, 3.2.1–204, 5.1
>   Fletcher: Prologue, 1.3–4, 2.1–2, 3.1, 3.2.204–460.1, 4.1–2, 5.2–4, Epi-
>   logue

The Two Noble Kinsmen (1613)

Written in direct collaboration with John Fletcher for the King's in late 1613, with the following attribution:

>   Shakespeare: 1.1–4, 2.1, 3.1–2, 5.1.19–68, 5.2–3, 5.5–6
>   Fletcher: Prologue, 2.2–6, 3.3–6, 4.1–2, 5.1.1–18, 5.4, Epilogue
>   Disputed: 1.5, 4.3

Middleton's Adaptations of Shakespeare

Titus Andronicus (1592/1616)

See above for original authorship; adapted in 1616 by Thomas Middleton for the King's, who added the 'fly scene', 3.2.

Macbeth (1606/1616)

Written originally by Shakespeare solus for the King's mid-1606; adapted for them in late 1616 by Thomas Middleton, who added:

>   the 'Hecate' scene, 3.5, including a song transposed from his own 1616 play, *The Witch*; some Hecate dialogue and another song from *The Witch* at 4.1.39–A1–17 '*Enter Hecate . . .* good keep out'; and 4.1.120–30.1 'Horrible sight . . . *dance, and vanish*'.

Gary Taylor in the Oxford Middleton attributes other linking phrases and dialogic passages at 1.1.8, 1.2.7–9, 20–3, 1.3.43–5, 4.1.79–80, 140–2, 153–5, 157–61, 163–7, 171–4, 4.2.39–57.

Measure for Measure (1603-4/1621)

Written originally by Shakespeare solus for the King's late 1603, probably into early 1604; adapted for them in late 1621 by Thomas Middleton, who most famously changed the play's location from an Italianate setting, possibly Ferrara, to Vienna, transposed the Duke's two soliloquies of 3.1 and 4.1 ('He who the sword of heaven will bear' and 'O place and greatness'), and added the following:

1.2.A1–67 (up to 'I am custom-shrunk'); 1.2.16.1–18 *'Enter Provost . . . Madam Juliet'*; 2.1.37–40 'Well, heaven . . . fault alone'; 2.1.166–72 'What trade . . . Nine!'; 2.1.232–43 'What's o'clock . . . Come, sir'; 4.1.0–23 *'Enter Mariana . . .* and welcome', including the first stanza of the song 'Take oh take those lips away', taken from *Rollo, Duke of Normandy* (1617–20); 4.2.113,150 'but here nursed up and bred', 'O, death's a great disguiser and you may add to it'; 4.3.0–14 *'Enter . . .* Lord's sake!' The 2007 *Oxford Middleton* also argues for three interjections by Lucio at 2.2.134,136,161 as Middletonian interpolations.

All's Well that Ends Well (1605/1622)

Written originally by Shakespeare solus for the King's in early 1605; adapted for them in early 1622 by Thomas Middleton, who added:

1.1.98–139 'Are you meditating . . . Not my virginity, yet . . .' comprising the 'virginity' dialogue; 2.3.117–30 'From lowest place . . . every grave' in the King's speech about Helena; and 4.3.90–9 'A plague . . . merciful general', 4.3.140–93 'Demand of him . . . in's forehead', 4.3.203–38 'Therefore once more . . . cramp', 4.3.260–4 'Good captain . . . yet', comprising Middleton's significant adaptation of the 'interrogation' scene.

Canon and Chronology

This book differs on select matters of Shakespeare's dramatic chronology from those of the 1986–7 and revised 2005 *Oxford Shakespeare* editions, the NOS (2016), and Wiggins' *British Drama* (2012–), tabulated below. Dates below are 'best-guess', reflecting Shakespeare's likely authorial work on a play rather than its known completion and/or staging.

Oxford (1986–7)	Oxford 2 (2005)	Wiggins (2013–15)	New Oxford (2016)	This Book (2023)
TGV (1590–1)	*TGV* (1589–91)	*2H6* (1591)	*TGV* (1588)	*TGV* (1590)
TS (1590–1)	*TS* (1590–1)	*3H6* (1591)	**AF (1588)**	**AF (1590)**
2H6 (1591)	*2H6* (1590–1)	*TS* (1592)	*TA* **(1589)** *	**2H6 (1591)**
3H6 (1591)	*3H6* (1591)	**TA (1592)**	**2H6 (1590)**	**3H6 (1591)**
1H6 (1592)	**1H6 (1592)**	*CE* (1593)	**3H6 (1590)**	*TA* **(1591–2)** *
TA (1592)	**TA (1592)**	*R3* (1593)	*TS* (1591)	*TS* (1592)
R3 (1592–3)	*R3* (1592–3)	**E3 (1593)**	**E3 (1592)**	*R3* (1592)
VA (1592–3)	*VA* (1592–3)	*TGV* (1594)	*R3* (1592)	*VA* (1593)
RL (1593–4)	*RL* (1593–4)	*1H6* ʾ/2&3 rev. **(1594)**	*VA* (1593)	**E3 (1593–4)** ·
CE (1594)	**E3 (1594)**	*RJ* (1595)	*RL* (1594)	*RL* (1594)
LLL (1594–5)	*CE* (1594)	*R2* (1595)	*CE* (1594)	*1H6* ʾ/2&3 rev. **(1594)**
R2 (1595)	*LLL* (1594–5)	*MND* (1595)	*LLL* (1594)	*CE* (1594)
RJ (1595)	*R2* (1595)	*LLL* (1596)	*LLW* (1595)	*LLL* (1594)
MND (1595)	*RJ* (1595)	*KJ* (1596)	*R2* (1595)	*RJ* (1595)
LLW (1595–6)	*MND* (1595)	*MV* (1596)	*1H6* ʾ/2&3 rev. **(1595)**	*R2* (1595)
KJ (1596)	*LLW* (1595–6)	*1H4* (1597)	*RJ* (1595)	*MND* (1595)
MV (1596–7)	*KJ* (1596)	*MWW* (1597)	*MND* (1596)	*LLW* (1596)
1H4 (1596–7)	*MV* (1596–7)	*2H4* (1597)	*KJ* (1596)	*KJ* (1596)

Continued

Continued

This Book (2023)	New Oxford (2016)	Wiggins (2013–15)	Oxford 2 (2005)	Oxford (1986–7)
MV (1596)	MV (1597)	LLW (1598)	1H4 (1596–7)	MWW (1597–8)
1H4 (1597)	1H4 (1597)	MA (1598)	MWW (1597–8)	2H4 (1597–8)
MWW (1597)	2H4 (1598)	H5 (1599)	2H4 (1597–8)	MA (1598)
2H4 (1597–8)	MA (1598)	JC (1599)	MA (1598–9)	H5 (1598–9)
MA (1598)	H5 (1599)	AYL (1600)	H5 (1598–9)	JC (1599)
H5 (1598–9)	JC (1599)	Ham (1600)	JC (1599)	AYL (1599–1600)
Span. Trag. (1599)*	Span. Trag. (1599)*	STM (1601)*	AYL (1599–1600)	Ham (1600–1)
JC (1599)	AYL (1600)	TN (1601)	Ham (1600–1)	TN (1601)
AYL (1600)	MWW (1600)	TC (1602)	TN (1601)	TC (1602)
Ham (1600–1)	TN (1601)	MM (1603)*	TC (1602)	**STM (1603–4)**
TN (1601)	TC (1602)	Oth (1604)	**STM (1603–4)**	MM (1603)*
TC (1602)	Ham (1602–3)	AWW (1605)	MM (1603–4)*	Oth (1603–4)
STM (1603–4)·	**Sej (1603)**	KL (1605–6)	Oth (1604)	AWW (1604–5)
MM (1603–4)*	**STM (1603–4)**·	Mac (1606)*	KL (1605–6)	**Tim (1605)**
Oth (1604)	Oth (1604)	AC (1606)	**Tim (1606)**	KL (1605–6)
AWW (1604–5)*	MM (1604)*	**Tim (1607)**	Mac (1606)*	Mac (1606)*
KL (1605–6)	AWW (1605)*	**Per (1607)**	AC (1606)	AC (1606)

Per (1607)	AWW (1606–7)	Cor (1608)	KL (1605)	**Tim (1606)**
Cor (1608)	**Per (1607)**	KL rev. (1610)	**Tim (1606)**	Mac (1606) *
WT (1609)	Cor (1608)	Cym (1610)	Mac (1606) *	AC (1606–7)
KL rev. (1610)	WT (1609–10)	WT (1611)	AC (1607)	**Per (1607–8)**
Cym (1610)	KL rev. (1610)	Temp (1611)	**Per (1608)**	Cor (1608)
Temp (1611)	Cym (1610–11)	**AIT/H8 (1612)**	Cor (1608)	WT (1609–10)
Card (1612–13)	Temp (1610–11)	**Card (1612)**	WT (1609)	KL rev. (1610)
AIT/H8 (1613)	**Card (1612–13)**	**TNK (1613)**	KL rev. (1610)	Cym (1610–11)
TNK (1613–14)	**AIT/H8 (1613)**		Cym (1610)	Temp (1611)
	TNK (1613)		Temp (1611)	**Card (1612)**
			Card (1612)	**AIT/H8 (1613)**
			AIT/H8 (1613)	**TNK (1613)**
			TNK (1613)	

Bold = written originally in direct or indirect collaboration

• = adapted by Shakespeare after original composition by others (dates reflect Shakespeare's revisions)

* = adapted by Thomas Middleton (dates reflect Shakespeare's original composition)

Notes

INTRODUCTION

1. *Bartholomew Fair* (1614), Induction; *Pimlico, or Run Red-Cap* (1609) and Robert Tailor's *The Hog Hath Lost his Pearl* (1614) reference *Pericles'* exceptional popularity. See Lukas Erne, *Shakespeare and the Book Trade* (Cambridge: Cambridge University Press, 2013), 33–4, for reprint rates of Shakespeare plays.
2. *The Oxford Shakespeare: The Complete Works* and *William Shakespeare: A Textual Companion*, gen. eds. Stanley Wells, Gary Taylor, John Jowett, and William Montgomery (Oxford: Oxford University Press, 1986–7).
3. *The New Oxford Shakespeare Modern Critical Edition*, gen. eds. Gary Taylor, John Jowett, Terri Bourus, and Gabriel Egan (Oxford: Oxford University Press, 2016); *The New Oxford Shakespeare Authorship Companion*, eds. Gary Taylor and Gabriel Egan (Oxford: Oxford University Press, 2017).

CHAPTER I

1. Gary Taylor, 'Collaborating with The Dead' TEDxFSU 31 March 2017, Tallahassee, Florida, https://www.youtube.com/watch?v=G_GZo7M9AKc
2. Suze Marsupial, 'Pragmatics for Pragmatists', https://newsocialist.org.uk/pragmatics-for–pragmatists/amp/; H.P. Grice, 'Logic and Conversation', in Peter Cole and Jerry L. Morgan (eds.), *Syntax and Semantics 3: Speech Acts* (London: Academic Press, 1975), 41–58.
3. D.F. McKenzie, *Bibliography and the Sociology of Texts* (Cambridge: Cambridge University Press, 1999), 15.
4. Diana E. Henderson, *Collaborations with the Past: Reshaping Shakespeare Across Time and Media* (Ithaca: Cornell University Press, 2006).
5. See Janet Clare, *Shakespeare's Stage Traffic: Imitation, Borrowing and Competition in Renaissance Theatre* (Cambridge: Cambridge University Press, 2014); Tom Rutter, *Shakespeare and the Admiral's Men: Reading across Repertories on the London Stage, 1594–1600* (Cambridge: Cambridge University Press, 2017).
6. Goran Stanivukovic, 'The Language and Style of Early Shakespeare', in Rory Loughnane and Andrew J. Power (eds.), *Early Shakespeare,*

1588–1594 (Cambridge: Cambridge University Press, 2020), 76–101 (pp. 77–8).

7. See Colin Burrow, *Imitating Authors: Plato to Futurity* (Oxford: Oxford University Press, 2019), and *Shakespeare and Classical Antiquity* (Oxford: Oxford University Press, 2013), 21–50; Lynn Enterline, *Shakespeare's Schoolroom: Rhetoric, Discipline, Emotion* (Philadelphia: University of Pennsylvania Press, 2012), 21–50.

8. Stanivukovic, 'Language and Style', 77.

9. Laurie Maguire and Emma Smith, 'What is a Source? Or, How Shakespeare Read his Marlowe', *Shakespeare Survey* 68 (2015), 15–31; Raphael Lyne, *Memory and Intertextuality in Renaissance Literature* (Cambridge: Cambridge University Press, 2016).

10. Harold Love, *Attributing Authorship* (Cambridge: Cambridge University Press, 2002).

11. John Kerrigan, *Shakespeare's Originality* (Oxford: Oxford University Press, 2018).

12. Jonathan Bate, *How the Classics Made Shakespeare* (Princeton, NJ: Princeton University Press 2019).

13. Stephen Greenblatt, *Renaissance Self-Fashioning: From More to Shakespeare* (Chicago: University of Chicago Press, 1980).

14. William Sleights, 'The Edifying Margins of Renaissance English Books', *Renaissance Quarterly* 42:4 (1989), 682–716. See also *Hamlet*, 5.2.127.

15. Claire M.L. Bourne suggests that early printed play-texts employed typographical forms of theatrical performance; *Typographies of Performance in Early Modern England* (Oxford: Oxford University Press, 2020).

16. See Adam Smyth, *Material Texts in Early Modern England* (Cambridge: Cambridge University Press, 2018), on the literary value of mistakes.

17. Gabriel Egan, 'What is Not Collaborative about Early Modern Drama in Performance and Print?', *Shakespeare Survey* 67 (2014), 18–28; Gary Taylor, 'Artiginality', in *Authorship Companion*, 3–26.

18. Jack Stillinger, *Multiple Authorship and the Myth of Solitary Genius* (Oxford: Oxford University Press, 1991). See also Sonia Massai, *Shakespeare and the Rise of the Editor* (Cambridge: Cambridge University Press, 2007), 30, on the role of 'annotating readers' who prepared copy for press, and Colin Burrow's 'Fictions of Collaboration: Authors and Editors in the Sixteenth Century', *Swiss Papers in English Language and Literature* 25 (2011), 175–98.

19. Eoin Price, *'Public' and 'Private' Playhouses in Renaissance England* (London: Palgrave Pivot, 2015).

20. Heather Hirschfield, 'Early Modern Collaboration and Theories of Authorship', *PMLA* 116:3 (2001), 609–22.

21. Jeffrey Masten, *Queer Philologies* (Philadelphia: University of Pennsylvania Press, 2016), 39–68.

22. Evelyn B. Tribble, *Cognition in the Globe: Attention and Memory in Shakespeare's Theatre* (New York: Palgrave Macmillan, 2011).

23. Taylor, 'Artiginality', 18; Nora Johnson, *The Actor as Playwright in Early Modern Drama* (Cambridge: Cambridge University Press, 2003).

24. See Richard Preiss, *Clowning and Authorship in Early Modern Theatre* (Cambridge: Cambridge University Press, 2014).

25. Simon Smith, *Musical Response in the Early Modern Playhouse, 1603–1625* (Cambridge: Cambridge University Press, 2017); Tiffany Stern, *Documents of Performance in Early Modern England* (Cambridge: Cambridge University Press, 2009).

26. Roslyn Lander Knutson, *The Repertory of Shakespeare's Company 1594–1613* (Fayetteville: University of Arkansas Press, 1991), 20–55; Holger Schott Syme, 'A Sharers' Repertory', in Tiffany Stern (ed.), *Rethinking Theatrical Documents in Shakespeare's England* (London: The Arden Shakespeare, 2020), 33–51.

27. Peter Holland, 'Reading to the Company', in Hanna Scolnicov and Peter Holland (eds.), *Reading Plays: Interpretation and Reception* (Cambridge: Cambridge University Press, 1991), 8–29.

28. Egan, 'What is Not?', 23.

29. See Grace Ioppolo, *Dramatists and Their Manuscripts in the Age of Shakespeare, Jonson, Middleton and Heywood: Authorship, Authority and the Playhouse* (Abingdon: Routledge, 2006), 34; the play was *Machiavel and the Devil* (1613).

30. Simon Palfrey and Tiffany Stern, *Shakespeare in Parts* (Oxford: Oxford University Press, 2007), 61–2; Lucy Munro, 'Writing a Play with Robert Daborne', in Stern (ed.), *Rethinking*, 17–32 (pp. 29–30).

31. Egan, 'What is Not?', 20–1.

32. Ibid., 21.

33. Egan, 'What is Not?', 22.

34. Tiffany Stern, *Rehearsal from Shakespeare to Sheridan* (Oxford: Oxford University Press, 2000), 76, 99.

35. Ibid., 106, 112.

36. Eric Rasmussen, 'The Revision of Scripts', in John D. Cox and David Scott Kastan (eds.), *A New History of Early Modern Drama* (New York: Columbia University Press, 1997), 441–60 (pp. 444–47).

37. Ibid., 446.

38. Paul Werstine, *Early Modern Playhouse Manuscripts and the Editing of Shakespeare* (Cambridge: Cambridge University Press, 2013), 398–400.

39. John Jowett, 'Exit Manuscripts: The Archive of Theatre and the Archive of Print', *Shakespeare Survey* 70 (2017), 113–122 (p. 114).
40. Wiggins, *British Drama* #908, argues Chettle's lines may have been added as part of a 1602 revival, at a time when 'superstition' plays were back in vogue.
41. John Jowett, 'Middleton's Early Readers', in Gary Taylor and John Lavagnino (gen. eds.), *Thomas Middleton and Early Modern Textual Culture* (Oxford: Oxford University Press, 2007), 286–327 (p. 292).
42. Jowett, 'Exit', 116.
43. James Purkis, *Shakespeare and Manuscript Drama* (Cambridge: Cambridge University Press, 2016).
44. Stephen Orgel, 'What is a Text?', in David Scott Kastan and Peter Stallybrass (eds.), *Staging the Renaissance* (London: Routledge, 1991), 83–7.
45. Paulina Kewes, *Authorship and Appropriation: Writing for the Stage in England, 1660–1710* (Oxford: Oxford University Press, 1998), 132.
46. Gary Taylor, 'Collaboration 2016', in Dympna Callaghan and Suzanne Gossett (eds.), *Shakespeare in Our Time: A Shakespeare Association of American Collection* (London: Bloomsbury, 2016), 141–49 (pp. 143, 146).
47. Gary Taylor, 'Thomas Middleton (1580–1627)' *ODNB*.
48. Martin Butler, 'Richard Brome (c.1590–1652)', *ODNB*; G.E. Bentley, *The Profession of Dramatist in Shakespeare's Time 1590–1642* (Princeton, NJ: Princeton University Press, 1971).
49. Katherine Duncan-Jones, *Shakespeare: Upstart Crow to Sweet Swan, 1592–1623* (London: Methuen Drama, 2011), 92–100.
50. Meryl Faiers and Martin Wiggins, 'The Economics of Authorship', in Rory Loughnane and Will Sharpe (eds.), *The Oxford Handbook of Shakespeare and Authorship* (Oxford: Oxford University Press, forthcoming).
51. Gary Taylor, 'Why Did Shakespeare Collaborate?', *Shakespeare Survey* 67 (2014), 1–17. Jeffrey Knapp, *Shakespeare Only* (Chicago: University of Chicago Press, 2009), counters the argument that collaboration was the norm in the early modern theatre; see also Brian Vickers, *Shakespeare, Co-author* (Oxford: Oxford University Press, 2002).
52. Jeffrey Masten, *Textual Intercourse: Collaboration, Authorship, and Sexualities in the English Renaissance* (Cambridge: Cambridge University Press, 1997).
53. Jeffrey Masten, 'Playwriting: Authorship and Collaboration', in J.D. Cox and D.S. Kastan (eds.), *New History*, 357–82 (p. 371).
54. 'Why Did Shakespeare Collaborate?', 2.
55. 'Authorship and Attribution', in Jonathan Bate and Eric Rasmussen, with Jan Sewell, Will Sharpe, Peter Kirwan, and Sarah Stewart (eds.),

William Shakespeare and Others: Collaborative Plays (Basingstoke: Palgrave Macmillan, 2013), 641–745.

56. 'Collaboration and Shakespeare's Early Career', in R. Loughnane and A.J. Power (eds.), *Early Shakespeare*, 54–75.

57. Dates here refer to the play's original composition in the first instance, and revisions in the second. Masten in *Textual Intercourse* credits W.B. Worthen with the origin of the term, borrowed from linguistics, in which diachronic is the study of change over time, and synchronic of a particular moment.

58. The leading figures in these attribution arguments have been Hugh Craig and John Burrows for *Henry VI*, MacDonald P. Jackson and Arthur Kinney for *Arden*, and Laurie Maguire and Emma Smith for *All's Well*.

59. Taylor and Loughnane, *Authorship Companion*, 538–42; Anne Barton, *Ben Jonson: Dramatist* (Cambridge: Cambridge University Press, 1984), 93–4.

60. Jonson suggests he has 'rather chosen to put weaker (and no doubt less pleasing) of mine own, than to defraud so happy a genius of his right by my loathed usurpation'.

61 John-Mark Philo, 'Ben Jonson's *Sejanus* and Shakespeare's *Othello*', *Shakespeare Survey* 75 (2022), 122–36.

62. William George Clark and William Aldis Wright (eds.), *Macbeth* (Oxford: Clarendon Press, 1869), xii; Alice Walker, 'The Text of *Measure for Measure*', *Review of English Studies*, 34 (1983), 1–20; Brian Vickers, 'Disintegrated: Did Thomas Middleton Really Adapt *Macbeth*?', *TLS* (28 May 2010), 14–15.

63. Richard Proudfoot and Nicola Bennett (eds.), *King Edward III* (London: Bloomsbury, 2017), 49–89.

64. Suzanne Gossett (ed.), *Philaster* (London: Methuen Drama, 2009), 16; Stanley Wells, *Shakespeare & Co.* (London: Penguin Books Ltd., 2006), 127.

65. Gordon McMullan, 'Stylistic Worlds: Shakespeare and his Collaborators', *TLS* (11 June 2021), 22–3; *Shakespeare and the Idea of Late Writing: Authorship in the Proximity of Death* (Cambridge: Cambridge University Press, 2007).

66. 'Stylistic Worlds', 23.

CHAPTER 2

1. R.A. Foakes (ed.), *Henslowe's Diary*, Second Edition (Cambridge: Cambridge University Press, 2002). Henslowe also records the Queen's and Sussex's together in 1594(?), the Chamberlain's at Newington Butts in June 1594, and the Pembroke's/Admiral's merger, Sept.–Oct. 1597.

2. David McInnis, *Shakespeare and Lost Plays: Reimagining Drama in Early Modern England* (Cambridge: Cambridge University Press, 2021).

3. Andrew Gurr, *The Shakespearean Stage 1574–1642*, Fourth Edition (Cambridge: Cambridge University Press, 2009), 52. Gurr suggests the company that broke in 1597 was a reconstituted version of the one that broke in 1593, while Holger Schott Syme, in 'Three's Company: Alternative Histories of London's Theatres in the 1590s', *Shakespeare Survey* 65 (2012), 269–89, contends it had survived since 1591.

4. Andrew Gurr, 'Three Reluctant Patrons and Early Shakespeare', *Shakespeare Quarterly* 44:2 (1993), 159–74; Roslyn L. Knutson, 'What's So Special about 1594?', *Shakespeare Quarterly* 61:4 (2010), 449–67; Holger Syme, 'I See Your Duopoly and. . .', *Dispositio* (20 September 2013).

5. While 'unknown' is more properly meant, 'Anon.' (anonymous) is used here as shorthand signifier.

6. Not counting Peele's lost *Iphigenia* (1582) and three Lord Mayor's shows, and Wilson's lost *Phyllida and Corin, Felix and Philomena,* and *Five Plays in One* (1584), apparently for the Queen's.

7. The chronology for non-Shakespearean drama is here tied to Martin Wiggins' *British Drama* catalogue, as are the company auspices for all plays where known or reasonably inferred, with the exception of *Richard III* which Wiggins places with Derby's. Dates reflect likely composition rather than first printing. Shakespearean chronology and authorship reflect the present study. Wiggins does not identify *Arden, Contention,* or *RDY* as collaborative Shakespeare plays.

8. Nashe's hand in *Dido*, suggested by title-page evidence, continues to divide scholars. Wiggins allows H.J. Oliver's identification of vocabulary evidence, while Marcus Dahl and Darren Freebury-Jones have argued against it. Gary Taylor and John V. Nance are noncommittal; see 'Imitation or Collaboration? Marlowe and the Early Shakespeare Canon', *Shakespeare Survey* 68 (2015): 32–47. Eoin Price in 2018 felt the evidence 'not strong enough to discount Nashe'; see 'Marlowe in Miniature: *Dido, Queen of Carthage* and the Children of the Chapel Repertory', in Kirk Melnikoff and Roslyn L. Knutson (eds.), *Christopher Marlowe, Theatrical Commerce, and the Book Trade* (Cambridge: Cambridge University Press, 2018), 41–55 (p. 42). More recently, Ruth Lunney and Hugh Craig, in 'Who Wrote *Dido, Queen of Carthage?*', *Journal of Marlowe Studies* 1 (2020), 1–31, have strongly discounted the possibility on stylometric grounds.

9. John Jowett, 'Shakespeare's Metamorphosis', *Shakespeare* 13 (2017), 318–32 (p. 326).

10. Wiggins, *British Drama* #1099.

11. Jennie Challinor, '"Pox on Kindred": the Anonymous *Counterfeit Bridegroom* (1677) and its Middletonian Source', *Restoration* 46:1 (2022), 37–64.

12. Warren Chernaik, 'Katherine Philips [née Fowler]' *ODNB*.

13. Jowett, 'Metamorphosis', 326.

14. Roslyn L. Knutson, 'Marlowe in Repertory, 1587–1593', in Melnikoff and Knutson (eds.), *Christopher Marlowe*, 26–40 (p. 39).

15. Neil Carson, *A Companion to Henslowe's Diary* (Cambridge: Cambridge University Press, 1988), 59–61.

16. *Volpone* (Prologue, 16–18); parentheses mine.

17. Paul Brown, 'The Geographies of the Professional Theatre before Shakespeare', unpublished essay, 2017.

18. Sharpe, 'Collaboration and Shakespeare's Early Career', 59–60.

19. Neil Carson, 'Collaborative Playwriting: The Chettle, Dekker, Heywood Syndicate', *Theatre Research International* 14:1 (1989), 13–23.

20. Paul Yachnin, 'Shakespeare's Problem Plays and the Drama of His Time', in Richard Dutton and Jean E. Howard (eds.), *A Companion to Shakespeare's Works Vol. 4: The Poems, Problem Comedies, Late Plays* (Oxford: Blackwell Publishing Ltd, 2003), 51.

21. The latter may have been a large-scale adaptation of another dramatist's work; Wiggins, *British Drama* #1217.

22. *Fortune by Land and Sea* (1623) and *A Woman Never Vexed* (1624); see Wiggins, *British Drama* #2069 and #2084.

23. From his 1633 address to *The English Traveller*.

24. David Nicol, *Middleton and Rowley: Forms of Collaboration in the Jacobean Playhouse* (Toronto: University of Toronto Press, 2012) offers the definitive account of their collaborative relationship.

25. Wells, *Shakespeare & Co.*, 114.

26. Thomas Heywood, *An Apology for Actors* (London, 1612), F3; but see Lucy Munro, Anne Lancashire, John Astington, and Marta Straznicky, 'Issues in Review: Popular Theatre and the Red Bull', *Early Theatre* 9:2 (2006), 99–156.

27. Webster's status as a professional dramatist is ambiguous, his father's coach-making business his main income source. Henry Fitzgeffrey's 'Notes from Blackfriars' refers to him as 'The playwright, cartwright: whether? Either!'

28 Kathleen McLuskie makes this wider argument about the theatre business in *Dekker and Heywood: Professional Dramatists* (Basingstoke: St. Martin's Press, 1994), 150.

29. Andrew Gurr, *The Shakespearean Stage 1574–1642*, Fourth Edition (Cambridge: Cambridge University Press, 2009), 31–3.

30. Kewes, *Authorship and Appropriation*, 131–4.
31. Alfred Harbage, rev. S. Schoenbaum, *Annals of English Drama— 975–1700* (London: Methuen & Co. Ltd, 1964).
32. https://cadredb.net/.
33. Dekker was released in 1620, collaborating immediately thereafter with Massinger on *The Virgin Martyr* for the Revels company at the Red Bull.
34. Foakes (ed.), *Henslowe's Diary*, 73.
35. *The Conquest of the Indies* by Day, Dekker, and Haughton—Rowley's letter dated 4 April 1601.
36. The number of sheets for a complete play recorded by Henry Herbert in 1623, the first year of his record-keeping, ranges between 9 and 17 (18 and 34 leaves).
37. William Ingram suggests the two things are not linked, and that the closure was routine; see *A London Life in the Brazen Age* (Cambridge, Mass., and London: Harvard University Press, 1978), 167–88; Wiggins, *British Drama* #1081.
38. *Lenten Stuff* (1599).
39. Nicol, *Middleton and Rowley*, fn. 139, quotes Edward Burns's idea that attributionists should not divide plays into scenes but into 'strands of rhetorical actions' associated with things that particular dramatists were good at; see Burns (ed.), *1 Henry VI* (London: Methuen Drama, 2000), 80–2.
40. Wiggins, *British Drama* #1202; Carson, *Companion*, 59.
41. 'Why Did Shakespeare Collaborate?', 4; Taylor and Lavagnino (eds.), *Textual Culture*, 440–1.
42. Sarah Wall-Randell, 'What Is a Staged Book?', in Stern (ed.), *Rethinking*, 128–52 (p. 132).
43. Possibly *The Maid's Tragedy* (1611).
44. Wiggins, *British Drama* #1719.
45. Cyrus Hoy, 'The Shares of Fletcher and His Collaborators in the Beaumont and Fletcher Folio I-VII', *Studies in Bibliography* 8–9, 11–15 (1956–1962), 129–46, 143–62, 85–106, 91–116, 77–108, 45–67, 71–90); data for *The Honest Man's Fortune* in *SB* 12 (1959), 100–8.
46. MacDonald P. Jackson argues that Cyril Tourneur is the likelier author of Acts 1 and 2 in 'Cyril Tourneur and *The Honest Man's Fortune*', *Medieval & Renaissance Drama in England* 32 (2019), 203–18.
47. Gossett (ed.), *Philaster*, 16–17.
48. John Jowett (ed.), *Sir Thomas More* (London: Methuen Drama, 2011), 422–6; MacDonald P. Jackson, 'Deciphering a Date and Determining a Date: Anthony Munday's John a Kent and John a Cumber and the Original Version of Sir Thomas More', EMLS, 15:3 (2011).

49. Ioppolo, *Dramatists*, 33–4; Carson, *Companion*, 59–60.

50. Andrew Gurr, *The Shakespeare Company 1594–1642* (Cambridge: Cambridge University Press, 2004), 106.

51. Wiggins, *British Drama* #1747.

52. Ioppolo, *Dramatists*, 35; Munro, 'Daborne', 17–18.

53. Grace Ioppolo, 'Robert Daborne's Foul Papers and Fair Copies', *Henslowe-Alleyn Digitisation Project*, online at https://henslowe-alleyn. org.uk/.

54. Ioppolo, *Dramatists*, 35.

55. Heather Wolfe, 'Was Early Modern Writing Paper Expensive?', *The Collation* (13 February 2018), https://collation.folger.edu/2018/02/writing-paper-expensive/; *National Archives Currency Converter: 1270–2017*, https://www.nationalarchives.gov.uk/currency-converter/.

56. Gary Taylor, 'Lives and Afterlives', in *Thomas Middleton: The Collected Works* (Oxford: Oxford University Press, 2007), 25–58 (p. 40).

57. Martin Wiggins, 'No Later Than Munday, Chettle', *Around the Globe* 31 (Autumn 2005), 26–7.

58. The *Groatsworth* was entered in the Stationers' Register to Chettle on 20 September, Greene having died on 3 September; see John Jowett, 'Johannes Factotum: Henry Chettle and *Greene's Groatsworth of Wit*', *PBSA* 87 (1993), 453–86; *Textual Companion*, 288–90.

59. *The Repentance of Robert Greene* (1592).

60. Jowett, 'Metamorphosis', 325; '. . . there is an upstart Crow, beautified with our feathers, that with his tiger's heart wrapped in a player's hide, supposes he is as well able to bombast out a blank verse as the best of you', playing on 'O tiger's heart, wrapped in a woman's hide' from *3 Henry VI* (1.4.137).

61. Ibid., 323–4.

62. Nashe, in *Pierce Penniless* (1592), says he was not friendly with Greene 'save for a carouse or two', but may have collaborated with him shortly afterwards, in May 1592; see Wiggins, *British Drama* #934.

CHAPTER 3

1. So-called because their publisher, Thomas Millington, found long-winded ways of including the word in their titles: 'THE First part of the Contention betwixt the two famous Houses of Yorke and Lancaster, with the death of the good Duke Humphrey' (1594, quarto); 'The true Tragedie of Richard *Duke of Yorke, and the death of* good King Henrie the Sixt, *with the whole contention betweene* the two Houses Lancaster and Yorke' (1595, octavo).

2. J. Dover Wilson (ed.), *2 Henry VI* (Cambridge: The New Shakespeare, 1952), xii–xiv; Andrew Gurr, *The Shakespearian Playing Companies* (Oxford: Oxford University Press, 1996), 267–8. Pembroke's son was a devoted friend to Burbage until the actor's death in 1619, and a dedicatee of the First Folio.

3. Its lease expired, forcing the Chamberlain's to use the nearby Curtain for a short time. They dismantled it that winter, using its materials to build the Globe.

4. Wiggins, *British Drama* #928.

5. Lawrence Manley and Sally-Beth MacLean, *Lord Strange's Men and Their Plays* (New Haven: Yale University Press, 2013).

6. Stanley Wells, private communication.

7. Taylor and Loughnane, in *Authorship Companion*, 513–17.

8. The NOS editors suggest *Shrew* is multi-authored, and John Nance has recently argued Marlowe as the likeliest author of 1.1.1–47; see *Early Shakespeare*, 261–83.

9. Gary Taylor, John V. Nance, and Keegan Cooper, 'Shakespeare and Who? Aeschylus, *Edward III* and Thomas Kyd', *Shakespeare Survey* 70 (2017), 146–53; Proudfoot and Bennett (eds.), *King Edward III*, 79–89.

10. *British Drama*, #952. Ferdinando Stanley, Lord Strange, became Earl of Derby on 25 September 1593 following his brother's death.

11. Knutson, *Repertory of Shakespeare's Company*, 12–13, 81; Syme, 'Three's Company', 285–6.

12. Charles Nicholl, 'Christopher Marlowe [Marley] (1564–1593)' *ODNB*.

13. *1* and *2 Tamburlaine* (1587), **Doctor Faustus** (1588), **Dido, Queen of Carthage** (1588), *The Jew of Malta* (1589), **Contention/2 Henry VI** (1591), **Richard Duke of York/3 Henry VI** (1591), *1 Henry VI/Harry VI* (1592), *Edward II* (1592), *The Massacre at Paris* (1593).

14. 'A Collaboration about a Collaboration: The Authorship of *King Henry VI, Part Three*', in Marilyn Deegan and Willard McCarty (eds.), *Collaborative Research in the Digital Humanities* (Burlington, VT: Ashgate, 2012), 27–65. Several pieces in the last two decades have supported the assertion, including Hugh Craig and Arthur F. Kinney eds., *Shakespeare, Computers, and the Mystery of Authorship* (Cambridge: Cambridge University Press, 2009), 40–77; Taylor and Nance, 'Imitation or Collaboration?'; Santiago Segarra, Mark Eisen, Gabriel Egan, and Alejandro Ribeiro, 'Attributing the Authorship of the *Henry VI* Plays by Word Adjacency', *Shakespeare Quarterly* 67:2 (2016): 232–56. Darren Freebury-Jones, 'Did Shakespeare Really Co-write *2 Henry VI* with Marlowe?', *American Notes and Queries* 30:3 (2017), 137–41, offers a rebuttal, as have others; see https://brianvickers.uk/the-new-oxford-shakespeare/ for a complete list.

15. Rory Loughnane, 'Shakespeare and the Idea of Early Authorship', in *Early Shakespeare*, 21–53 (pp. 26–7).

16. Stanley Wells, 'The Failure of *The Two Gentlemen of Verona*', *Shakespeare Jahrbuch* 99 (1963), 161–73; MacDonald P. Jackson, 'Pause Patterns and Shakespeare's Verse: Canon and Chronology', *Literary and Linguistic Computing* 17 (2002), 36–47.

17. Jowett, 'Metamorphosis', 329.

18. Martin Wiggins (ed.), *A Woman Killed with Kindness and Other Plays* (Oxford: Oxford World's Classics, 2008).

19. Brian Vickers, 'Thomas Kyd, Secret Sharer', in *Times Literary Supplement*, 18 April 2008, 13–15; Darren Freebury-Jones, 'In Defence of Kyd: Evaluating the Claim for Shakespeare's Part Authorship of *Arden of Faversham*', *Authorship* 7:2 (2018). MacDonald P. Jackson has disputed the Kyd claim in, 'New Research on the Dramatic Canon of Thomas Kyd', *Research Opportunities in Renaissance Drama* 47 (2008), 107–27, and *Determining the Shakespeare Canon: Arden of Faversham and A Lover's Complaint* (Oxford: Oxford University Press, 2014).

20. Gary Taylor, 'Shakespeare, Arden of Faversham, and Four Forgotten Playwrights', *The Review of English Studies*, 71 (2020), 867–95; Pervez Rizvi, 'The Unsoundness of the Stylometric Case for Thomas Watson's Authorship of *Arden of Faversham*', *ANQ: A Quarterly Journal of Short Articles, Notes and Reviews* (2020), 261–70.

21. MacDonald P. Jackson, 'New Research on the Dramatic Canon of Thomas Kyd', *RORD* 47 (2008), 107–27.

22. Michael J. Hirrel, 'Thomas Watson, Playwright: Origins of Modern English Drama', in David McInnis and Matthew Steggle (eds.), *Lost Plays in Shakespeare's England* (Basingstoke: Palgrave Macmillan, 2014), 187–207 (pp. 187, 204).

23. Ibid., 198–9.

24. Albert Chatterley, 'Thomas Watson (1555/6–1592)', *ODNB*.

25. Catherine Richardson (ed.), *Arden of Faversham* (London: Bloomsbury, 2022), 46–7.

26. Ibid., 59.

27. 'Why Did Shakespeare Collaborate?', 7.

28. Richardson (ed.), *Arden*, 60.

29. Jowett, 'Metamorphosis', 325.

30. Frank S. Hook, in Charles Tyler Prouty (gen. ed.), *The Life and Works of George Peele* (New Haven and London, 1952–70), 2: 1–212; Wiggins, *British Drama* #881.

31. Marlowe/Unknown* (Acts 1–2): 1x29, 1x25, 1×46 (York), 1x21* (Hume), 1×23 (Margaret), 1x31*(Duchess). Shakespeare (Act 3): 1×38 (Margaret),

1×30 (Gloucester), 1×25 (Henry), 1×53 (York), 1×49 (Margaret), 1×28 (Salisbury), 1×20 (Suffolk).

32. Randall Martin, '*The True Tragedy of Richard Duke of York*: Report and Revision', *RES*, 209 (2002), 8–30; (ed.) *Henry VI Part 3* (Oxford: Oxford World's Classics, 2001); John Jowett, 'The Origins of Richard Duke of York', in *Early Shakespeare*, 235–60.

33. *New Oxford Shakespeare: Critical Reference Edition Vol. 2*, 2562.

34. *Authorship Companion*, 491; Taylor, 'Why Did Shakespeare Collaborate?', 7–8.

35. Paola Pugliatti, *Shakespeare the Historian* (London: Macmillan Press Ltd, 1996).

36. Stanley Wells and Gary Taylor, 'No Shrew, A Shrew, and The Shrew: Internal Revision in *The Taming of the Shrew*', in Bernhard Fabian and Kurt Tetzeli von Rosador (eds.), *Shakespeare, Text, Language, Criticism: Essays in Honour of Marvin Spevack* (New York: Olms-Weidmann), 351–70.

37. Of the five suspected 'bad' quartos already printed by then—*The Troublesome Reign of King John*, *Arden of Faversham*, *Fair Em*, *Jack Straw*, and *Edward I*—only *Fair Em* shows signs of potential memorial contamination. Marlowe's *Massacre at Paris*, the worst example of a memorially reconstructed text outside Shakespeare, may also have been printed by then; apparent small-scale borrowings from *Richard, Duke of York* and *Edward II* may be authorial.

38. Jowett, 'Origins', 235–60.

39. *Authorship Companion*, 490–3; Rory Loughnane, 'Re-editing Non-Shakespeare for the Modern Reader: The Murder of Mutius in *Titus Andronicus*', *Review of English Studies* (2017), 268–95, also argues for Shakespeare's light revision of Peele's opening scene.

40. Jonathan Bate and Eric Rasmussen (eds.), *The RSC Shakespeare: The Complete Works* (Basingstoke: Macmillan Publishers Ltd., 2007), 1618; Paulina Kewes, '"I ask your voices and your suffrages": The Bogus Rome of Peele and Shakespeare's *Titus Andronicus*', *The Review of Politics*, 78:4 (2016), 551–70.

41. Vickers, *Shakespeare Co-author*, 191.

42. Jonathan Bate (ed.), *Titus Andronicus* (London: Bloomsbury, 1995), 18.

43. From *Hippolytus* (*Phaedra*) in *Titus*' case (2.1.134–6 and 4.1.80–1); Burrow, *Classical Antiquity*, 165.

44. Victoria Moul, 'Virgil as a Poet', in C. Martindale and F. Mac Góráin (eds.), *The Cambridge Companion to Virgil: Revised Edition* (Cambridge: Cambridge University Press, 2019), 345–67, 363–4.

45. Lukas Erne, *Beyond* The Spanish Tragedy*: A Study of the Works of Thomas Kyd* (Manchester: Manchester University Press, 2001), 5.
46. Tamara Atkin makes a related point in 'Medieval Inheritance', Loughnane and Sharpe (eds.), *Handbook of Shakespeare and Authorship* (Oxford: Oxford University Press, forthcoming).
47. Randall Martin, private communication.
48. Jowett, 'Metamorphosis'; Alexandra Halasz, *The Marketplace of Print: Pamphlets and the Public Sphere in Early Modern England* (Cambridge: Cambridge University Press, 1997).
49. Albeit his name did not appear on a play's title page until 1598, in the first imprint of *Love's Labour's Lost*.
50. Jowett, 'Metamorphosis', and 'Credulous to False Prints', in John Batchelor, Tom Cain, and Claire Lamont (eds.), *Shakespearean Continuities* (Basingstoke: Macmillan Press, 1997), 93–103.

CHAPTER 4

1. Clara Calvo and Jesús Tronch (eds.), *The Spanish Tragedy* by Thomas Kyd (London: Methuen Drama, 2013), 328.
2. *Authorship Companion*, 246–60, 261–77, 528–31.
3. Clare Smout, 'Actor, Poet,Playwright, Sharer . . . Rival? Shakespeare and Heywood, 1603–4', *Early Theatre* 13:2 (2010), 175–89.
4. Heywood, *Apology*, G4v, tells us Shakespeare 'was much offended with M. Jaggard that (altogether unknown to him) presumed to make so bold with his name' in printing *The Passionate Pilgrim*.
5. *Textual Companion*, 595; John Jowett, 'Whose Hamlet Mocks the Warm Clown?', *Papers of the Bibliographical Society of America* 113:3 (2019), 341–70.
6. Sharpe, '*The Spanish Tragedy*' in *Collaborative Plays*, 671–80; David Kathman, 'Thomas Heywood (*c*.1573–1641)', *ODNB*; Holger Syme, 'Shakespeare and *The Spanish Tragedy*', *Dispositio* (31 August 2013) offer fuller accounts.
7. Jowett, 'Whose Hamlet . . .?', 346.
8. Historically More's promotion came in 1529, so the dramatists' 'impression of causality is fabricated'; Jowett (ed.), *More*, 54.
9. These letters refer to designations provided by W.W. Greg, who transcribed the manuscript in *The Book of Sir Thomas More* (Oxford: The Malone Society, 1911). Greg labelled the revisers A–E, Tilney's being the only hand he could identify confidently. He originally thought Munday a scribe, not a dramatic author, hence S. Digitized images of the whole manuscript can be viewed at http://www.bl.uk/manuscripts/FullDisplay. aspx?ref=Harley_MS_7368/.

10. Rationale for the dating of the OT and additions can be found in Jowett (ed.), *More*, 424–58; see also Sharpe, 'Sir *Thomas More*', *Collaborative Plays*, 683–97. Wiggins dates both the OT and its revisions to 1601.

11. Jowett (ed.), *More*, 426.

12. Carson, 'Collaborative Playwriting'.

13. Ibid., 102.

14. Addition I, containing a long speech by More in Chettle's hand to replace two deleted speeches on the first side of fol. 19, is wrongly placed in the manuscript; see Peter W.M. Blayney, '*The Booke of Sir Thomas Moore* re-examined', *Studies in Philology* 69:2 (1972), 167–91.

15. Jowett (ed.), *More*, 327–43, offers a transcript of the surviving original material and describes how the revisions replace it.

16. Werstine, in *Early Modern Playhouse Manuscripts*, is notably agnostic on the identification. Arguments in favour include Giles E. Dawson, 'Shakespeare's Handwriting', *Shakespeare Survey* 42 (1990), 119–28; MacDonald P. Jackson, 'The Date and Authorship of Hand D's Contribution to *Sir Thomas More*: Evidence from Literature Online', *Shakespeare Survey* 59 (2006), 69–78; MacDonald P. Jackson, 'Is "Hand D" of *Sir Thomas More* Shakespeare's? Thomas Bayes and the Elliott-Valenza Authorship Tests', *EMLS* 12:3 (2007), 1.1–36; Jowett (ed.), *More*, 437–69.

17. Jowett (ed.), *More*, 70–7.

18. Greg, *More*, p. x.

19. John Jowett, *Shakespeare and Text*, Revised Edition (Oxford: Oxford University Press, 2019), 32–3.

20. Jowett (ed.), *More*, 380; C writes, 'Enter Lincoln. Doll. Clown. Georg Betts williamson others / And a sergaunt at armes' to guide Shakespeare's revision.

21. Ibid., 378–9.

22. Jowett assumes Shakespeare did not know Heywood would create Clown Betts, or at least not call him that; 382–3.

23. Ibid., 453–8.

24. Erin Sullivan, 'Sir Thomas More', unpublished essay, 2011.

25. Jowett (ed.), *More*, 458.

26. Ibid., 392.

27. Anna Pruitt (ed.), in *Critical Reference Edition Vol. 1*, 1101.

28. Jowett (ed.), *More*, 362.

29. The passages in question are: 1.1.166–79, 1.1.189–209, 1.3.21–4, 1.3.36–55, 1.3.85–108, 2.3.23–45, 3.1 (entire scene absent from the first impression of the quarto (QA), and added in the second state (QB)), 4.1.55–79, 4.1.101–37.

30. John Jowett and Gary Taylor, 'The Three Texts of *2 Henry IV*', *Studies in Bibliography* 40 (1987), 31–50 (pp. 35–6).
31. Ibid., 36–7.
32. *Textual Companion*, 351. Characteristic spellings common to Hand D are also preserved, the two texts used as mutually corroborative evidence for Shakespeare's authorial hand and papers: 'scilens' (silence) and 'Iarman' (German), the latter appearing only once elsewhere in sixteenth and seventeenth-century English drama, in the manuscript play *John of Bordeaux*, attributed to Robert Greene, the former in two much earlier poems, and nowhere else in drama of the period.
33. Ioppolo, *Dramatists*, 102–9, argues the manuscript shows Shakespeare making adjustments on a copy he is making; Jowett, *Shakespeare and Text*, 202, n.12, suggests 'the more usual view is that it shows Shakespeare in the process of initial composition'.
34. Bate and Rasmussen (eds.), *Collaborative Plays*, 23.
35. Roger Holdsworth, 'Shakespeare and Middleton: A Chronology', *Authorship Companion*, 366–84.
36. F.P. Wilson, *The Plague in Shakespeare's London* (Oxford: Clarendon Press, 1927), 125.
37. Theatres were closed for seven months from 10 July 1606; see Wilson, *Plague*, 124.
38. Gary Taylor, 'Shakespeare's Midlife Crisis', *The Guardian*, 3 May 2004.
39. Charlton Hinman, *The Printing and Proof-Reading of the First Folio of Shakespeare*, 2 vols. (Oxford: Oxford University Press, 1963), 2:231–85; John Jowett (ed.), *Timon of Athens* (Oxford: Oxford World's Classics, 2004), 120–32.
40. Jowett (ed.), *Timon*, 6; MacDonald P. Jackson, *Studies in Attribution: Middleton and Shakespeare* (Insitut Für Anglistik und Amerikanistik, 1979), 50.
41. Jowett (ed.), *More*, 394.
42. These adaptations for revival have been conjecturally dated to 1616 for *Titus* and *Macbeth*, late 1621 for *Measure*, and 1622 for *All's Well*; see *Authorship Companion*.
43. Middleton's adaptation of *Measure for Measure* and *Macbeth* is most comprehensively articulated in *Middleton: Collected Works* and its companion volume. See also *Authorship Companion* for his adaptation of *Titus* and *All's Well*, and Laurie Maguire and Emma Smith 'Many Hands. A New Shakespeare Collaboration?', *TLS* 20 April 2012, 13–15, which first posited Middleton's hand, as collaborator rather than reviser, in *All's Well*.
44. Jowett (ed.) *Measure for Measure*, in *Middleton: Collected Works*, 1545; Gary Taylor, 'Shakespeare's Mediterranean *Measure for Measure*', in Tom

Clayton, Susan Brock, and Vicente Forés (eds.), *Shakespeare and the Mediterranean* (Newark: University of Delaware Press, 2004), 243–69.

45. Gary Taylor and John Jowett, *Shakespeare Reshaped* (Oxford: Oxford University Press, 1993).

46. Laurie Maguire and Emma Smith, 'Many Hands', 14; see also Loughnane, Bourus, Karim-Cooper, Taylor, and Nance in *Authorship Companion*, 278–365.

47. *Authorship Companion*, 364.

48. Gary Taylor and Doug Duhaime, 'Who Wrote the Fly Scene (3.2) in *Titus Andronicus*?', *Authorship Companion*, 67–91 (p. 91); see also Taylor and Nance, 'Imitation or Collaboration', 33.

CHAPTER 5

1. *Shakespeare: A Critical Study of His Mind and Art* (Cambridge: Cambridge University Press, 1875, repr. 2009); McMullan, *Idea of Late Writing*.

2. Masten, *Textual Intercourse*, 84–89.

3. *Critical Reference Edition Vol. 1*, 1346–48.

4. MacDonald P. Jackson, *Defining Shakespeare: Pericles as Test Case* (Oxford: Oxford University Press, 2003), 25.

5. Ibid., esp. pp. 11–39, 166.

6. Doreen DelVecchio and Anthony Hammond (eds.), *Pericles* (Cambridge: Cambridge University Press, 1998), 14–15.

7. Jackson, *Defining*, 188.

8. Charles Nicholl's *The Lodger: Shakespeare on Silver Street* (London: Penguin Books Ltd., 2007) focuses heavily on Wilkins' life and art.

9. *Miseries* was entered into the Stationers' Register on 31 July 1607 and published sometime later that year.

10. Roslyn L. Knutson, 'The Repertory', in Cox and Kastan (eds.), *New History*, 461–80, discounts the notion of blocking entries, while Lukas Erne, in *Shakespeare as Literary Dramatist* (Cambridge: Cambridge University Press, 2003), suggests the company's publishing strategies may have changed 'after February 1603', 108. Suzanne Gossett (ed.), *Pericles* (London: Thomson Learning, 2004), 16–18, offers an alternative discussion of the Blount evidence.

11. Erne, *Book Trade*; Richard Preiss, 'Natural Authorship', *Renaissance Drama* NS 34 (2005), 69–104.

12. *Textual Companion*, 558.

13. Preiss, 'Natural Authorship'; Erne, *Literary Dramatist*; Jowett, *Shakespeare and Text*, 10–12. Apart from *Lear* and *Pericles*, *Troilus* was the only other authentic Shakespeare play to be printed that decade, again with

some problems over entitlement to publish; *Critical Reference Edition Vol. 2*, 3449–57.

14. *Textual Companion*, 557.

15. *Authorship Companion*, 569–71.

16. Jackson, *Defining*, 84.

17. Martin Wiggins, *Shakespeare and the Drama of His Time* (Oxford: Oxford University Press, 2000), 102. The preliminaries drew on Giambattista Guarini's *Il Pastor Fido* (*c.*1568–98), the archetype of tragi-comic form, to reclaim it from its application as a term of abuse for plays indecorously crossing the boundaries between the two classical genres.

18. Wiggins, *Drama of His Time*, 111–18 (esp. p. 117).

19. Raphael Lyne, *Shakespeare's Late Work* (Oxford: Oxford University Press, 2007), 124–37.

20. Ibid., Chapter 7.

21. David Lindley, 'Blackfriars, Music and Masque: Theatrical Contexts of the Last Plays', in Catherine M.S. Alexander (ed.), *The Cambridge Companion to Shakespeare's Last Plays* (Cambridge: Cambridge University Press, 2010), 29–45 (pp. 32–3).

22. *Critical Reference Edition Vol. 2*, 2746.

23. The hired men 'Curtis' (Curtis Greville) and 'T. Tucke' (Thomas Tuckfield), acting as Messengers and Attendants in 4.2 and 5.3, are named across two stage directions; G.R. Proudfoot and Eric Rasmussen (eds.), *The Two Noble Kinsmen* (Oxford: The Malone Society Reprints, 2005), TLN 2436, 3009. Tuckfield is identified in a list of 'Musitions and other necessary attendantes' of the King's company in Henry Herbert's records; G.E. Bentley, *The Jacobean and Caroline Stage* (Oxford: Oxford University Press, 1941–1968), 7 vols., 2:606.

24. Stylistic and stylometric data in *Double Falsehood* point to Shakespeare as the author of the first half of the play (everything up to and including 3.2 according to the NOS), and Fletcher the remainder; see also Stephan Kukowski, 'The Hand of John Fletcher in *Double Falsehood*', *Shakespeare Survey* 43 (1991), 81–9; Jonathan Hope, *The Authorship of Shakespeare's Plays: A Sociolinguistic Study* (Cambridge: Cambridge University Press, 1994), 100; Brean Hammond (ed.), *Double Falsehood* (London: Methuen Drama, 2010), 102–3.

25. Cf. the different spellings of Apemantus and Ventidius in the Shakespeare/Middleton sections of *Timon*.

26. Lois Potter (ed.), *The Two Noble Kinsmen* (London: Thomson Learning, 2002), 25.

27. 557/465/467/513/615 = 2617 (1622 B/995 F); attribution data and line numbering are keyed to Gossett (ed.), *Philaster*. Hoy's studies show

Fletcher taking many different combinations of authorial share across his career.

28. Wiggins #1522 and #1724; both were printed from scribal transcripts. NOS follows Q *Kinsmen* in assigning 2.1 and 2.2 as separate scenes.

29. Stephen Greenblatt et al. (eds.) *The Norton Shakespeare* (W.W. Norton & Co., 1997), 3118.

30. Annabel Patterson, *Reading Holinshed's Chronicles* (Chicago: University of Chicago Press, 1994).

31. Hoy, 'Shares', *SB* 15 (1962), 71–90; see Vickers, *Shakespeare Co-author*, for a comprehensive survey of work done up to 2002.

32. For the likely authenticity of Theobald's claim that the manuscript from which he worked—albeit adapted by Thomas Betterton and transcribed by the prompter John Downes some time in the 1660s—was descended from an original collaboration by Shakespeare and Fletcher, see Hammond (ed.), *Double Falsehood*; David Carnegie and Gary Taylor (eds.), *The Quest for Cardenio: Shakespeare, Fletcher, Cervantes, & the Lost Play* (Oxford: Oxford University Press, 2012); Sharpe, 'Double Falsehood', in *Collaborative Plays*, 717–24.

33. Dobson, Wells et al., *The Oxford Companion to Shakespeare*, Second Edition (Oxford: Oxford University Press), 492.

34. Munro, 'Daborne', 19.

35. Jowett, 'Credulous', 93–103.

36. *Strange News* (London, 1592), E4v.

37. The Second Part of Coney-Catching',in Alexander B. Grosart (ed.), *The Life and Complete Works in Prose and Verse of Robert Greene*. 15 vols. (Huth Library, 1881–6; reprinted New York: Russell & Russell, 1964), 10:161.

38. Dis is often equated with the chthonic deity, Hades, or his Roman equivalent, Pluto.

39. Viv Thomas, 'Plants', in *Oxford Companion to Shakespeare*, 435.

40. Jowett, 'Metamorphosis', 322–4.

41. Ibid., and 'Credulous'.

CHAPTER 6

1. Tara L. Lyons, 'Richard Jones, *Tamburlaine the Great*, and the Making (and Remaking) of a Serial Play Collection in the 1590s', in Melnikoff and Knutson (eds.), *Christopher Marlowe*, 149–64.

2. Eight others had appeared in quarto that were silent on his authorship, including *1 Honest Whore* attributed solely to his co-author, Dekker, and *A Yorkshire Tragedy*, falsely attributed to Shakespeare.

3. Erne, *Book Trade*, argues for Shakespeare's particular popularity in early modern print. See also Appendix to Maureen Bell, 'Booksellers without an Author 1627–1685' in Taylor and Lavagnino (eds.), *Textual Culture*, 260–85, which tabulates a marked increase in the popularity of printed authorial collections from the late 1630s onwards.

4. Bell, 'Booksellers', 280; Alan B. Farmer and Zachary Lesser, 'Vile Arts: The Marketing of English Printed Drama, 1512–1660', *RORD* 39 (2000), 77–165; Jeffrey Masten, 'Ben Jonson's Head', *Shakespeare Studies* 28 (2000), 160–8.

5. Lois Potter, *Secret Rites and Secret Writing: Royalist Literature, 1641–1660* (Cambridge: Cambridge University Press, 1989) discusses the matter of 'literature' during the Interregnum; Martin Butler, *Theatre and Crisis 1632–1642* (Cambridge: Cambridge University Press, 1984) offers an extended discussion of the Folio's explicitly pro-Royalist position.

6. *The Coxcomb* (1609); *The Captain* (1612); *The Masque of the Inner Temple and Gray's Inn* (1613).

7. Hoy, 'Shares'.

8. *A Very Woman* (1634, printed 1655), with Fletcher, attributed to Massinger alone; the others are listed on pp. 148–9.

9. Masten, *Textual Intercourse*, 134.

10. Jowett, 'Metamorphosis', 329.

11. Jeffrey Todd Knight, 'Invisible Ink: A Note on Ghost Images in Early Printed Books', *Textual Cultures* 5.2 (2010): 53–62.

12. Erne, *Book Trade*, 56. Tara L. Lyons has argued the collection was marketed not on Shakespeare's status as an author, but his association with serial histories; see 'Serials, Spinoffs, and Histories: Selling "Shakespeare" in Collection before the First Folio', *Philological Quarterly* 91.2 (2012): 185–220.

13. *Ralph Roister Doister* and *Gammer Gurton's Needle* were printed in 1566 and 1575 respectively. For data on the extant post-Reformation drama, see Wiggins, *British Drama* Vols. 1–2, and Tamara Atkin, *Reading Drama in Tudor England* (London: Routledge), 2018.

14. Brian Vickers, 'The Two Authors of *Edward III*', *Shakespeare Survey* 67 (2014), 102–18.

15. Bracketed material conjecturally supplied by W.W. Greg, 'Three Manuscript Notes by Sir George Buc', *The Library* 12 (1931), 307–21.

16. '*Locrine*', *Collaborative Plays*, 657–63. Knutson is generally sceptical of the identification; 'Ur-Plays and Other Exercises in Making Stuff Up', in McInnis and Steggle (eds.), *Lost Plays*, 31–54. Darren Freebury-Jones attributes the play to Greene in *Reading Robert Greene: Recovering Shakespeare's Rival* (Abingdon: Routledge, 2022).

17. His name was first attached to them when they were reprinted together in 1632 as the collection *Six Court Comedies*.
18. Dates refer to printing rather than composition. *Dido* is unusual in this list as the only single-authored play advertised as a collaboration. *Doctor Faustus* A is the original collaboration between Marlowe and Nashe, B the Q4 imprint containing 1602 revisions by, perhaps, Samuel Rowley and William Birde (Wiggins #810); they are here counted as one play.
19. Of the two 1613 imprints of the play, the first names John Marston—who began it *c.*1608—only; the second drops his name, and supplies those of Lewis Machin and William Barkstead, who finished it off. This was likely at Marston's behest.
20. *Collaborative Plays*, 697–710.
21. The cryptic '&c.' raises the possibility of another, unknown, collaborator.
22. An expansion of the one in the 1656 edition of Thomas Goffe's *The Careless Shepherdess*, published by London booksellers Richard Rogers and William Ley; see Taylor in *Textual Culture*, 405–08, listing work by Greg (1946) and Masten (2000), who between them establish the extent of Archer's inexactitude, and that authorship was not his primary concern.
23. It attributes *The Old Law* to Massinger alone, contrary to the title page of the book to which it is appended. Heywood may have been an original co-author, or may have adapted the play in the 1630s; see Masten in *Middleton: Collected Works*, 1331–4 (p. 1333).
24. Stern, *Documents*, 36–62.
25. Syme, 'The Strange Case of Thomas Dekker', *Dispositio* (30 March 2012).
26. Zachary Lesser, 'Shakespeare's Flop: John Waterson and *The Two Noble Kinsmen*', in Marta Straznicky (ed.), *Shakespeare's Stationers* (Philadelphia: University of Pennsylvania Press, 2013), 177–96.
27. Potter (ed.), *Kinsmen*, 6.
28. It was certainly revised, and annotated for performance, from its first stagings *c.*1613–14 to a revival in 1625–6; *Textual Companion*, 625–9; *Critical Reference Edition Vol. 2*, 3547–53.
29. Burns (ed.), *Henry VI Part 1*, 84.
30. Michael Taylor (ed.), *Henry VI Part 1* (Oxford: Oxford World's Classics, 2003), 11.
31. *The Spanish Tragedy* also appeared in the AEMD series, given to Thomas Kyd solus on the cover, albeit its editors in the apparatus cautiously averred Shakespeare's presence as reviser.
32. Peter Kirwan, *Shakespeare and the Idea of Apocrypha* (Cambridge: Cambridge University Press, 2015), offers an important examination of the concept of 'apocrypha' in the Shakespeare canon.
33. Andrew Murphy, *Shakespeare in Print*, Second Edition (Cambridge: Cambridge University Press, 2021), 319.

34. Paperweights are measured in gsm (grammes per square metre); see Marshall Lee, *Bookmaking: Editing, Design, Production*, Third Revised Edition (New York: W.W. Norton, 2009), 199–206.

CHAPTER 7

1. An unusual hold-up in printing the play suggests the Folio printers were made to wait for a copy to be made; *Critical Reference Edition Vol. 2*, 2744–6.
2. *Textual Companion*, 618–24; R.A. Foakes (ed.), *King Henry VIII* (London: Methuen, 1957).
3. Fredson Bowers (ed.), *Henry VIII*, in *The Dramatic Works in the Beaumont and Fletcher Canon* (Cambridge: Cambridge University Press, 1989), Vol. 7; A.C. Partridge, *The Problem of 'Henry VIII' Reopened* (Cambridge: Cambridge University Press, 1949).
4. MacDonald P. Jackson, 'Is "Hand D" . . .?'; Giles E. Dawson, 'Shakespeare's Handwriting', *Shakespeare Survey* 42 (1990): 119–28.
5. Jackson, 'Is "Hand D" . . .?'.
6. Jowett, *Shakespeare and Text*, 79–89.
7. McKenzie, *Making Meaning*; Paul Werstine, 'Close Contrivers: Nameless Collaborators in Early Modern London Plays', in C.E. McGee and A.L. Magnusson (eds.), *The Elizabethan Theatre* XV (Canada: P.D. Meany, 2002), 3–20; Bourne, *Typographies*.
8. Anthony Graham-White, *Punctuation and Its Dramatic Value in Shakespearean Drama* (Newark: University of Delaware Press, 1995).
9. Jowett, 'Origins', 235–60.
10. Ibid., 246–51.
11. Ibid., 250; John Burrows and Hugh Craig, in 'The Joker in the Pack? Marlowe, Kyd and the Co-authorship of *Henry VI, Part 3*', *Authorship Companion*, 194–217, note 'broad similarity' between O and F in their profiles of proposed authorial shares (216).
12. Potter (ed.), *Kinsmen*, 128.
13. Jeffrey Masten, 'More or Less: Editing the Collaborative', *Shakespeare Studies*, 29 (2001), 109–31, 116; Suzanne Gossett, 'Editing Collaborative Drama', *Shakespeare Survey* 56 (2006), 213–24 (p. 218).
14. Masten (ed.), *An/The Old Law*, in *Middleton: Collected Works*, 1331–96.
15. See *Textual Companion*; Vickers, *Shakespeare, Co-author*; Sharpe, 'Authorship and Attribution', in *Collaborative Plays*, 641–745; Gabriel Egan, 'A History of Shakespearean Authorship Attribution', in *Authorship Companion*, 27–47; also Alysia Kolentsis, *Shakespeare's Common Language* (London: Bloomsbury, 2020).

16. MacDonald P. Jackson, 'Authorship Attribution and the New Oxford Shakespeare: Some Facts and Misconceptions', *ANQ*, Volume 33 (2020), 148–55.

17. See especially Craig and Kinney (eds.), *Computers*.

18. James Gleick, *The Information* (New York: Pantheon Books, 2011).

19. Segarra et al., 'Attributing'.

20. Taylor and Nance, 'Imitation or Collaboration?'; Hugh Craig and Brett Greatley-Hirsch, *Style, Computers, and Early Modern Drama: Beyond Authorship*, (Cambridge: Cambridge University Press, 2017).

21. Eric Sams, Shakespeare's *Edmund Ironside: The Lost Play* (Wildwood House Ltd, 1986); Mark Dominik, *William Shakespeare and The Birth of Merlin* (Philosophical Library, 1987); Michael Egan (ed.), *The First Part of the Tragedy of King Richard the Second: A Newly Authenticated Play by William Shakespeare* (Edwin Mellen Press, 2006). Randall Martin's edition of *Edmond Ironside* (New York: Garland Press, 1991), convincingly refutes Shakespeare's authorship of the play.

22. Jackson, *Determining*.

23. Matthew Reisz, 'Scholars feud over Shakespeare co-authorship', *THE* (15 December 2017).

24. E.K. Chambers' 1924 British Academy lecture, 'The Disintegration of Shakespeare', spoke pejoratively of early efforts—chiefly those of F.G. Fleay and J.M. Robertson—to attribute parts of Shakespeare's accepted canon to other writers; see John Jowett, 'Disintegration, 1924', *Shakespeare* 10:2 (2014), 171–87.

25. *Notes & Queries* 65:1 (2018), 131–4; see also Jackson, 'Authorship Attribution'.

26. Reisz, 'Scholars Feud'.

27. E.K. Chambers, *William Shakespeare: A Study of Facts and Problems* (Oxford: Oxford University Press, 1930); Karl Wentersdorf, 'Shakespearean Chronology and Metrical Tests', in W. Fischer and K. Wentersdorf (eds.), *Shakespeare-Studien* (Marburg: Verlag N.G. Elwert, 1951), 161–93.

28. Kenneth Muir, *Shakespeare as Collaborator* (New York: Barnes & Noble, 1960); Cyrus Hoy, 'Critical and Aesthetic Problems of Collaboration in Renaissance Drama', *RORD* 19 (1976), 3–6; S. Schoenbaum, *Internal Evidence and Elizabethan Dramatic Authorship* (London: Edward Arnold Ltd, 1966).

29. McMullan, *Idea of Late Writing*, 243.

30. Eric Rasmussen, 'Collaboration', in *Oxford Companion to Shakespeare*, 72.

31. Gary Taylor, 'Empirical Middleton: *Macbeth*, Adaptation, and Microauthorship', *Shakespeare Quarterly*, 65:3, (2014), 239–72.

32. Taylor, 'Shakespeare, *Arden of Faversham*'; Taylor and Duhaime, 'Fly Scene'.
33. Brian Vickers, 'Infecting the Teller: Rebutting a Mathematical Method of Attribution', *TLS* (17 April 2020).
34. Craig and Greatley-Hirsch, *Style*, 164–201.
35. Siobhan Keenan, *Acting Companies and Their Plays in Shakespeare's London* (London: Arden Shakespeare, 2014), 66; Roslyn L. Knutson, 'The Start of Something Big', in Helen Ostovich, Holger Schott Syme, and Andrew Griffin (eds.), *Locating the Queen's Men, 1583–1603* (Farnham: Ashgate, 2009), 99–108.
36. William Scott, *The Model of Poesy* (1599).
37. Mary Thomas Crane, *Shakespeare's Brain: Reading with Cognitive Theory* (Princeton, NJ: Princeton University Press, 2001).
38. Edward Pechter, 'Against Attribution', *Shakespeare Quarterly* 69:4 (2018), 228–55 (p. 255).
39. John Burrows, 'A Second Opinion on "Shakespeare and Authorship Studies in the Twenty-First Century"', *Shakespeare Quarterly* 63:3 (2012), 355–92 (p. 367).
40. Lunney and Craig, 'Who Wrote *Dido*?'
41. Elaine Hobby, Claire Bowditch, Gillian Wright, and Mel Evans (gen. eds), *The Cambridge Edition of the Works of Aphra Behn* (Cambridge: Cambridge University Press, 2021–); Darren Freebury-Jones, 'Determining Robert Greene's Dramatic Canon', *Style* 54:4 (2020), 377–98. Many others are detailed in *Collaborative Plays*, 641–745.
42. Jeffrey Masten, 'Beaumont and/or Fletcher: Collaboration and the Interpretation of Renaissance Drama', *English Literary History* 59 (1992), 337–56.
43. Aaron Pratt, comment on Andy Kesson, 'Shakespeare, Attribution and Attrition: At Tribute Zone', *Before Shakespeare* (12 April 2017), https://beforeshakespeare.com/2017/04/12/shakespeare-attribution-and-attrition-at-tribute-zone/.
44. Nicol, *Middleton and Rowley*, 14.
45. Kesson, '. . . At Tribute Zone' (17 April 2017).
46. B.K. Adams, 'Fair / foul', in Claire M.L. Bourne (ed.), *Shakespeare / Text* (London: Bloomsbury, 2021), 29–49.
47. Ibid., 30.
48. Masten, comment on '. . . At Tribute Zone' (15 April 2017).
49. Adams, 'Fair / foul', 44.

APPENDIX I

1 See Jowett (ed.), *Sir Thomas More*, 101–3; this overall reconstruction is indebted to Jowett's edition.

Further Reading

Collaboration

Richard Proudfoot's *Shakespeare: Text, Stage & Canon* (London: Blooms-bury, 2001) offers an accessible guide to the main issues of authorship, canon, and collaboration. Jeffrey Masten's *Textual Intercourse: Collaboration, Authorship, and Sexualities in the English Renaissance* (Cambridge: Cambridge University Press, 1997) is a hugely influential, foundational study that challenges many orthodoxies, seeing collaboration as a kind of indivisible poetics; his essay 'Playwriting: Authorship and Collaboration', in John D. Cox and David Scott Kastan (eds.), *A New History of Early Modern Drama* (New York: Columbia University Press, 1997), 357–82, examines and rethinks lots of early evidence for practices of, and attitudes towards, authorial collaboration. Heather Hirschfield's *Joint Enterprises: Collaborative Drama and the Institutionalization of the English Renaissance Theater* (Amherst: University of Massachusetts Press, 2004), challenged Masten's ideas and did much to rehabilitate the theatre-historical evidence of institutional collaborative writing, offering rich theoretical insight of its own. Gary Taylor's 'Artiginality: Authorship after Postmodernism', in Gary Taylor and Gabriel Egan (eds.), *The New Oxford Shakespeare Authorship Companion* (Oxford: Oxford University Press, 2017), 3–26, offers a rebuttal to Masten's ideas, restating the case for recognizing individual authors within any collaboration. Laurie Maguire and Emma Smith's 'What Is a Source? Or, How Shakespeare Read his Marlowe', *Shakespeare Survey* 68 (2015), 15–31, is a fascinating, compelling account of precursory authorship and intertextual influence as a form of collaboration.

David Nicol's *Middleton and Rowley: Forms of Collaboration in the Jacobean Playhouse* (Toronto: University of Toronto Press, 2012) offers the definitive account of the two dramatists' collaborative relationship, and an excellent thinking through of the major disputes around, and figurations of, collaborative playwriting in the early theatres. Brian Vickers' *Shakespeare, Co-author* (Oxford: Oxford University Press, 2002) offers a lengthy chapter on collaborative playwriting in the period, while Jeffrey Knapp's *Shakespeare Only* (Chicago: University of Chicago Press, 2009), counters the argument that collaboration was the norm in the early modern theatre. A number of collaborative plays associated with Shakespeare, along with extended discussion of their authorship and of collaboration in general can be found together in the volume *William Shakespeare and Others: Collaborative Plays* (Basingstoke: Palgrave Macmillan, 2013), edited by Jonathan Bate and Eric Rasmussen, with Jan Sewell, Will Sharpe, Peter Kirwan, and Sarah Stewart. *Shakespeare Survey 67* (Cambridge University Press, 2014), is devoted entirely to the subject of Shakespeare's collaborative work, and MacDonald P. Jackson has an excellent chapter on collaboration in Arthur Kinney (ed.), *The Oxford Handbook of Shakespeare* (Oxford: Oxford University Press, 2012), 31–52. The open-access site *Co-authored Drama in Renaissance England* (CADRE), online at https://cadredb.net, is a searchable database of all co-authored plays from the period.

Early Theatre

Much work has been done both to reconstruct the practices of collaborative labour, including playwriting, though contextualizing it within wider knowledge of the early theatres is vital. E.K. Chambers' *The Elizabethan Stage*, 4 vols. (Oxford: Clarendon Press, 1923) and G.E. Bentley, *The Jacobean and Caroline Stage*, 7 vols. (Oxford: Oxford University Press, 1941–1968) are monumental studies, available free online at https://archive.org, and Bentley's *The Profession of Dramatist in Shakespeare's Time 1590–1642* (Princeton, NJ: Princeton University Press, 1971) is a superb supplement. G.K. Hunter's *English Drama 1586–1642: The Age of Shakespeare* (Oxford: Oxford University Press, 1997) is another particularly rich study. Andrew Gurr's many foundational overviews of early theatrical practice over the last fifty years include *The Shakespearean Stage 1574–1642*, Fourth Edition (Cambridge: Cambridge University Press, 2009); *Playgoing in Shakespeare's London*, Third Edition (Cambridge: Cambridge University Press, 2004); *The Shakespearian Playing Companies* (Oxford: Oxford University Press, 1996); *The Shakespeare Company* (Cambridge: Cambridge University Press, 2004); and *Shakespeare's Opposites: The Admiral's Company 1594–1625* (Cambridge: Cambridge University Press, 2009). John D. Cox and David Scott Kastan's edited collection, *A New History of Early English Drama* (New York: Columbia University Press, 1997) has been the most transformative reappraisal of the conditions of playwriting of the last thirty years, and Tiffany Stern (ed.), *Rethinking Theatrical Documents in Shakespeare's England* (London: The Arden Shakespeare, 2020) is another vital collection. Stern's other major work includes *Documents of Performance in Early Modern England* (Cambridge: Cambridge University Press, 2009)—which explores the collaborative relationships between authors and a range of other makers of texts relating to, and relaying, authorial texts for the stage, *Rehearsal from Shakespeare to Sheridan* (Oxford, 2000), and *Shakespeare in Parts* (Oxford: Oxford University Press, 2007), with Simon Palfrey. Roslyn Lander Knutson's *The Repertory of Shakespeare's Company 1594–1613*

(Little Rock: University of Arkansas Press, 1991), puts collaboration in the context of a company's work, and David Bradley, *From Text to Performance in the Elizabethan Theatre: Preparing the Play for the Stage* (Cambridge: Cambridge University Press, 1992) is a very useful complement. Martin Wiggins in association with Catherine Richardson, *British Drama 1533–1642: A Catalogue*, 9 vols. (Oxford: Oxford University Press, 2012–) is a major guide to the chronology of the early drama, offering detailed entries on each play, including lost plays. David McInnis's *Shakespeare and Lost Plays: Reimagining Drama in Early Modern England* (Cambridge: Cambridge University Press, 2021) examines the influence on Shakespeare's work and practices of a number of lost works, including collaborations, and the *Lost Plays* Database online at https://lostplays.folger.edu, to which McInnis contributes, is an excellent free resource. The *Henslowe-Alleyn Digitisation Project*, online at https://henslowe-alleyn.org.uk, is another. Holger Schott Syme's 'The Theatre of Shakespeare's Time', in Stephen Greenblatt et al. (eds.), *The Norton Shakespeare: Third Edition* (New York: W. W. Norton, 2015), 93–118, offers a number of fresh perspectives.

Shakespeare's Career

Some of the many works devoted to this subject that have inspired this book include E.K. Chambers' *William Shakespeare: A Study of Facts and Problems*, 2 vols. (Oxford: Oxford University Press, 1930), a compendious, classic gathering of the documentary evidence relating to Shakespeare's works. Lukas Erne's *Shakespeare as Literary Dramatist* (Cambridge: Cambridge University Press, 2003) and *Shakespeare and the Book Trade* (Cambridge: Cambridge University Press, 2013) examine Shakespeare's authoriality and popularity through his working life via bibliographic means. Gary Taylor's 'The Canon and Chronology of Shakespeare's Plays', in Stanley Wells and Gary Taylor (eds.), *William Shakespeare: A Textual Companion*, with John Jowett and William Montgomery (Oxford: Oxford University Press, 1987), 69–144, is probably the most influential twentieth-century rethinking since Chambers, and see also Taylor and Rory Loughnane's revised version in *The New Oxford Shakespeare Authorship Companion*, 417–602. The NOS in general has been hugely influential in changing our sense of early Shakespearean collaboration with Marlowe in particular, and Loughnane and Andrew J. Power's edited collections *Early Shakespeare, 1588–1594* (Cambridge: Cambridge University Press, 2020) and *Late Shakespeare, 1608–1613* (Cambridge: Cambridge University Press, 2013) are extremely useful collections of essays, rethinking the contexts and activities of the two extreme ends of Shakespeare's career where collaboration dominates. John Jowett's editions of *Timon of*

Athens (Oxford: Oxford World's Classics, 2004) and *Sir Thomas More* (London: Methuen Drama, 2011) are superb accounts of Shakespearean mid-career collaboration, and Gary Taylor and John Lavagnino (gen. eds.), *Thomas Middleton: The Collected Works* (Oxford: Oxford University Press, 2007), and *Thomas Middleton and Early Modern Textual Culture* (Oxford: Oxford University Press, 2007) offer a wealth of material on early modern authorship alongside detailed editorial accounts of Middleton's adaptations of Shakespeare. Charles Nicholl, *The Lodger: Shakespeare on Silver Street* (London: Penguin Books Ltd., 2007) is very useful on Shakespeare's connections with Wilkins, and Gordon McMullan's excellent edition of *King Henry VIII* (London: Bloomsbury, 2000) is a timely account of Shakespeare's work with Fletcher and of collaboration study in general. McMullan's *Shakespeare and the Idea of Late Writing* (Cambridge: Cambridge University Press, 2007) is a compelling antidote to the romanticism that has often attended accounts of Shakespeare's late authorship, and Raphael Lyne's *Shakespeare's Late Work* (Oxford: Oxford University Press, 2007) is more congenial, but no less useful. David Carnegie and Gary Taylor (eds.), *The Quest for Cardenio: Shakespeare, Fletcher, Cervantes, & the Lost Play* (Oxford: Oxford University Press, 2012), is a major collection on Shakespeare's 'lost' collaboration.

Print

W.W. Greg's *A Bibliography of the English Printed Drama to the Restoration* 4 vols. (London: Bibliographical Society, 1939–1959) is the original comprehensive catalogue of all the printed drama, though Alan B. Farmer and Zachary Lesser's *Database of Early English Playbooks* online at http://deep.sas.upenn.edu is far more easily accessible, and usefully searchable. Lesser's essay 'Shakespeare's Flop: John Waterson and *The Two Noble Kinsmen*', in Marta Straznicky (ed.), *Shakespeare's Stationers* (Philadelphia: University of Pennsylvania Press, 2013), 177–96, is an excellent book-history study of the one early modern imprint to identify Shakespearean collaboration correctly. Julie Stone Peters, *Theatre of the Book: 1480–1880* (Oxford: Oxford University Press, 2000) is a forerunner of Erne's stage-to-page criticism, examining the tensions between theatrical performance and printed plays as artforms, while Claire M.L. Bourne's *Typographies of Performance in Early Modern England* (Oxford: Oxford University Press, 2020) provocatively explores the idea that early printed play-texts employed typographical means of recapturing theatrical performance. Bourne has also edited *Shakespeare/Text* (London: Bloomsbury, 2021), an important new collection of essays including entries on 'Canon / apocrypha' by Aleida Auld, and 'Book / theatre' by Holger Schott Syme. Valerie Wayne (ed.), *Women's Labour and the History of the Book in Early*

Modern England (London: Bloomsbury, 2020), is a timely gender-focused study of forms of female collaboration with drama in an era of male-only playwrights, and Sonia Massai's *Shakespeare and the Rise of the Editor* (Cambridge: Cambridge University Press, 2007) is an excellent study on the collaborative roles of publishers and annotators who prepared copy for press. Andrew Murphy, *Shakespeare in Print: Second Edition* (Cambridge: Cambridge University Press, 2021) features a chapter on 'Collecting Shakespeare', 43–82, focusing on Shakespeare's authorial presentation in the so-called Pavier quartos and the landmark First Folio. Emma Depledge and Peter Kirwan (eds.), *Canonising Shakespeare: Stationers and the Book Trade, 1640–1740* (Cambridge: Cambridge University Press, 2017) looks at the formation of Shakespeare's identity in print from the closure of the theatres in the 1640s to the early eighteenth century, including a short chapter by Kirwan on 'Consolidating the Shakespeare Canon', 81–88. Kirwan's *Shakespeare and the Idea of Apocrypha* (Cambridge: Cambridge University Press, 2015), is an important examination of the concept of 'apocrypha' in the Shakespeare canon, including plays legitimately part-ascribed to Shakespeare, and John Jowett's 'Shakespeare Supplemented', in Douglas A. Brooks (ed.), *The Shakespeare Apocrypha* (Lampeter: Edwin Mellen Press, 2007), 39–73, gives an excellent overview of the changing margins of the Shakespeare canon.

Stylometry and Editorial Theory

Gabriel Egan's 'A History of Shakespearean Authorship Attribution', in *The New Oxford Shakespeare Authorship Companion*, 27–47, offers a comprehensive overview of the development of stylistic and stylometric approaches to ascertaining Shakespearean authorship in disputed plays since the rise of serious scholarly editing in the eighteenth century. His monograph, *The Struggle for Shakespeare's Text: Twentieth-Century Editorial Theory and Practice* (Cambridge: Cambridge University Press, 2010) does the same for the development of technical scholarly editing since the New Bibliography. Jerome J. McGann's *Critique of Modern Textual Criticism* (Chicago: University of Chicago Press, 1983) and D.F. McKenzie's *Making Meaning: 'Printers of the Mind' and Other Essays* (Boston: University of Massachusetts Press, 2002) are stimulating provocations against received editorial orthodoxies. John Jowett's *Shakespeare and Text*, Revised Edition (Oxford: Oxford University Press, 2019) is an invaluable guide to the complex history of Shakespeare editing, including attempts to categorize theatrical manuscripts from the New Bibliography to the present day. Grace Ioppolo's *Dramatists and Their Manuscripts in the Age of Shakespeare* (Abingdon, 2004), Paul Werstine's *Early Modern Playhouse Manuscripts and the Editing of Shakespeare* (Cambridge, 2012), and

James Purkis, *Shakespeare and Manuscript Drama* (Cambridge: Cambridge University Press, 2016), are important interventions in questions around authorship and collaboration in the extant manuscript record. Major works on stylometry and attribution study include S. Schoenbaum, *Internal Evidence and Elizabethan Dramatic Authorship* (Edward Arnold Ltd, 1966); Marina Tarlinskaja, *Shakespeare's Verse* (New York: Peter Lang Inc., 1987); Jonathan Hope, *The Authorship of Shakespeare's Plays: A Sociolinguistic Study* (Cambridge: Cambridge University Press, 1994); Harold Love, *Attributing Authorship* (Cambridge: Cambridge University Press, 2002); Brian Vickers, *Shakespeare, Co-Author* (Oxford: Oxford University Press, 2002); Hugh Craig and Arthur F. Kinney (eds.), *Shakespeare, Computers, and the Mystery of Authorship* (Cambridge: Cambridge University Press, 2009); Lene B. Petersen, *Shakespeare's Errant Texts* (Cambridge: Cambridge University Press, 2010); Hugh Craig and Brett Greatley-Hirsch, *Style, Computers, and Early Modern Drama: Beyond Authorship* (Cambridge: Cambridge University Press, 2017); and Gary Taylor and Gabriel Egan (eds.), *The New Oxford Shakespeare Authorship Companion* (Oxford: Oxford University Press, 2017). Will Sharpe, 'Authorship and Attribution', in *William Shakespeare and Others: Collaborative Plays* (Basingstoke: Palgrave Macmillan, 2013), 641–745, introduces readers to attribution study and considers Shakespeare's authorship of a number of 'apocryphal' plays attributed to him. The many works of MacDonald P. Jackson, undoubtedly the most influential and prominent figure in the development of modern Shakespearean stylometry, include *Studies in Attribution: Middleton and Shakespeare* (Insitut Für Anglistik und Amerikanistik, 1979); *Defining Shakespeare: Pericles as Test Case* (Oxford: Oxford University Press, 2003); 'Early Modern Authorship: Canons and Chronologies', in Gary Taylor and John Lavagnino (gen. eds.), *Thomas Middleton and Early Modern Textual Culture* (Oxford: Oxford University Press, 2007), 80–97; and *Determining the Shakespeare Canon* (Oxford: Oxford University Press, 2014), which considers Shakespeare's authorship in *Arden of Faversham*. Laurie Maguire's *Shakespearean Suspect Texts* (Cambridge: Cambridge University Press, 1996) is a rich meditation on textual 'badness' in the critical imagination.

Index